Professional Wrestling
and the Law

Professional Wrestling and the Law

Legal Battles from the Ring to the Courtroom

ALEX B. LONG

McFarland & Company, Inc., Publishers
Jefferson, North Carolina

ISBN (print) 978-1-4766-9297-5
ISBN (ebook) 978-1-4766-5200-9

LIBRARY OF CONGRESS AND BRITISH LIBRARY
CATALOGUING DATA ARE AVAILABLE

Library of Congress Control Number 2024017201

© 2024 Alex B. Long. All rights reserved

No part of this book may be reproduced or transmitted in any form or by any means, electronic or mechanical, including photocopying or recording, or by any information storage and retrieval system, without permission in writing from the publisher.

Front cover images © Shutterstock

Printed in the United States of America

*McFarland & Company, Inc., Publishers
Box 611, Jefferson, North Carolina 28640
www.mcfarlandpub.com*

To Nancy Long,
who would have had decidedly mixed feelings
about seeing this book published
but who would have supported me anyway

Table of Contents

Acknowledgments	vi
Preface	1
CHAPTER 1 An Introduction to Kayfabe in the Law of Wrestling	5
CHAPTER 2 Kayfabe and the Doctrine of Unclean Hands	15
CHAPTER 3 Negligence and Battery	33
CHAPTER 4 Antitrust and Interference with Contractual Relations	52
CHAPTER 5 Labor and Employment Law	95
CHAPTER 6 Sex Discrimination, Constitutional Law, and Lady Wrestlers	120
CHAPTER 7 Defamation	150
CHAPTER 8 Breach of Contract	168
CHAPTER 9 Concussions, Fraud, and Statutes of Repose	181
CHAPTER 10 Race Discrimination	196
Chapter Notes	221
Bibliography	243
Index	247

Acknowledgments

Thanks to Dalton Howard, Emily Gould, Savannah Hall, Brandon Townsend, and Peyton Annoni for their research assistance. It probably wasn't what they imagined they would be doing when they enrolled in law school. Thanks to Joe Slater and Fiona McQuarrie for their helpful comments on an earlier draft. (Academic wrestling fans of the world unite!) Thanks to Kassidy McBride for helping to put it all together. Thanks also to reference librarian extraordinaire Becca Kite for finding stuff that was hard to find. Thanks to Phillip Smith at the Knox County Archives, Shane Bell at the National Archives in Atlanta, and the good folks at the Knox County Courthouse.

Thanks to Tom Prichard, Akio Sato, Patrick Helvey, Lucas Middlebrook, Jim Cox, and Greg Oliver for taking the time to respond to my questions. And thanks to Robert Rogan, Bob Layman, Vern Hall, and others for going to wrestling matches with me back in the day.

Preface

I'm a law professor. I've taught and written about the law for over 20 years. I also grew up as a wrestling fan.

I'm not sure, but I think the idea for this book probably started when wrestler Hulk Hogan sued the internet site Gawker for posting part of a sex tape featuring Hogan and his best friend's wife. I don't think my students knew then I was a wrestling fan, but we were covering invasion of privacy in my Torts class around the time the case went to trial and a student asked about it.

The case generated a bunch of mainstream media coverage, so a lot of people were interested in it. But as someone who had spent a lot of time watching Hulk Hogan on television and who taught about the exact legal theory Hogan was asserting in court, I was particularly interested. I don't remember thinking at the time, "I should write a book about legal cases involving professional wrestling." But the case probably planted a seed in my brain.

Now, eight years later, I've written that book.

Professional Wrestling and the Law is a detailed history of legal cases involving professional wrestling. But hopefully, it is more than that. The book uses legal disputes involving professional wrestling as a means of exploring different legal theories and discussing them in a manner that non-lawyers and lawyers alike should find interesting. In doing so, the book also sheds on light on events in the world of professional wrestling—some famous, some less well known—that helped shape the evolution of the business. In the process, the book examines professional wrestling's role within popular culture more generally.

As this book illustrates, professional wrestling has long been the subject of legal commentary. Fittingly enough, one of the first references to professional wrestling in an academic law journal was in 1960, in reference to the ability of the Federal Communications Commission to regulate deceptive television programming. (The *University of Pennsylvania Law Review* article referred to wrestling as a form of entertainment that "our culture generally regards as unobjectionable.")* Since then, there have been over 500 law journal articles that reference professional wrestling in some capacity. Professional wrestling has also been the subject of dozens of academic writings in other disciplines, including biographies of famous performers as well as Ph.D. theses on gender identity, the role of race in the world of professional wrestling, and other topics. So, clearly, I'm not the only academic who is interested in this sort of stuff.

Of course, courts had been dealing with legal issues involving the world of professional wrestling for decades before legal academics began to turn their attention to the business. One of the recurring themes of many of the cases involving professional wrestling in the 20th century was whether wrestling was "fake." Given wrestling's somewhat unusual relationship with reality, it is perhaps fitting that the first published judicial opinion in the United States to reference professional wrestling involved a case of fraud. *Fleming v. State*,† an Indiana case from 1910, involved (in the words of the Indiana Supreme Court) "a consummate set of rogues and thieves" who engaged in an elaborate con. The con involved separating the victim from his $10,000 by tricking him into betting on a "pretended wrestling match." During the match, Blair, one of the wrestlers who was in on the con, threw his supposed opponent, Wilson, to the ground. At this point, "[s]ome kind of a fluid which looked like blood, which had been prepared for the occasion, ran from Wilson's mouth, and the latter writhed and twitched and pretended to be unconscious, and every one present appeared to be very much excited and rushed to his assistance." Fearing arrest, the victim (minus his $10,000) fled the scene. The legal question facing the Indiana Supreme Court was whether to sustain the con men's conviction under Indiana's "bunko steering" statute. The court upheld the convictions.

The modern business of professional wrestling has its origins in these types of unsanctioned (or barely sanctioned) staged matches. And while the scam in *Fleming* was more elaborate than the trickery employed by early wrestling promoters in traveling carnivals, the basic idea was the same. Early chapters in *Professional Wrestling and the Law* explore what it means to say that wrestling is "fake" and how the "fake" nature of the business impacted the resolution of legal disputes prior to the revelation to the public in the 1980s that professional wrestling was entertainment and not competition.

The book also focuses on how promoters used the law to build and

---

* "Federal Communications Commission: Control of 'Deceptive Programming,'" 108 *U. Pa. L. Rev.* 868, 869 (1960).
† 91 N.E. 1085 (Ind. 1910).

maintain their businesses in the face of competition and changing times. One way promoters were able to ward off competitors was simply by violating state and federal competition laws. One chapter examines a series of antitrust cases filed against wrestling promoters during the 20th century (including a largely unexplored case involving Randy "Macho Man" Savage) and explores how some of the same tactics employed by older promoters are still allegedly being used today. Another chapter discusses how wrestling promoters were able to build the industry by structuring their businesses so as to avoid the reach of labor and employment law. Many of the legal concepts at issue in these earlier decisions are increasingly timely today. Several chapters examine the contracts that promoters used when hiring their talent and discuss how the terms within the contracts were interpreted by the courts.

Other chapters place professional wrestling within the broader framework of important legal and social changes during the 20th century. Long before the wrestling business got caught up in the #MeToo movement that brought to light disturbing incidents of sexual harassment involving high-profile figures, "lady wrestlers" fought a number of legal battles against institutionalized sexual discrimination in the business. As discussed in one chapter, some of these battles took place against the backdrop of the women's liberation movement of the 1960s and 1970s. Professional wrestling also has a shameful history with race discrimination. The role that the integration of sports and entertainment world played in the civil rights movement was significant. A later chapter discusses the role that wrestling (and its more acceptable cousin, boxing) played inside and outside the courtroom in helping to integrate the sports and entertainment world.

* * *

Some of the individual cases addressed in *Professional Wrestling and the Law* have been the subject of prior academic discussion, internet message board arguments, and podcast retellings. But this book attempts to place the cases within the broader context of the law and society. Several chapters rely upon actual court filings and trial transcripts to shed new light on longstanding controversies and urban folklore concerning the wrestling business.

As I have taught and written about the law for over 20 years (and have been a wrestling fan for much longer than that), my hope is that lawyers, non-lawyers, wrestling fans, and maybe even non-wrestling fans will be entertained and learn as much from reading *Professional Wrestling and the Law* as I did while writing it.

Chapter 1

An Introduction to Kayfabe in the Law of Wrestling

> **Kayfabe:** *term used to describe the illusion (and up-keep of the illusion) that professional wrestling is not staged (i.e., that the on-screen situations between performers represent reality). Also used by wrestlers as a signal to close ranks and stop discussing business due to an uninformed person arriving in earshot. The term is said to have been loosely derived from the Pig Latin pronunciation of the word "fake" ("akefay").*
> —Pro Wrestling Fandom.com,
> Glossary of Professional Wrestling Terms

During the course of an interview conducted in 1984, John Stossel, host of the ABC news show *20/20*, suggested to professional wrestler "Dr. D" David Schultz that professional wrestling was fake. Schultz responded by smacking Stossel on the right side of his head and asking, "Is that fake?" as Stossel lay on the floor. Stossel apparently didn't provide the correct response, because after Stossel got back up, Schultz smacked him again, this time on the left side of the head. "You think it's fake?" asked Schultz. Stossel then proceeded to run away from Schultz after he picked himself off the floor for a second time. Eight weeks after the incident, Stossel told the *New York Times* that he was still experiencing pain and a buzzing in his ears.[1]

* * *

Not too long after the Stossel/Dr. D incident, wrestler Hulk Hogan appeared on a television show hosted by actor/comedian Richard Belzer to promote the upcoming Wrestlemania pay-per-view event. After several minutes of conversation, in which Belzer made little effort to conceal his disdain for professional wrestling, Belzer asked Hogan to demonstrate one of his famous wrestling moves. Hogan demurred, telling Belzer, "I'm gonna stick to the basics because the floor's a little hard here and I don't want you getting hurt." Hogan then applied what he called a "front chin lock" on Belzer. After only a few seconds, Belzer's arms went limp and Hogan released the hold. Belzer immediately fell to the floor in a heap, unconscious. Judging from the awkward silence and audible gasps in the video of the incident, it is clear that the audience appeared to not know whether what they were witnessing was real or fake as Belzer lay unconscious on the floor. Belzer eventually came to, but the pool of blood on the floor and on the back of his jacket demonstrates that Belzer had legitimately cracked his head open when he fell. Belzer ended up getting nine stitches as a result of the incident. Despite the injury, Belzer bounced up from the ground and, adopting the persona of a schlocky television host, pointed to the camera and told the home audience, "We'll be right back after this word from you-know-who!" Belzer did not return after the commercial.[2]

* * *

As one might imagine, both Stossel and Belzer sued following their respective incidents. A doctor hired by the defendants to examine Stossel for his claimed ear damage told Stossel that he had a "jurosomatic illness." In other words, Stossel was holding on to his pain only because he was involved in a lawsuit. Stossel eventually settled the case and received $280,000 for his pain and suffering. Reflecting on the incident years later, Stossel told an interviewer that the doctor may have had a point about his jurosomatic illness because, according to Stossel, his pain went away "when I got paid."[3]

Belzer ended up suing Hulk Hogan (and others) for $5 million. Once again, the case settled before going to trial. Belzer used the proceeds to purchase a house in Nice, France, which he dubbed "Chez Hogan."[4] Following the settlement, Belzer and his attorneys got into a spat over the attorneys' legal fees. This dispute actually did make it to court. Belzer had originally agreed to a one-third contingency fee, meaning that his lawyers would receive one-third of whatever proceeds there were from the lawsuit. If Belzer received nothing, however, his lawyers would also receive nothing. But somehow Belzer's lawyers persuaded Belzer to increase the fee to a whopping 50 percent of the recovery. Belzer then to tried to back out of the agreement, claiming he had agreed to the increase under duress. Belzer's lawyers professed to be outraged. They informed the court that they were entitled to the 50 percent because of the "angst, aggravation and life's blood which this case caused" them and complained that Belzer was a "paradigm of ingratitude." In support of their claim, the lawyers produced an affidavit previously signed by Belzer after agreeing to increase his lawyers' fee to 50 percent in which Belzer "spoke in glowing terms of the dedication and devotion of his attorneys, as well as the hardship and risks undertaken by them in order to confer the benefit upon him of an enhanced settlement." The judge was unimpressed and dryly observed that Belzer's affidavit "could not have been more supportive of the application for additional fees and more lavish in praise of the attorneys' efforts if the attorneys themselves had drafted it." The judge denied the lawyers' application for a greater fee.[5]

* * *

So, which of these individuals were being "fake?" Which ones were attempting to create and maintain illusions? Or, to use the wrestling vernacular, who was trying to maintain kayfabe in these situations? Schultz and Hogan, when they legitimately physically abused a couple of smart alecks who questioned the legitimacy of professional wrestling? Stossel, with his possible "jurosomatic illness" that miraculously cleared up when he got paid? Belzer, when he tried to create the illusion that his falling on the floor was all just show biz (when the reality was that he was suffering from a very real head injury)? Belzer's lawyers, when they portrayed themselves as the victims of a client's inexplicable lack of gratitude in not wanting to give them half of his settlement for having his head split open on national television? Who was trying to maintain kayfabe?

* * *

To enter the world of professional wrestling is to enter a world based on illusions and secrets. The business has its roots in the traveling carnivals of the late 19th century. Promoters would put on wrestling exhibitions in which locals could test their skill against the carnival's resident tough guy (known as "the hooker"). While the carnival wrestlers were legitimate tough guys who would legitimately and routinely defeat audience members, these were, after all, carnivals.* So, sometimes the promoters would employ a little deception, perhaps by installing a "plant" in the audience in

---

* There is at least one reported judicial decision involving a wrestler at a carnival being convicted of a crime for breaking the leg of a customer who decided to test his luck against a wrestler. The promoter offered to pay any fan who could last ten minutes in the ring with wrestler Dobie Osburn. According to newspaper accounts, Osburn "clamped a head-hold" on a fan who decided to take up Osburn's challenge. This prompted the fan's brother to enter the ring and protest the referee's control of the match. A fight eventually broke out between the fan and his brother, on one side, and a number of wrestlers, including Texas Red Allen, on the other. "3 Side Show Men Charged in Affray, *Fort Worth Star-Telegram*," March 8, 1932, at 8. According to the court, Allen, "jump[ed] up and down on the injured party with his feet while he (the injured party) was being beaten by the other participants in the difficulty. At the same time someone twisted the injured party's leg and broke it." Allen was convicted of aggravated assault and sentenced to 60 days in jail. *See Allen v. State*, 54 S.W.2d 810 (Tex. Ct. Crim. App. 1932).

order to encourage volunteers or increase the amount of money bet. Customers were targets (or "marks") and it was the job of the carny to separate the mark from his money. Since it was important to maintain the deception that all of the carnival's attractions were on the level, carnies would often speak a secret carny language in order to keep outsiders in the dark as to what was going on, hence the term "kayfabe."[6]

Questions about whether professional wrestling was "fake" dogged the sport almost from its inception. News stories from the 19th century would sometimes question and outright dismiss the legitimacy of some matches.[7] There were plenty of legitimate wrestling contests early on. The problem was that some of them were likely quite boring to watch. For example, a 1914 match between Tony Stecher and Wesley Cobb in 1914 reportedly lasted five hours and 18 minutes.[8] If wrestling was going to draw patrons, it was going to have to be more entertaining. One of the most important demarcation points in the professional wrestling's shift from sport to entertainment occurred in 1925 when champion Ed "Strangler" Lewis was defeated by Wayne "Big" Munn in a shocking upset in Kansas City. Lewis, a true wrestler who had made a name for himself by winning hours-long wrestling contests, was considered virtually unbeatable. In contrast, Munn had no real wrestling training. So, when Munn defeated Lewis—aided, in part, by a blatant foul in the second fall out of three when Munn threw Lewis out of the ring—the result was met with disbelief. As well it should have been. By this point, Lewis had joined forces with two other individuals (Billy Sandow and Toots Mondt) to form "the Gold Dust Trio," a group that transformed the business by injecting theatricality into the sport.[9] Sensing that more money could be made by having Lewis suddenly appear beatable, the Trio decided to put the world championship belt on Munn. So, Lewis agreed to lose to Munn in order to increase profits.* By the 1930s, the sport was increasingly perceived as no longer being on the level, with *The New Yorker* stating in 1932 that professional wrestling "had been exposed more times than Santa Claus."[10]

Professional wrestling increasingly developed a reputation for being "fake" as the theatricality of the events took on more importance. But up until the 1980s at least, there were still paying customers who believed that at least some of what they witnessed in the ring was on the level. And those in the business went to great lengths to protect the illusion.

* * *

---

* The Trio sold the result and the blatant nature of Munn's foul even after the match. A newspaper article at the time reported that Lewis was hospitalized following the match after suffering "a badly injured back." "'Strangler' Lewis Still in Hospital," *San Pedro News Pilot*, Jan. 9, 1925, available at https://cdnc.ucr.edu/?a=d&d=SPNP19250109.2.76&e=------en--20--1--txt-txIN--------.

But sometimes the illusory world of professional wrestling would come face to face with the often cold, hard reality of the legal world. Sometimes fans are accidentally (or intentionally) injured by wrestlers. Sometimes wrestlers are injured through the negligence of others. Sometimes there are disputes between the wrestling talent and the promoters as to who has creative control over plots or matches and who owns the rights to a wrestler's persona or character. Sometimes outsiders invade the privacy of the performers who have labored so hard to create an alternate reality. In each of these situations, the law might provide a remedy to the injured party. But to do that, the law has to get to the truth.

A law school dean once remarked that the first-year law school curriculum "teaches that tough-minded analysis, hard facts, and cold logic are the tools of a good lawyer, and it has little room for emotion, imagination, and morality."[11] He didn't say this in an admiring way, and it's definitely an overly dramatic depiction of the law school curriculum. But it's not completely off base either. There are numerous references in the legal literature to the "cold logic of the law."[12] Equally common is the notion that "the law is a quest for truth."[13] The rules of criminal and civil procedure are designed to permit the parties and their lawyers to discover as many relevant facts as possible before trial begins. There are few secrets or surprises when it comes to the facts that are presented at trial.

All of which is entirely at odds with the nature of professional wrestling, which thrives on secrets and surprises. In delving into the history of legal cases involving professional wrestling, it's fascinating to see how those in the legal profession and those in the wrestling business seek to find some sort of uneasy compromise between the need for truth and the need for illusion. For example, there are several older legal cases involving the question of whether professional wrestlers were employees of the companies for whom they worked—in which case the company could be held liable and forced to pay damages for the wrongdoing of the wrestlers committed in the scope of employment—or whether wrestlers were independent contractors—in which case the company could not be held liable. The key question in all of these cases is how much control the company had over the wrestlers? The greater the control, the more likely it is that an individual is an employee. It is fascinating to read how those inside of this business at this time, which was still fundamentally based on kayfabe, attempted to navigate the competing values of their profession (deception) and the law (truth).

By the 1990s, the truth about professional wrestling was widely known among the public, so this truth sometimes came out during the course of legal proceedings.[14] But prior to that, wrestling promoters were willing to risk legal sanctions to maintain kayfabe. Some promoters, on the advice of counsel, simply refused to answer whether the outcomes of matches were pre-determined.[15] Others insisted, under penalty of perjury, that wrestling was on the level. For example, in one 1969 case from Massachusetts, the president of a wrestling organization testified that "[n]o wrestler was told who was to win or lose, and the only instruction given was in regard to the time limit for each bout."[16] To be charitable, this is literally almost impossible to believe; everyone who is familiar with the history of professional wrestling knows that wrestlers were (and still are) given instructions on how matches will proceed and end. The fact that the promoter's devotion to maintaining kayfabe was still so intense that he was willing to risk criminal conviction by saying under oath that wrestling matches were on the level should provide the reader with some sense of how strong the code of kayfabe was at the time.

There were practical reasons why someone in the wrestling business might be willing to risk a perjury charge when asked about the true nature of the business. In a 1953 case from Washington, a wrestling promoter was asked under oath about the extent of a promoter's control over a match. A state statute at the time specifically made it a criminal offense to put on a "fake or sham" wrestling event.* So, if the promoter admitted that promoters determined in advance who would win or lose a match, the promoter would have theoretically been opening himself up to criminal prosecution. In addition, wrestling was regulated by state athletic commissions in many states, so a promoter who admitted that his shows were not true athletic competitions ran the risk of losing his promoter's license. If, however, he lied about the extent of his control, he would have theoretically been subject to conviction for perjury. The Washington promoter apparently decided to risk the potential perjury charge because he ended up testifying that he did not exercise control over the matches.[17]

There was also the risk that by bringing a complaint before the courts that a judge might expose the true nature of the wrestling business in front of jurors (or at least cause jurors to doubt the legitimacy of the business). In a 1959 case, a local promoter charged that the National Wrestling Alliance, a nationwide coalition of promoters, had established a monopoly that prevented him from earning a living. At trial, the judge regularly mocked the promoter's case and the wrestling business in general in front of the jury. The judge referred to paying customers as "suckers," said that professional wrestling was "the art of acting," and asked another promoter

---

* There are still similar statutes on the books in some states that prohibit sham boxing or mixed martial events. *See* La. Rev. Stat. § 75; Hawaii Rev. Stat. § 440–22. Some statutes continue to reference wrestling. *See* Md. Code, Bus. Reg. § 4–316. Ohio's statute prohibits "sham or fake" boxing matches but specifically allows sham or fake professional wrestling matches. *See* Ohio Rev. Code. § 3773.46(C).

1. An Introduction to Kayfabe in the Law of Wrestling   11

how he "[kept] his religion" promoting wrestling matches.[18] Not surprisingly, the jury sided against the promoter.[19]*

* * *

Despite these sorts of incidents where the curtain was pulled back on the world of professional wrestling, people in the wrestling business during this time believed it was necessary to preserve the illusion of reality in order to maintain the business. The thinking was that if too many people in the audience stopped believing that what they saw was on the level, they might stop buying tickets. So, promoters and wrestlers did their best to maintain the illusion of reality, albeit a highly stylized version of reality. The moves wrestlers used may not have been designed to injure an opponent, but the simulated violence still needed to look as real as possible. And insiders would still close ranks and speak carny when in the presence of outsiders. Throughout most of the 20th century, kayfabe was the wrestling business' form of *omerta*, the Mafia code of silence.

The kayfabe era officially came to an end on February 19, 1989. This was the day that the *New York Times* published a story disclosing the fact the WWF's Linda McMahon, wife of Vince McMahon, had testified before the New Jersey legislature that professional wrestling was entertainment and not a legitimate athletic competition.[20] For a while, other wrestling organizations circled the wagons and tried to maintain the fiction that it was only the WWF that was "fake." But the jig was up. By 1993, second-generation wrestler Eddie Gilbert felt comfortable enough about the death of kayfabe to give what is generally considered to be the first "shoot" interview, in which he discussed events occurring behind the scenes.[21] Ten years later, it was common for wrestlers to speak publicly about the realities of professional wrestling.

Why would McMahon, whose father had previously run the family business and was as devoted to maintaining kayfabe as anyone, expose the business like this? Because he wanted to get away from the law. Specifically, he no longer wanted his product to be subject to regulation by state athletic commissions, which imposed restrictions on how McMahon ran his business and took money out of his pocket.[22] In addition to controlling the licenses as to who could promote an event (for a fee), state commissions might impose other requirements, such as requiring performers to undergo a physical examination before a match. They also sometimes collected a cut from the gate. For example, the Tennessee Athletic Commission around this time collected four percent of the gross of ticket sales.[23]

---

* Despite losing at trial, the promoter was granted a new trial on appeal on the grounds that the judge's mockery was so bad that the promoter had been denied a fair trial.

The more the wrestling business had to contend with the law, the more expensive and cumbersome it was to do business. So, McMahon exposed the business in order to avoid the restrictions imposed by the law.

* * *

Eventually, wrestling's façade gradually gave way to reality—or at least a form of reality. No one actually believes professional wrestling is real anymore, at least in the sense that matches are legitimate competitions. Yet, the business survives. So, it's not as if those in the business are trying to deceive the audience into believing that professional wrestling storylines and matches are 100 percent real. Everyone knows that the violence is simulated. Kayfabe isn't what it used to be.

But illusions remain critical to the success of professional wrestling. There is an unspoken contract between performers and audience members. For their part, performers will create an illusion of competition and violence that advances an interesting plot. As their part of the deal, audience members will suspend disbelief and respond appropriately to what transpires in order to aid the performers in their task (provided the performers do a good job of it). Wrestling fans accepted the fact that when Brock Lesnar administered his famed F-5 finishing move, his opponent was not going to get up. Wrestling fans accepted the fact that when Dwayne "the Rock" Johnson delivered the People's Elbow to his opponent, the match was over. Wrestling fans accepted these things, not because they believed that the moves had actually injured the other wrestlers, but because everyone involved—performers and audience members alike—understood that acceptance of this fake reality was necessary to the orderly resolution of the matches.

* * *

Even inside the cold, logical world of the law, there are professionally maintained illusions. For example, a "legal fiction" is an assertion that judges and lawyers accept as true, knowing full well that the assertion really isn't true. Judges and lawyers accept the assertion as true because it is necessary to do so in order for the law to operate smoothly. For example, the law treats a corporation as a person, not because anyone actually believes corporations are people, but because the law would be unable to deal with disputes involving corporations unless we accepted the assertion that corporations are people and enjoy the same rights that individuals enjoy. Legal fictions aren't meant to deceive; instead, they require an agreed-upon suspension of disbelief so that the legal process can function.[24]

Wrestling fans should be able to intuitively grasp this concept. Fans accept the idea that lawyers often play roles or characters. Professional wrestlers need fan favorites and someone to root against in order for a match to work. Within the roles of good guys and bad guys, there are also various archetypes that wrestling fans are familiar with.* For example, there is the "badass-good-guy-who-takes-no-crap-from-authority-figures" character (*see* Stone Cold Steve Austin); the "cowardly bad guy" character (*see* the Honky Tonk Man); and "the egotistical bad guy" character (*see* Gorgeous George, Ric Flair, Chris Jericho, Maxwell Jacob Friedman, and others too numerous to list).

Just as professional wrestlers adopt a persona or character in the ring and interviews, lawyers have their own roles that they must play in order for the system to function. While it may not always be clear during a trial which lawyer is the good guy and which is the bad guy, lawyers are well aware that they have roles to play within the system. It is essential for the system to function that lawyers play the roles of "zealous advocate," "officer of the court," or "minister of justice" (if the lawyer is a prosecutor). There are also various lawyer archetypes that books and Hollywood have presented us with and that many lawyers emulate, not because the system depends on it, but because—to use a wrestling term—they want to "get over" with the jury. Some lawyers gladly play the part of "the simple country lawyer" (*see Matlock*), "the champion of the underdog" (*see* Atticus Finch from *To Kill a Mockingbird*), and "the no-nonsense prosecutor" (*see Law & Order*) in order to make a connection with jurors.

Lawyers involved in litigation and negotiation also engage in role-playing and choreographed actions designed to prevent the need to ever enter into a courtroom. As observed by Ryan Holiday, the author of a book about one of Hulk Hogan's lawsuits, most lawsuits are kayfabe. "There is tough talk and occasionally a good show. But in the end, the outcome is usually predetermined: the case will settle, because the law is settled, and the lawyers on both sides will win."[25]

None of these things that lawyers do make their jobs any less "real." Lawyers have a job to do; it is just one that sometimes requires playacting and posturing in order to arrive at a result that most everyone knows is inevitable. And while the legal system certainly has its flaws and inherent biases, nothing about trial is "fake" (except, perhaps, the occasional false testimony that a witness provides). The legal system is "real" despite the fictions it sometimes relies upon.

It's also a mistake to think of modern professional wrestling as being

---

* From time to time, this book will use wrestling jargon as appropriate. For the uninitiated, "bad guys" in wrestling are known as "heels." "Good guys" are called "faces" or "babyfaces."

"fake." Wrestling is based upon agreed-upon suspension of disbelief, not deception. Even back in the time when professional wrestlers did try to deceive their audiences, the blood the wrestlers spilled and the concussions they sometimes suffered were (and are) most definitely real.

* * *

Also real are the legal troubles professional wrestlers and promoters sometimes find themselves in. This book is all about those legal troubles and the uneasy relationship between the law and professional wrestling. Part of what makes the cases in this book interesting is the collision between the "fake" and secretive world of professional wrestling, on the one hand, and the "real" and sometimes brutally open nature of legal proceedings on the other. Adding to the entertainment value is the fact that many of the real-life people involved are every bit as colorful (and prideful and vengeful and reckless) as the characters they portray. As every lawyer knows, those kinds of people make for interesting clients. (They also tend to get into trouble a lot, which makes them potentially lucrative clients.) But readers should also remember that each case discussed in this book involves real people with real problems that the law seeks to address— even if those problems originally stemmed from the "fake" world of professional wrestling.

Chapter 2

Kayfabe and the Doctrine of Unclean Hands

NWA Southeastern Wrestling, Inc. v. Garvin (1979)

Kayfabe, the practice of maintaining the illusion that professional wrestling was a competitive athletic contest, was still alive and well into the 1970s. One of the most frequently cited examples of how seriously wrestlers took kayfabe at the time was the story of a plane crash in Wilmington, North Carolina, in 1975. The small commuter plane was carrying several wrestlers, including babyface Tim Woods (a.k.a. Mr. Wrestling) and heels Johnny Valentine and Ric Flair. The crash left Woods with broken ribs and a concussion, Flair with a broken back, and Valentine paralyzed. Aside from the obvious physical consequences for the individuals involved, the crash posed a particular problem for the wrestling promotion that employed them. According to the storyline at the time, Woods hated the evil Valentine and Flair. If the public learned that Woods was on the same small plane as his hated rivals, the reality of professional wrestling would be exposed. So, while lying in the hospital, Woods used his real name (George Burrell Woodin) and falsely claimed to be a promoter in order to hide his identity. When rumors emerged that Woods really had been on the flight, Woods returned to the wrestling ring, still injured, in order to sell the "reality" that he hadn't been on the flight.

But kayfabe was more difficult to maintain when the legal process was at issue. Lawyers are subject to professional discipline (including up to disbarment) for making frivolous legal or factual assertions, knowingly making false statements of fact to a judge, and knowingly offering evidence the lawyer knows to be false.[1] Witnesses are sworn to tell the truth, the whole truth, and nothing but the truth. These were generally foreign concepts for people in the wrestling business at the time.

One of the examples of where kayfabe ran into the reality of legal proceedings is a legal action brought by promoter/wrestler Ron Fuller* against wrestler "Hands of Stone" Ronnie Garvin in Knoxville, Tennessee, in 1979. As internet lore has it, Fuller sued Garvin over a wrestling-related dispute but lost the case because he was unwilling to admit at trial that wrestling was not on the level. The reality is a bit more complicated and illustrates the legal doctrine of "unclean hands."

* * *

Part 1: In Which Ronnie Garvin (Allegedly) Takes the Money and Runs

In 1979, Ron Fuller, a.k.a. "the Tennessee Stud," ran Southeastern Championship Wrestling out of Knoxville under the National Wrestling Alliance (NWA) banner. In June, a group of Southeastern wrestlers, including Bob Roop, Bob Orton, Jr., Professor Boris Malenko, and Southeastern heavyweight champion Ron Garvin, walked out of the company to form a new company, All Star Championship Wrestling, to compete with Fuller in East Tennessee.[2]† Garvin, in particular, had been a fan favorite in the area for years.

Like all wrestling promotions, the heavyweight champion of Southeastern Championship Wrestling carried a championship belt, symbolizing his status as champion. According to Fuller, he had personally paid $175 for Southeastern's belt two years earlier.[3] One of the time-honored practices in professional wrestling at the time was for the champion of a promotion to "drop the belt" to another wrestler prior to leaving to join another promotion so the other wrestler would be the champion of the promotion. Garvin had become the Southeastern champion the night before he and his cohorts (or co-conspirators if you prefer) left the promotion. But rather than leaving the belt behind, Garvin took the belt with him.

What's more, according to Fuller, Garvin took a bunch of Fuller's money with him when he left. According to Fuller, Garvin had wanted to buy a new boat. Garvin already owned a boat but was in the market for a new one. So, Garvin came up with the idea for an angle in which Southeastern Championship Wrestling would hold a "Bayliner Boat Tournament." The idea was that Southeastern would announce that it had

---

* Fuller's real last name was Welch, which was the name he used in the legal proceeding.

† More details concerning the legal fallout from this split are covered in a later chapter.

purchased a brand new Bayliner boat, and that the winner of the tournament would win the boat. Not surprisingly, Garvin's plan called for Garvin to win the tournament. While the boat was advertised on TV as having been bought by Southeastern, in reality, the plan was for Fuller to loan Garvin $12,000 on behalf of Southeastern Wrestling for Garvin to use as a down payment on a new boat. Garvin would use the loan from Fuller to buy the new boat, sell his other boat, and use the proceeds from the sale to repay Fuller (at eight percent interest).[4] So, in reality, Garvin would win the tournament but not actually win the boat.* Fuller withdrew $12,000 from the bank, placed it in a brown paper bag, and gave it to Garvin.[5]

According to Fuller, Garvin then went ahead and bought the boat, left the company before the conclusion of the tournament, and left Fuller holding the bag. Despite Fuller's requests, Garvin never repaid Fuller for the loan. So, Fuller sued Garvin in Chancery Court in Knoxville.

* * *

Part 2: In Which Ron Fuller Sues Ronnie Garvin

Fuller maintained kayfabe in his initial complaint. Fuller's complaint did not identify Fuller or Garvin as professional wrestlers, and it said nothing about the Bayliner Boat Tournament. Instead, Fuller simply alleged that he loaned Garvin the $12,000 and had not been paid back. He sought to recover the $12,000 he had loaned Garvin and asked the court to issue a Writ of Attachment commanding the local sheriff "to attach a 27 foot Bayliner boat and trailer, said boat presently being docked at the Norris Dam Marina located on Norris Lake, just above the Norris Dam."[6] In other words, Fuller asked the court to direct the local sheriff to seize Garvin's boat until trial as a means of ensuring Garvin had sufficient funds to pay any judgment in the case. Despite Garvin's objections, the court issued the writ.

Less than two weeks after Fuller filed suit, Garvin's cohorts who had left Southeastern with him wrote a letter to the editor of the *Knoxville News-Sentinel* in which they broke kayfabe by referring to Fuller as the promoter of the organization and noting that the Tennessee Athletic Commission prohibited one from being both a promoter and a participant

---

* Fuller had previously employed this same basic gimmick when the company ran a "Cadillac tournament" in which the winner would supposedly receive a new Cadillac. *NWA Southeastern Wrestling Inc. v. Garvin*, No. 66591, Trial Transcript at 18–20 (Knox County Chancery Court, Feb. 13, 1980). This "Cadillac tournament" concept was a fixture among wrestling promotions around this time.

in a wrestling exhibition.⁷ Whether in response to the letter or as a matter of coincidence in time, Fuller subsequently amended his complaint the next day to include the following language:

> Plaintiff owns a belt known as the Southeastern Championship Belt which is in the wrongful possession of the defendant. The Plaintiff has demanded return of the belt and the defendant has refused and continues to refuse to return the belt to the Plaintiff. The defendant is guilty of conversion of the belt and should be ordered by this court to return belt [sic] and be responsible for any damages sustained to said property.⁸

So, Fuller and the NWA were now seeking to recover his $12,000 and the championship belt.

* * *

Trial was held on February 13, 1980, in Knox County Chancery Court before Chancellor Frederick D. McDonald. Some 40 years after the trial, Garvin remembered the case this way:

> The only way Ron could have won that case was to expose the business and admit that the belt was given to us through prearranged matches. In those days, you didn't do that, so Ron was between a rock and a hard place.⁹

Garvin's recollection of events is (understandably) somewhat hazy. As it played out, Fuller was willing to do what he and his lawyer thought was necessary to win the case, including exposing the true nature of the Bayliner Boat Tournament.

After announcing that he thought that this would be a "rather quick lawsuit," Fuller's attorney asked Fuller about the Bayliner Boat Tournament within the first minute or two of the trial. Fuller explained Garvin's idea behind the tournament and that Garvin needed a loan in order to make a down payment on the boat. Fuller's lawyer then had Fuller elaborate on the details of the tournament:

> Q: Was it pre-determined who was going to win that tournament?
> A: Yes.
> Q: Who was that going to be?
> A: Ron Garvin.¹⁰

On cross-examination, Garvin's attorney asked Fuller about the details of the loan to Garvin. Did he insist on a date of repayment? Did he have any receipts showing his withdrawal of the money that he gave to Garvin? Did he ask for any kind of security interest to verify his interest in the boat? But Garvin's attorney focused most heavily on Fuller's admission that the result of the Bayliner Boat Tournament had been pre-determined:

> Q: Now, I believe that you used this boat in the advertisement of Southeastern Championship Wrestling?

2. Kayfabe and the Doctrine of Unclean Hands

> **A:** Yes.
> **Q:** And the advertisement stated that Southeastern Championship Wrestling had bought a boat, and they were going to give it to the winner of the tournament, and that was an elimination tournament; isn't that correct?
> **A:** Right.
> ....
> **Q:** I'm familiar with the way the matches are actually won, but the general principle was that Southeastern Championship Wrestling had a boat, and whoever won the boat was going to get from Southeastern the championship for winning the boat, is that right?
> **A:** Right.
> **Q:** That wasn't really the way it was?
> **A:** Actually, we did not buy the entire boat for Southeastern Wrestling.
> **Q:** Actually, it was pre-determined who was going to win the boat, wasn't it?
> **A:** Yes.
> **Q:** And therefore, the advertisement in this entire transaction of Southeastern Wrestling owning the boat and giving it to a wrestler was actually a fraud to the public, wasn't it?
> **A:** To a certain extent.
> **[FULLER'S LAWYER]:** I object to that.
> **COURT:** Inadmissible.
> **Q:** Let me rephrase it. Isn't it a fact that the public was being told this was a tournament, and there was going to be a winner?
> **A:** Right.
> **Q:** And that winner was going to get the boat from Southeastern Wrestling?
> **A:** Right.
> **Q:** But it had already been pre-determined who was going to win that tournament; wasn't it?
> **A:** Yes.[11]

Garvin's lawyer later focused on the details of the departure of Garvin and his cohorts from Southeastern and how that departure related to the boat:

> **Q:** Now, after they had withdrawn and after Mr. Garvin had used his boat and after this lawsuit was filed and an attachment was issued for this boat, you continued to use this boat in your advertising, did you not?
> **A:** Yes.
> **Q:** And, in fact, you continued to run the tournament with the boat, did you not?
> **A:** Yes.
> ....
> **Q:** So, after this boat was under attachment for this court, you continued to use the boat. In fact, one time you had it down at the Civic Coliseum for one of the occasions, for one of the elimination matches, didn't you?
> **A:** I had it down there once. I'm not sure it was after that time, but it was there on one occasion.[12]

* * *

The parties also focused some attention on the Southeastern Heavyweight Championship Belt in Garvin's possession. Fuller's complaint charged Garvin with the offense of conversion, which involves the wrongful exercise of control over the property of another. By keeping the belt, Garvin was clearly exercising control of the belt and treating it as his own. Thus, the key legal questions should have been (1) was the belt the property of Fuller and Southeastern Championship Wrestling? and (2) if so, did Garvin nonetheless have the legal right to retain possession?

Regarding the first question, Fuller testified that he, the sole shareholder of Southeastern Championship Wrestling, had paid for the actual belt. So, it seems farfetched to argue that Garvin legally owned the physical belt. Instead, Garvin was more likely what the law refers to as a "bailee," one who is given temporary possession, but not ownership, of a piece of property until the agreement between the parties ends. As the Tennessee Court of Appeals has explained, "bailees are not owners of the property, but merely temporary possessors."[13] (For example, when you take your clothes to the dry cleaner, the dry cleaner is a bailee of your clothes.) Fuller/Southeastern would have been the "bailor," the party that actually owns the property in question. Under the law, a bailor has the right to demand the return of the property from the bailee at any time. Thus, as the bailee, Garvin should have been legally obligated to return the belt to Fuller once Fuller demanded it.* The failure to do so amounts to an unlawful conversion.[14]

This, then, should have been a simple matter for Fuller. But for some reason, the parties descended into a discussion about the "rules" in the fictional world of professional wrestling regarding when a champion loses physical possession of a championship belt. It is unclear from the trial transcript whether the parties were trying to maintain kayfabe concerning transfer of the championship belt (despite having earlier exposed the business when it came to the boat tournament) or whether, for some reason, the parties thought the fictitious rules of professional wrestling contests might actually make a difference in a court of law.

Fuller explained on direct examination that if the champion loses a championship match, the belt is given to the winner. Also, if the champion refuses to participate in a match, the belt would be forfeited and there would a tournament to determine the new champion.[15] Reflecting on these

---

* While there is a long history of departing champions "dropping the belt" for leaving a promotion, there is also something of a history of champions doing what Garvin did: taking the belt with them to another promotion or, in some cases, making a public display of throwing away the belt.

2. Kayfabe and the Doctrine of Unclean Hands

IN THE CHANCERY COURT FOR KNOX COUNTY, TENNESSEE

NWA SOUTHEASTERN WRESTLING, INC.)
)
    Plaintiff,)
)
v.) No. 66591
)
RONNIE GARVIN)
) 3:20 P.M.
    Defendant.)

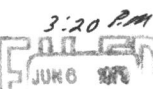

COMPLAINT

1. Plaintiff is a domestic corporation with its principal place of business located in Knoxville, Knox County, Tennessee.

2. Defendant is a resident of Knoxville, Knox County, presently residing at Apt. 1, Sunset Real Apts., Magnolia Avenue, Knoxville, Tennessee.

3. Recently plaintiff advanced to the defendant the sum of twelve thousand dollars ($12,000), with the understanding that the defendant would use said $12,000 as a down payment on the purchase of a 27 foot Bayliner pleasure boat and trailer. Plantiff avers that defendant in fact did use said $12,000 as a down payment on the purchase of such a boat and trailer.

4. Plaintiff has made demand upon defendant to repay to plaintiff said $12,000, but defendant has refused and the debt for which plaintiff sues is just, due, and unpaid.

5. Plaintiff avers that the defendant is about to remove himself and said 27 foot Bayliner boat and trailer from the State of Tennessee. Plaintiff further avers that if said 27 foot Bayliner boat and trailer is not attached, thus preventing the defendant from removing the same from the jurisdiction of this Court, then plaintiff will suffer irreparable harm.

PREMISES CONSIDERED, PLAINTIFF PRAYS AS FOLLOWS:

1. That the process issue and be served upon the defendant requiring him to appear and answer this Complaint, but his oath to his Answer is hereby expressly waived.

2. That the plaintiff recover from the defendant the sum of $12,000, plus interest.

The first court filing in Southeastern Championship Wrestling's suit against Ronnie Garvin in the Bayliner boat litigation. Garvin was extremely popular in Knoxville at the time, which may be how the local newspaper ended up covering the case.

```
            IN THE CHANCERY COURT FOR KNOX COUNTY, TENNESSEE

NWA SOUTHEASTERN WRESTLING, INC.,     :
                                      :
            PLAINTIFF,                :
                                      :
                                      :
VS.                                   :   NO. 66591
                                      :
                                      :
RONNIE GARVIN,                        :
                                      :
            DEFENDANT.                :
```

FILED MAR 1 7 1980
H. DAVID CATE, C. & M.

TRANSCRIPT OF PROCEEDINGS

FEBRUARY 13, 1980

WAGNER—BROWN COURT REPORTING
524-2841
P.O. BOX 2347
301 CUMBERLAND AVE.
KNOXVILLE, TN 37901

The trial transcript in the Bayliner boat litigation. Ron Fuller's lawyer referred to Fuller by his real name (Ronald Welch) during the trial.

2. Kayfabe and the Doctrine of Unclean Hands 23

events some 40 years later, Garvin agreed with this version of how championship belts were won and lost but argued that he had done nothing that should have required him to relinquish the belt: "I was always told that when I won the wrestling belt, it would be my property until somebody beat me for it.... The only other way I could lose the belt was if I refused to defend it against a legitimate challenger, and I never refused to defend it."[16]

Garvin's lawyer tried to advance this same theme during his cross-examination of Fuller. Garvin's lawyer suggested that Garvin had neither forfeited a match nor refused to defend the Southeastern title:

> **Q:** And Mr. Garvin won that belt, and he was the holder of that belt when he and the others left the employment of Southeast Championship Wrestling?
> **A:** Right.
> **Q:** Now, he has never forfeited a match, has he?
> **A:** Actually, yes, he did, the next night, Morristown, Tennessee. After he left, he forfeited the match. ... He did not show up, and he was the champion. He would have lost the belt by forfeit that night.
>
> ....
>
> **Q:** I believe that Mr. Garvin and some of the others have continued to offer to wrestle and make themselves available to wrestle and defend their championship titles, have they not?
> **A:** Not for Southeastern Wrestling, Incorporated, no.
> **Q:** They had the challenges in the newspapers to various of the members of Southeastern Championship Wrestling, had they not, and offered to defend their ability to win these matches?
> **A:** Yes.

The point Garvin's lawyer was attempting to make here was a weak one, even within the fictional world of professional wrestling. If, as Fuller claimed, Garvin failed to show up for a scheduled title defense, he forfeited the match and was no longer the champion under the fictional rules of professional wrestling competitions. And the fact that Garvin may have expressed a willingness to defend the Southeastern title after leaving Southeastern made little sense.* By this point, Garvin was a member of the rival organization All Star Championship Wrestling. He no longer had the right to defend the title of an organization he was no longer a member of. If, for example, the University of

---

* According to the allegations in a separate lawsuit that Fuller filed, All-Star Championship Wrestling continued to advertise Garvin as being the "Southeastern Champion" despite the fact that he no longer worked for the company. So, according to Fuller, not only was Garvin in wrongful possession of the physical belt, he and All Star were trading on the Southeastern name. *NWA Southeastern Wrestling, Inc. & Robert Welch a/k/a Robert Fuller v. All Star Championship Wrestling, Inc., Ronnie Garvin, Bob Orton, Jr., Bob Roop, and Ron Wright*, No. 67652, Complaint at 6–7 (Knox County Chancery Court Oct. 3, 1979).

Ronnie Garvin's receipt for the Bayliner.

Tennessee won the football championship for the Southeastern Conference (SEC) and then quit the SEC to join the Big 10, Tennessee could no longer claim to be able to defend the SEC championship. Yet, this is essentially what Garvin was doing.

But the point Garvin's lawyer was trying to make was also a weak one as a legal matter. Championship belts in the world of professional wrestling are purely symbolic devices used to further the fiction that there is actually a champion who has won a legitimate athletic competition. The reality, of course, is that the results of championship matches are predetermined. Professional wrestling also has a long history of choosing not to recognize title changes when, as in Garvin's case, it was inconvenient for an organization to do so.* Finally, wrestling promotions would sometimes publicize "phantom" title changes—title changes in matches that never actually occurred—when it was necessary to further some fictional storyline. In short, it made little sense from a legal standpoint for the lawyers in this case to argue about the fictional rules governing title changes in the world of professional wrestling. All that should have mattered is whether there was a bailor/bailee relationship between Fuller/the NWA and Garvin, in which case Garvin didn't have a legal leg to stand on.†

* * *

Part 3: In Which "Hands of Stone" Ronnie Garvin Accuses Ron Fuller of Having Unclean Hands

The plaintiff in a civil case bears the burden of presenting enough evidence that the finder of fact—usually the jury, but in this particular case, the judge—could find in the plaintiff's favor. Usually, once the plaintiff in a civil case presents their case, the defendant gets a chance to introduce their own evidence. But here, Garvin's lawyer made a motion to dismiss the case without even introducing any of his own evidence.

Instead, Garvin's lawyer argued that the case should be dismissed on the equitable doctrine of "unclean hands." This ancient principle is founded on the idea that, as expressed by a New Jersey court in 1793, "those who come into a court of justice must come with clean hands."[17] The United States Supreme Court has explained that "whenever a party who, as actor, seeks to set the judicial machinery in motion and obtain some remedy, has violated conscience, or good faith, or other equitable principle, in his prior conduct, then the doors of the court will be shut against him …; the court will refuse to interfere on his behalf, to acknowledge his right, or

---

* In fact, Southeastern Championship Wrestling did not publicly acknowledge that Garvin had won the title the night before he left the organization. Instead, the promotion pretended as if the title change had not occurred. Bobby Matthews, "Ron Garvin and Bob Roop: How Stealing the Title Led to a Rebellion," *Pro Wrestling Stories* https://prowrestlingstories.com/pro-wrestling-stories/ron-garvin-boob-roop-rebellion/.

† Interestingly, Garvin recalled having taken the witness stand and being asked how a wrestler can lose a title after winning it. According to the trial transcript, this never occurred; Garvin never testified at trial.

to award him any remedy."[18] In short, a court will not help a party when that party comes to the court with unclean hands concerning the matter in question.

One of the primary purposes of the unclean hands doctrine is to protect the integrity of the courts. As explained by one court, "allowing a plaintiff with unclean hands to recover in an action creates doubts as to the justice provided by the judicial system."[19] Examples of the application of the doctrine might include a breach of contract action where the plaintiff sues a defendant for breach of contract after persuading the defendant to enter into the contract through fraud or coercion or a legal malpractice claim against an attorney where the client had committed perjury in the original legal action.[20]

According to Garvin's lawyer, the entire transaction involving the boat was "full of deceit" and Fuller had come to the court seeking help with unclean hands.

> The public, by the own admission of the plaintiff's agent was going to be told that this boat had been purchased by Southeastern Championship Wrestling. The public was going to be told ... that this was a tournament.... It was being advertised as a tournament, when in actuality, even taking the plaintiff's testimony, it was pre-determined from the very beginning who was going to win the boat.
> The transaction is in deceit from its very beginning. The person seeking equity and seeking recovery in this court of equity has unclean hands.[21]

Whatever the weaknesses of Garvin's argument concerning ownership of the championship belt, the unclean hands argument was a strong one. Caught off guard, Fuller's lawyer responded by arguing that the unclean hands doctrine should not apply, but if it did, it applied with equal force to Garvin. After all, the lawyer argued, the boat tournament was Garvin's idea to begin with. He needed the money to get a boat, and he used the idea of a fictitious tournament to get his boat.[22]

Ultimately, Chancellor McDonald agreed with both parties. The court observed that the unclean hands argument raised a question of public policy.

> Should the courts of Tennessee be used as a means of enforcing contracts to carry out fixed wrestling matches? Viewed in that light the answer to the question certainly must be apparent. We don't think that the court should have any part of enforcing for Plaintiff or Defendant, for that matter, this type of contract. The public would lose all confidence in the courts if they became a part of this transaction.[23]

Instead, Chancellor McDonald concluded that the appropriate solution was to "leave the parties in exactly where they were when they came into the court." The court dismissed Fuller's complaint and resolved the attachment, giving Garvin his boat back. The court observed that normally where there had been a wrongful attachment, the victim would have a right to recover for any losses. But given the fact that Garvin himself had unclean hands, he would not be entitled to recover any such damages.[24]

Interestingly, the question of what should happen to the championship belt went unresolved. Chancellor McDonald failed to specifically address the issue, thus leaving Garvin in possession of the belt by default. Garvin managed to hold on to the belt over the ensuing decades before eventually selling it on eBay for $2,500 in 2005.[25]*

* * *

The *Knoxville News-Sentinel* reported on the trial at the time, noting Fuller's concession that the results of the Bayliner Boat Tournament had been pre-determined. In an article entitled "Judge Pins Fake Wrestling Scheme," the *News-Sentinel* accurately reported most of the details concerning Fuller's loan to Garvin.[26] Despite this, the lore surrounding this dispute has always been that Ron Fuller was unwilling to break kayfabe in order to prevail in his lawsuit.

In reality, *NWA v. Garvin* represents the beginning of the end of the kayfabe era. Prior to this case, active wrestlers and promoters were generally willing to commit perjury (or at least refuse to provide an answer) on the question of whether the results of wrestling matches were fixed. But the wrestling business was exposed that day in Chancery Court in Knoxville. Fuller apparently decided that he probably shouldn't lie under oath. Or perhaps he thought originally that he could avoid discussing the details of his "fake wrestling scheme" when he first filed suit. The complaint that Fuller initially filed with the court was lacking in details concerning the loan to Garvin. The complaint made no mention of the Bayliner Boat Tournament or even professional wrestling, other than to list NWA Southeastern Championship Wrestling as a party. Instead, it simply alleged that Fuller had loaned money to Garvin for the purchase of a boat and that Garvin had refused to repay the loan.[27] So, Fuller was initially able to avoid making any false statement to the court simply by omitting details concerning the loan. But when Fuller was sworn in as a witness and asked about the tournament, he went into the details of his arrangement with Garvin, including the true details of the Bayliner Boat Tournament.

---

* Looking back on the case, Garvin reportedly said that Chancellor McDonald threw out the case and suggested that Fuller and Garvin wrestle for the title. Bobby Matthews, "Ron Garvin and Bob Roop: How Stealing the Title Led to a Rebellion," *Pro Wrestling Stories* https://prowrestlingstories.com/pro-wrestling-stories/ron-garvin-boob-roop-rebellion/. If this happened, it doesn't appear in the trial transcript.

Court proceedings are designed to uncover the truth. The United States Supreme Court has explained that false testimony is a "flagrant affront to the truth-seeking function of adversary proceedings."[28] At Fuller's trial that day, the inherently false nature of kayfabe gave way to the truth-finding function of legal proceedings. What's more, by admitting that the outcomes of wrestling matches were pre-determined, Fuller had admitted to the court that he had "unclean hands," thereby precluding the ability to recover the $12,000 that Garvin clearly seems to have owed Fuller.

It is unclear why Fuller and his lawyer made the tactical decision to disclose the truth behind the pre-determined nature of the Bayliner Boat Tournament. Arguably, the fact that the boat was part of a promotion was irrelevant to the question of whether Garvin owed Fuller the money; as a legal matter, all that mattered was that Fuller had loaned money to Garvin and Garvin had not repaid the loan. So, theoretically, Fuller could have simply discussed the basic facts concerning his loan of the $12,000 to Garvin at trial without getting into the origins and details of the arrangement. By doing so, Fuller could have maintained kayfabe, protected the wrestling business, and testified truthfully.

There are several possibilities as to why the facts came out. One is that Fuller's lawyer simply didn't realize the significance of asking Fuller about the fact that the outcomes of the matches were pre-determined and caught Fuller off guard. Another is that Fuller didn't want to commit perjury and he and his lawyer didn't think that a newspaper reporter would show up to cover the trial and report what Fuller said.

A final possibility is that they concluded that if they didn't discuss the details surrounding the tournament, Garvin and his lawyer would have brought out those details themselves on cross-examination anyway. In theory, this should not have been a concern for Fuller. Garvin was still in the business and was bound by the code of silence as much as Fuller. But Fuller might have had reason to suspect that Garvin was willing to let the truth come out. For one thing, Garvin's cohorts had previously exposed the reality in the local paper that Fuller was actually the promoter of Southeastern. So, they had already demonstrated a willingness to break kayfabe. For another, Fuller might have surmised that Garvin was genuinely angry about the fact that Fuller had taken possession of Garvin's boat and was using it to promote the tournament. Garvin had unsuccessfully filed a motion seeking to prevent Fuller from attaching the boat and was undoubtedly unhappy when he learned that Fuller was using the boat as part of his promotion. Indeed, Garvin's lawyer was quick to bring up this point during cross examination, which might suggest that it was the strategy of Garvin's lawyer all along to raise the unclean hands defense.

Perhaps the clearest proof that Garvin might be willing to expose the true nature of the business was revealed some forty years later. Unbeknownst to Fuller at the time, Garvin and his cohorts recorded a bizarre video they referred to as "Plan B."[29] Each member of the group, including Garvin, stood before the camera and explained that the results of matches were pre-determined and that they had never had a "real" wrestling match in their professional lives. At the end, one of the members, Bob Roop disclosed the group's plans to record more videos in which more dark secrets of the business would be revealed. The video did not see the light of day for another forty years. The most logical explanation for why Garvin's group would record such a video in the first place would be to release the video to Fuller and other promoters he was aligned with as leverage in their ongoing territorial war. Fuller claims not to have known of the existence of the video at the time. While Fuller may have had no idea that the video existed, its existence supports any doubts that Fuller may have had at the time about Garvin's willingness to maintain kayfabe.

Regardless, at the end of the day, by deciding to sue Garvin, Fuller ensured that the truth behind the wrestling business would come out in court. In short, kayfabe fought the law that day. And the law won.

* * *

Conclusion

In February of 1989, the *New York Times* published a story reporting that a spokesperson for Vince McMahon's WWF had testified before the New Jersey legislature that professional wrestling was entertainment and not a legitimate athletic competition.[30] Wrestling was "sports entertainment." McMahon's willingness to let the cat out of the bag stemmed from his desire to no longer be subject to regulation by state athletic commissions. Following the *New York Times* story, the *New York Post* reported that just a few years earlier, Vince's wife Linda had testified under oath in Richard Belzer's lawsuit against Hulk Hogan that professional wrestling was entertainment rather than competition and that Vince McMahon had testified in the John Stossel case involving "Dr. D." David Schultz that the outcomes of wrestling matches were pre-determined.[31] In 1994, Vince McMahon and Hulk Hogan both testified as part of a trial involving the use of steroids by WWF wrestlers that professional wrestling was scripted. By the early 1990s, old-school promoters and performers were willing to acknowledge the truth about wrestling in court proceedings.

Ron Fuller's disclosure of the true nature of professional wrestling in a small promotion in East Tennessee didn't generate the same kind of headlines as the WWF's disclosure nearly a decade later. But the disclosures of Fuller and McMahon illustrate how the legal process helped bring about the death of kayfabe. Fuller's case also marked one of the last times that the legal doctrine of "unclean hands" could effectively be asserted in a legal proceeding involving professional wrestling. Once the wrestling business acknowledged that professional wrestling was entertainment and not sport, no party could argue that the business was committing a fraud upon the public and that any contracts that had been entered into were unenforceable.

Postscript: Kayfabe and Negligence

Crass v. Welch (1987)

Eight years after the Bayliner Boat Litigation, Ron Fuller found himself on the other side of a lawsuit in Knoxville. Now, he was the one being sued. But this time, Fuller went to great lengths to maintain kayfabe.

By 1986, Fuller had moved back to Knoxville and started a new promotion. One night in at the Knoxville Civic Coliseum, Fuller appeared as a manager for Mr. Wrestling 2, who was wrestling as a heel against babyface "the Bullet" Bob Armstrong. After Armstrong prevailed against Mr. Wrestling 2, Fuller dressed in a tuxedo, wearing a top hat, and carrying a cane, climbed into the ring to confront Armstrong. Fuller "accidentally" dropped his cane, Armstrong picked it up, and whacked Fuller over the head with it. The cane broke (or "exploded" as later alleged in court filings), and a piece flew out and injured a spectator. According to the spectator's complaint, a piece of the cane hit her "in the area of the eye causing her to suffer serious and permanent damage to her eye."[32] The spectator alleged that Fuller was negligent in allowing the piece of the cane to strike the plaintiff and in failing to guard against her injury.[33]

Prior to trial, the plaintiff's lawyer conducted a deposition of Fuller in which the lawyer asked numerous questions of Fuller under oath concerning the incident. Part of the lawyer's strategy appears to have involved exposing some of the realities of professional wrestling. Eight years earlier, Fuller had admitted under oath that the outcome of the matches he promoted were pre-determined. But this time around, Fuller wasn't having any of it.

Fuller explained under oath (and presumably with a straight face) that his job as Mr. Wrestling 2's manager that night was simply to "stay at ringside and offer advice."[34] Fuller would use the cane "if [he] could help the man [he] was managing."[35] And he "sure didn't" know in advance that Armstrong was going to hit him with the cane.[36] What made that last answer particularly unbelievable was that Armstrong was actually a part owner of Fuller's promotion, a fact the plaintiff's lawyer picked up on:

2. Kayfabe and the Doctrine of Unclean Hands   31

Q: Where did he hit you at?
A: He hit me in the side of the head.
Q: In the side of the head. Did you know that was going to happen?
A: No, I sure didn't.
Q: That had not been planned to happen that way?
A: No, it sure hadn't.
Q: Had it been planned to happen a different way?
A: It hadn't been planned at all. I would have been a fool to let a man hit me in the side of the head.
Q: So, you're telling me your business partner hit you on the side of the head with a cane over this wrestling match?
A: He sure did.
Q: Is that right?
A: He sure did.
Q: Well, did you go to the Police and make out an assault report on him?
A: I sure didn't, because immediately following that I think I got back in the ring and took the rest of the cane and hit him with, broke it on his back.[37]

Fuller had testified that the cane in question was made out light wood, "[a]lmost like a particle type, particle board" and that Fuller had purchased several of them at the same time.[38] When the plaintiff's lawyer suggested that one reason why a wrestler might buy one particle board cane (let alone several) is because such a cane would do less damage than a hard, wooden cane when he hit someone with it, Fuller testified that he never considered whether he was going to hit somebody with it (although he did acknowledge that he had hit multiple wrestlers with multiple canes in the past).[39]

Finally, the plaintiff's lawyer asked the question that everyone sitting in the deposition already knew the answer to and the question that Fuller had answered truthfully eight years earlier:

Q: ... Did you know who was going to win this match before it started?
A: No.[40]*

* * *

Trial in the matter was scheduled for two months after the deposition. Fuller made one more attempt to protect the business. He filed what is known as a motion *in limine*, a motion to exclude evidence from being introduced at trial. Specifically, Fuller sought to prevent the plaintiff's

---

* Bob Armstrong was also deposed, and his testimony was consistent with Fuller's. He testified (presumably with a straight face) to the incident as being triggered by Fuller being upset that Mr. Wrestling 2 had lost and that Armstrong and Fuller had exchanged insults following the match. *Kathleen Crass v. Ronald Welch a/k/a Ron Fuller & Southeastern Gulf Coast Wrestling, Inc.*, No. 1-141-87, Deposition of Joseph M. James, a/k/a Bob Armstrong at 30–31, Nov. 21, 1988.

lawyer from questioning Fuller "as to whether wrestling is a purely entertainment-oriented event."[41] The case never made it to trial, however, so Fuller never wound up being asked the question at trial. Perhaps realizing that he might be asked questions under oath about the wrestling business and that his lawyer could not ethically allow him to give knowingly false testimony, Fuller ended up settling the case.* Presented with a second opportunity, Fuller managed to maintain kayfabe (even if it probably cost him a little bit of money).

---

* By this point, Fuller was in the process of putting together an expansion minor league hockey team in Nashville and was perhaps eager to resolve the lawsuit. *Knoxville News-Sentinel*, March 1, 1989, at 34.

Chapter 3

Negligence and Battery

Massey v. Jim Crockett Promotions, Inc. (1990)

"The timorous may stay at home."
—*Murphy v. Steeplechase Amusement Co.*,
166 N.E. 173 (N.Y. 1929)

* * *

Part 1: Beautiful Bobby Gets Hit by a Foreign Object and Sweet Stan Beats Up a Fan

"It's great to be back here in Beckley, West Virginia ... home of black lung disease."

So Jim Cornette announced to the crowd on May 29, 1987, at the Raleigh County Armory in Beckley, West Virginia. Over 4,000 professional wrestling fans were on hand that night to watch the Midnight Express, managed by Cornette, take on the Rock 'n' Roll Express. It is tough to imagine a scenario that better encapsulates what professional wrestling was like in the 1980s, at least south of the Mason-Dixon line, than a match in a National Guard Armory between the Rock 'n' Roll Express and the Midnight Express. In many ways, this match and the events that transpired after it represent the last gasp of old-school professional wrestling before the flashier, safer, and more sanitized form of "sports entertainment" came to dominate the market and pave the way for modern professional wrestling.

The Rock 'n' Roll Express and the Midnight Express had feuded for years across various wrestling territories. The Rock 'n' Roll Express, consisting of Ricky Morton and Robert Gibson, were the babyfaces. While it was their job as babyfaces to make the entire crowd root for them, the team had special appeal to females and, in particular, teenage girls. One of the greatest tag teams of all time, the Rock 'n' Roll Express made getting beaten up by their opponents an art form. Neither Morton nor Gibson were particularly big, a fact they used to their advantage in getting over with fans. Ricky Morton in particular was gifted at eliciting sympathy from the crowd as opponents would use whatever deceptive tactics were necessary to pummel Morton into near-unconsciousness before he finally made the inevitable "hot tag" to Gibson, who would substitute in for Morton and clean house on the opponents.*

The Midnight Express were the heels that night in Beckley (and almost every night throughout their careers). The team consisted of "Beautiful" Bobby Eaton and "Sweet" Stan Lane, with Lane having replaced "Loverboy" Dennis Condrey in the team a few months earlier. As heels, it was their job to draw a negative reaction—or "heat"—from the crowd. To that end, Eaton and Lane were two of the best cheaters in the history of professional wrestling. But the Midnight Express also had a heat-generating machine in the form of manager Jim Cornette. Cornette was a motor-mouth manager with 1,001 insults at his disposal who did the talking for the team. Adopting the character of a spoiled mama's boy, Cornette accompanied the Midnight Express to the ring with a tennis racquet, which he would sometimes use (when the referee wasn't looking) to whack over the head of the babyfaces.

The organizational structure of the NWA was somewhat confusing at the time (and is discussed in more detail in the chapter covering Antitrust), but the biggest promoter in the Alliance at the time was, hands down, Jim Crockett Promotions, an organization based out of Charlotte, North Carolina. Crockett would sometimes run two shows a night, with the A-show featuring most of the promotion's biggest draws performing in larger venues and the B-show taking place in smaller towns in high school gymnasiums and National Guard Armories. The A-show that night (featuring Ric Flair and Dusty Rhodes among others), was taking place in Gainesville, Florida. The Rock 'n' Roll Express v. the Midnight Express match headlined the B-show in Beckley. Despite the fact that the teams were on the B-show, a match between the two remained a big draw in this part of the country.

* * *

It may be difficult to imagine today, but there was a time when a significant percentage of any professional wrestling crowd believed that at

---

* Morton was so skilled at this routine that the practice of allowing oneself to be beaten up in order to generate fan enthusiasm is still referred to in the business as "playing Ricky Morton."

least some of what they saw was on the level. Some fans were "smart" and knew that the outcomes of matches were pre-determined and that the performers were cooperating with each other rather than competing against each other. But there were still some fans who accepted that most of the violence they saw in the ring was legitimate. In the parlance of the business, these fans were "marks." And if a mark of that era believed that he or she was witnessing a violent injustice taking place in the ring, that fan was capable of being angered to the point of taking action. In 1974, for example, there had been what could legitimately be termed a riot at a professional wrestling event in Cleveland, Ohio, brought on by an attack by wrestler Johnny Powers and notorious heel Ox Baker on babyface Ernie Ladd.* Fans hurled folding chairs into the ring. Some entered the ring to get to Powers and Baker. One fan entered the ring brandishing a folding chair as a weapon and another attacked Powers before Powers made a run for it, running through the crowd toward the back of the arena. Baker also made a run for it, but ended up getting struck in the back of the head by a folding chair thrown by a fan as Baker attempted to jump a barricade.[1]

The Midnight Express: "Sweet" Stan Lane, Jim Cornette, and "Beautiful" Bobby Eaton circa 1987. From the author's collection.

By 1987, however, it had grown increasingly difficult to maintain the illusion that professional wrestling was on the level. Vince McMahon and his rival organization, the World Wrestling Federation (WWF) (later to become WWE) had softened professional wrestling's rough edges and

---

* There are videos of the incident on YouTube.

made his product more cartoonish and family friendly. It was tough to watch a WWF match during this time and think that there was much "real" about it. But in 1987, NWA wrestlers and promoters still adhered to kayfabe, the practice of creating the illusion for fans that the competition in the ring was legitimate. And there was still a sizable contingent of wrestling fans who believed that the wrestlers involved often legitimately hated each other. Real violence, at least outside the ring, remained a possibility.

Four thousand paying customers in Beckley, West Virginia, that night was a good draw. And at least some of those customers legitimately hated the collective guts of Cornette, Beautiful Bobby, and Sweet Stan.

* * *

The Rock 'n' Roll Express prevailed that night in Beckley. Things turned ugly after the match. There were four security guards stationed on the floor at each corner of the ring. After the match, these guards escorted the Rock 'n' Roll Express back to the locker room. The Midnight Express remained in the ring with Cornette, who, in the words of the West Virginia Supreme Court, was "inciting the passions of the crowd."[2] Fans responded by pelting the trio with "balled up paper cups with ice in them, coins, [and] general refuse."[3] At one point, an intoxicated fan jumped the barrier between the crowd and the ring and went after Cornette, telling security that no one was going to stop him from getting to Cornette. A security guard was able to put the would-be attacker in a full nelson while three other guards grabbed ahold of his arms and legs and removed him from the arena.[4] It was during this time that someone from the crowd threw a wooden "aisle marker" into the ring, hitting Beautiful Bobby Eaton in the neck and shoulder. Sweet Stan Lane immediately charged out into the crowd to confront the individual who he believed had thrown the aisle marker, one Roy Massey, a 61-year-old, 5'6" disabled coal miner weighing 149 pounds.[5] Massey was sitting near the aisle, some 15 rows up in the stands.[6] Witnesses would later attest that Massey hadn't thrown the marker, that it was instead some teenager who had fled the arena, never to be identified.[7] But Lane, believing Massey to be the offender, struck Massey in the face, fracturing the orbit of Massey's left eye and other facial bones.* Massey was hospitalized for eight days following the incident and underwent surgery.[8]

Following the incident, a security guard was told that the Midnight Express wanted to see Massey in their locker room. Several people accompanied Massey to the locker room. Massey assumed the team wanted to

---

* According to Lane, he grabbed Massey and then Massey struck out at Lane, prompting Lane to hit Massey.

apologize to him. If Massey actually believed that, he didn't realize that there wasn't that big of a difference between the character of Jim Cornette and the real-life Jim Cornette. It's clear that the Midnight Express continued to believe that Massey had thrown the aisle marker, because instead of apologizing, Cornette verbally abused Massey, calling him "a dirty son-of-a-bitch [who] ought to be kicked off the face of the earth," "a drunken hillbilly [who had] never worked a day in his life," and other insults.[9] The evidence was disputed as to whether Sweet Stan joined in the verbal abuse, but according to one witness, both Sweet Stan and Beautiful Bobby were "drawing back" like they were going to hit Massey.[10]

At this point, the legal system in Beckley began to get a workout. Lane, of all people, actually filed criminal charges against Massey for supposedly having thrown the aisle marker.[11] Massey ended up suing the group on a variety of theories, including a claim of malicious prosecution for the criminal charges Lane had filed against him and a claim of defamation for the assertion that he had thrown the aisle marker.* He also sued the security company on hand that night for the allegedly poor job it did. The case would eventually make its way to the West Virginia Supreme Court, but there were only two of Massey's claims that the court would discuss at any length: (1) the claim that Jim Crockett Promotions was negligent in failing to provide adequate security to protect Massey from injury and (2) the claim that Jim Crockett Promotions should be held liable for the battery committed by Lane since he was acting within the scope of his employment at the time. All totaled, Massey's claims amounted to over $6 million in alleged damages.[12]

After a complaint is filed in a civil action, the parties usually engage in "discovery," a process in which all of the parties engage in fact-finding under the supervision of the court. But here, the security company made a motion to dismiss the claims against it even before the discovery process began. The trial court granted the security company's motion, eliminating the company as a party. After discovery was complete, Jim Crockett Promotions moved for summary judgment. Summary judgment is a time-saving device that prevents claims from going to trial when there is no doubt as to how the decision should come out. This motion effectively argues that none of the material facts are in dispute and that based on the facts, no reasonable jury could find in favor of the party bringing the lawsuit. The trial court granted Crockett's summary judgment motion on the

---

* Massey also alleged that Cornette and the Midnight Express were negligent in making the crowd hate them so much that violence was likely to erupt. In other words, Massey claimed that Cornette and the Midnight Express did their jobs as heels so well that they were to blame for the violent atmosphere that eventually led to Massey's injuries. Sadly, this claim wasn't resolved in the ensuing litigation.

IN THE SUPREME COURT OF APPEALS OF WEST VIRGINIA

ROY MASSEY and RUBY MASSEY,

    Plaintiffs,

vs.   APPELLATE NO:

JIM CROCKET PROMOTIONS, INC., a North
Carolina corporation, licensed to do
business in the State of West Virginia;
STAN LANE a/k/a "Sweet Stan," Individually;
BOBBY LEE EATON a/k/a "Beautiful Bobby,"
Individually; JIM CORNETTE, Individually;
and STAN LANE a/k/a "Sweet Stan," and BOBBY
LEE EATON a/k/a "Beautiful Bobby," and JIM
CORNETTE, all doing business as "THE MIDNIGHT
EXPRESS" and FREEDOM SECURITY & DETECTIVE
AGENCY, INC., a West Virginia corporation;

    Defendants.

PETITION FOR AN APPEAL FROM A FINAL ORDER
OF THE CIRCUIT COURT
OF RALEIGH COUNTY, WEST VIRGINIA

Submitted by:

J. Robert Rogers, Esquire
801 Charleston National Plaza
Charleston, West Virginia 25301

Counsel for Plaintiffs;
ROY MASSEY and RUBY MASSEY

PETITION FOR AN APPEAL FROM A FINAL ORDER

OF THE

CIRCUIT COURT OF RALEIGH COUNTY, WEST VIRGINIA

AND

MOTION TO DOCKET APPEAL ON BEHALF OF PLAINTIFFS

Roy and Ruby Massey appeal the trial court's order in their claim against Jim Crockett Promotions and the Midnight Express.

grounds that Sweet Stan's attack upon Massey was not foreseeable and that he was not acting within the scope of his employment at the time.[13] Massey then appealed the decisions of the trial court to the West Virginia Supreme Court of Appeals.

* * *

Part 2—The Negligence Claims

Tort law is the area of law that is designed to provide a monetary remedy to those who suffer personal injuries.* The most common tort action is a negligence claim. To succeed on a negligence claim, a plaintiff (the person suing) must first establish that the defendant owed the plaintiff a duty of care and that the defendant breached that duty before establishing that the defendant's negligence caused the plaintiff's injuries.

Ordinarily, the law does not impose upon an individual any duty to affirmatively act on behalf of another person unless that individual's conduct has created a risk of harm to the person. So, if you see a person walking down the street about to fall into a large hole, you don't owe that person any duty to try to keep him or her from falling into the hole. If you dug the hole, thereby putting the other person at risk, that would be a different matter. But assuming your conduct didn't create the risk of the person falling into the hole to begin with, you probably don't owe him or her any duty of care.

That general rule is also true when an individual faces a risk of harm posed by some third person. So, if you see a car driving recklessly and about to crash into a pedestrian, you are probably under no obligation to do anything to try to prevent the accident from occurring. It might be a simple thing for you to pull the pedestrian out of the way or to try to get the attention of the driver to prevent the accident. But, again, generally speaking, the law doesn't impose upon you any duty to do a good deed.

One exception to both of those rules is where there is some sort of special relationship between the parties. As a paying customer, Massey was what the law refers to as a *business invitee*—someone on the premises to provide an economic benefit to the defendant. As a business invitee, Massey was owed a duty of reasonable care by Jim Crockett Promotions, which had rented out the Raleigh County Armory that night. That duty arguably included a duty not just to avoid conduct that creates an unreasonable risk of harm to the customers (say, for example, by having them sit on unstable chairs or rickety old bleachers that might collapse, as actually happened at several wrestling events over the years).[14] It would also include a duty to take reasonable steps to prevent harm from occurring from risks that Crockett *didn't* create—including a duty to *protect* the customers/business invitees from a risk of harm posed by the wrestlers and other spectators—at least where harm was foreseeable.[15]

What qualifies as "reasonable care" depends on the circumstances.

---

* A "tort" is a wrongful act for which the law allows monetary recovery. The word "tort" derives from the French language.

Where it is foreseeable that an incident might occur that could result in an injury, "reasonable care" would mean taking some sort of reasonable precaution to prevent the injury from occurring. The greater the risk of injury (or the more serious the injury might be) to a business invitee, the greater precaution the defendant should be expected to incur.

Massey alleged that the precaution Crockett should have taken that night was having more security present than just the fifteen guards who were there. Actually, Massey claimed that only four of the fifteen security guards were really providing security. The rest were taking tickets and guarding the entrances to make sure that no fans snuck in without paying. But whether Crockett was negligent in not having more security present depended on just how foreseeable it was that a spectator might be at risk of physical injury at the event.

* * *

> *The invitor could not reasonably assume that the instant invitees would comport themselves as would staid adults witnessing a religious drama.*
> —*Wright v. Downing*, 211 P.2d 211 (Utah 1949).

Past history would suggest that while injuries suffered by fans at wrestling events weren't exactly common, they weren't exactly rare either. Massey's lawsuit was hardly the first suit brought by a fan against a wrestler or a promoter.

In several older reported cases, spectators were injured as a result of fans becoming angered at events occurring in the ring. For example, in *Whitfield v. Cox*, a 1949 case, the plaintiff and her two young children attended a professional wrestling event in Norfolk, Virginia, home to a large naval base. There was a good-sized crowd of two to three thousand that night. The plaintiff had attended numerous matches in the past and was sitting ringside on this occasion. At some point during the night, there was a match between a wrestler with a sailor gimmick and a wrestler by the name of Coffield.* Coffield generated some heat that night by sticking the sailor with a pin during the match. This apparently angered some of the real sailors in the audience to the point that, in the words of the plaintiff, "it seemed like the whole crowd wanted to get in and fight."[16] One sailor in particular marched toward the ring, threatening to kill Coffield. In order to calm herself, the plaintiff did what anyone would do in these circumstances—buy some popcorn. While buying the popcorn, she was struck in the face by an empty whiskey bottle thrown by an unidentified member of the crowd.

---

* "Coffield" was probably Jim Coffield, an old-time heel who worked in Kansas City and the southeast during this time.

The plaintiff sued the promoter, alleging that the promoter was negligent either in not having enough security present or in not maintaining order during the matches.* The courts in these kinds of cases generally had some sympathy for promoters, stating that promoters were only required to exercise *reasonable* care for the safety of their customers, not *perfect* care. For example, in another case involving a spectator injured by a flying whiskey bottle, a Florida appellate court explained that a wrestling promoter cannot realistically be expected to guarantee the safety of their customers. "To apply such a high degree of vigilance would make a public amusement impossible because of the expense of guards, time for searching customers to discover possible weapons, etc."[17]

In *Whitfield*, the Virginia Supreme Court pointed to the fact that the promoter had thirteen police officers and nine other individuals providing security that night as evidence of the fact that the promoter had exercised reasonable care. While there was conflicting testimony about whether drinking was taking place among the crowd (and the fact that the plaintiff was hit with an empty whiskey bottle would certainly tend to support the position that there was at least some drinking going on), the court noted that no alcoholic beverages were sold on the premises; soft drinks were served in paper cups instead of bottles; patrons found to have whiskey on their person were required to check it; and the crowd was no more disorderly than on any other night.[18] Short of searching every patron for objects that might be used to injure other patrons or "having enough employees to watch each patron and prevent one from injuring another," the court believed that "the measures taken by the defendant to protect his patrons were all that could reasonably be required."[19]

There is also some suggestion in the court decisions in these kinds of cases that spectators at professional wrestling events assume a certain amount of risk by attending an event. In *Whitfield*, for example, the Virginia Supreme Court stated, "It was not the duty of the defendant to keep the crowd quiet," and "[t]he antics of the crowd seemed to be part of the attraction."[20] The plaintiff, a regular attendee of the matches, knew that "these wrestling matches are not quiet and dignified affairs" and that the behavior of the spectators "was not always gentle, nor their speech always refined."[21] The court cited a famous New York decision from two decades earlier involving a customer who was injured on an attraction (known as "the Flopper") at an amusement park.[22] The plaintiff had watched other customers ride "the Flopper" and flop to the ground. So, as the New York

---

* The promoter, James Whitfield, was also a wrestler who went by the ring names "Bill Lewis," "Captain Bluebeard," and "Billy Whiskers" and promoted shows in the area under the NWA banner.

Court of Appeals observed, "[a] fall was foreseen as one of the risks of the adventure."[23] Despite this, the plaintiff sued the operator of the Flopper when he flopped. The court was unmoved and explained that the plaintiff could not recover because he had knowingly assumed the risk of flopping. The plaintiff boarded the Flopper to experience a thrill associated with the risk of falling; he "was not seeking a retreat for meditation."[24] In the court's view, "The very name, above the gate, 'the Flopper,' was warning to the timid. ... The timorous may stay at home."[25] In *Whitfield*, the Virginia Supreme Court viewed the two cases as being similar.[26] By attending a professional wrestling match which she knew to be unruly affairs, the plaintiff had assumed some risks, presumably, including being hit by flying whiskey bottles.

This, of course, is nonsense. It is one thing to say that one who watches multiple patrons fall down on a ride called "the Flopper" knowingly assumes the risk of falling. It is something else to say that one who pays to attend a professional wrestling event—even at the time when the rough edges of professional wrestling had not been smoothed—knowingly takes his or her chances of getting hit in the head by a flying whiskey bottle or injured through some other random act of violence. That's not to say that the promoters in these cases were negligent; they may not have been. But it's quite a stretch to say that a wrestling fan assumed the risk of being injured by some drunken fan just by buying a ticket.

This argument that paying customers assumed some risk of being injured by attending a wrestling event arguably carried more weight in cases in which a spectator chose to sit at ringside and was injured when the action in the ring spilled out to ringside. For example, in a 1965 case from North Carolina, a fan sitting at ringside was injured when one of the wrestlers was tossed over the top rope and into the space between the ring and the front row of spectators. There was no barrier between the ring and the crowd, and the wrestler lost his balance and "staggered into and fell against" the spectator, resulting in injuries to the spectator.[27] The spectator alleged that the promoter was negligent in failing to have installed any type of barrier between the ring and the crowd. The North Carolina Supreme Court observed that the plaintiff was aware that there were no barriers at ringside by virtue of having attended live wrestling events once a week basis for several months prior. And it was also common for wrestlers to be thrown out of the ring at matches. With little analysis, the North Carolina Supreme Court concluded that the promoter had not breached any duty of reasonable care by failing to install a barrier.[28] What ultimately seems to be driving the decision is the assumption that the spectator assumed some risk of being injured by choosing to sit in the front row. In the court's view, being fallen upon by a 240-pound wrestler

3. Negligence and Battery 43

was apparently one of the inherent risks one assumes when one decides to sit front row at a professional wrestling event, much in the same that getting hit by a foul ball is an inherent risk of going to a baseball game.* Sitting ringside at a professional wrestling event is dangerous. The timorous may stay home.

Similarly, some courts displayed a tendency to let the customs of the wrestling business dictate what qualified as reasonable care, thereby allowing promoters to set low safety standards. In *C. & M. Promotions v. Ryland*, another case from Virginia in 1967, a jury awarded a plaintiff $7,500 for injuries suffered at a professional wrestling event in Henrico, Virginia.[29] Following a match, the manager for one of the tag teams, Homer O'Dell, came into ring and began beating the opposing team with a cane.† This apparently enraged a large number of spectators to the point that they headed toward the ring, filling up the space between the ring and the ringside seats. While attempting to remove a rowdy fan from the area, a police officer who was providing security accidentally bumped into the plaintiff, causing the plaintiff to fall out of his chair and injure himself.

The plaintiff alleged that the promoter failed to exercise reasonable care by failing to install a railing or a barrier between the ring and the ringside seats to keep the customers safe. On appeal, the Virginia Supreme Court held that the exercise of reasonable care did not require the installation of a barrier.[30] In reaching this conclusion, the court relied heavily upon the fact that such barriers were not customary at wrestling matches. Since it was not customary for promoters to install barriers, the exercise of reasonable care did not require the promoter in this case to install one.[31] The court reversed the decision and threw out the jury verdict.

This is also nonsense. Industry custom may certainly help determine what care is reasonable under the circumstances. But an industry cannot define for itself what qualifies as reasonable care.[32] If it could, it might set dangerously low safety standards for itself with impunity. The fact that

---

* Other courts disagreed with the idea that being landed upon by a wrestler or a referee while at ringside is an inherent risk of attending a wrestling show. *See Dusckiewicz v. Carter*, 52 A.2d 788, 791 (Vt. 1947) (concluding fan did not assume the risk of being injured by a wrestler who had been thrown outside the ring and onto the fan); *Klause v. Nebraska State Bd. of Agriculture* 35 N.W.2d 104 (Neb. 1948) ("While it is shown that participants and referee often get out of the ring yet it is not shown that a known characteristic of such a departure from the regular wrestling precincts is the knocking of the referee into the laps of spectators."); *Silvia v. Woodhouse*, 248 N.E.2d 260 (Mass. 1969) (stating that "the risk of a wrestler being thrown out of the ring was much less open and obvious" than the risk of getting hit by a foul ball at a baseball game).

† O'Dell was a noted heel manager in the territory, who, according to legend, had, in real life, once been arrested for firing a gun into a fresh-water lake in an attempt to ward off invading submarines.

other promoters failed to install barriers doesn't mean that it was reasonable to not install barriers.

The more important questions were how foreseeable it was that a spectator might be injured at an event and how much effort would it take for the promoter to prevent the injury. Again, there is a long history in professional wrestling of angry fans causing injury to those around them, including wrestlers. There are dozens of stories from the kayfabe era involving professional wrestlers being attacked by fans. In 1976, for example, heel wrestler Ole Anderson was stabbed by a 79-year-old woman sitting at ringside as Anderson left the ring and headed back to the locker room in Greenville, South Carolina. Anderson was in surgery for four hours following the attack.[33] In an incident in Greeneville, Tennessee (not South Carolina), East Tennessee heel Ron Wright so incensed the crowd that he was attacked by multiple spectators on his way to the dressing room, resulting in a stabbing that required 192 stitches.[34]* In 1971, a fan jumped a guardrail at the Boston Garden, climbed into the ring, and stabbed heel Blackjack Mulligan, resulting in Mulligan receiving 100 stitches. Another wrestler at the Garden was injured when a fan threw a dart into the ring, hitting the wrestler in the leg. Promoters eventually placed plexiglass barriers around the ring at the Garden to prevent similar incidents from occurring.[35] And, of course, there is the Ox Baker/riot story mentioned earlier.

Admittedly, all of these incidents resulted in injuries to wrestlers, not spectators.† But there were plenty of lawsuits filed as a results of injuries sustained by fans from flying whiskey bottles, attacks by one fan upon another, and attacks by wrestlers upon fans where wrestlers believed they had been attacked by fans.[36] In light of the lawsuits, it probably wasn't too hard for promoters to imagine innocent bystanders getting injured near ringside in a melee as fans decided to take justice into their own hands and wrestlers defended themselves. In fact, in the Massey case, Jim Crockett himself testified in a deposition that Jim Crockett Promotions had actually been sued several times by fans who had been injured at wrestling matches.[37]

* * *

---

* Reports conflict as to how many stitches Wright received, but since this is a book about professional wrestling where tall tales are common, I went with the highest number that I found. Suffice it to say, Wright required some stitches that night. Videos on YouTube show Wright with a long scar down his back later in life.

† It's worth noting that sometimes the wrestlers themselves filed claims against unruly fans. For example, a September 16, 1979, story in the *Knoxville News-Sentinel* reported that heel wrestler Boris Malenko filed suit against one Dennis J. Jump of Madisonville, TN, after Jump allegedly "reached across the restraining ropes and assaulted and battered" Malenko following a match in the Knoxville Civic Coliseum.

3. Negligence and Battery 45

I got a special announcement, by the way. Would the woman who left her eleven kids over at the football stadium please go pick 'em up? They're beating the West Virginia University Mountaineers 21–7.
—Jim Cornette, taunting wrestling fans in West Virginia.[38]

So, did Jim Crockett Promotions exercise reasonable care toward business invitees like Massey? Or did it breach this duty by failing to provide adequate security?

There were fifteen security guards on duty that night. According to a stockholder of the security company, the Raleigh County Armory (presumably via Jim Crockett Promotions) had originally requested only twelve security guards. But the stockholder knew from past experience that he needed fifteen. While there may have been fifteen security guards in the building, according to Massey, there were actually only four guards actively providing security that night. The rest were guarding the doors to the arena or taking tickets.* What's more, the four security guards were busy escorting the Rock 'n' Roll Express back to their locker room when the incident with Massey and Sweet Stan Lane occurred. Indeed, the reason why Jim Cornette and the Midnight Express were still in the ring when Beautiful Bobby Eaton was struck by the aisle sign is because they were waiting for security to return and escort them back to their locker room. So, while it is not entirely clear how many security guards were available to provide security when the incident occurred, it sounds like most, if not all, of them were otherwise occupied when the sign was thrown. As a result, there were no security guards in the area at the time the aisle marker was thrown and Lane pummeled Massey.[39]

What's more, it was actually common at the time for promoters to arrange for law enforcement to provide some security at wrestling events. Indeed, some venues required that a promoter hire off-duty uniformed officers to provide security.[40] Jim Cornette himself says it was customary for police officers to escort wrestlers to and from the ring based on the very real potential for danger.† While an industry cannot insulate itself from liability by establishing its own safety standards, when a member of that industry fails to follow the industry's standard, that is typically considered quite strong evidence of the failure to exercise reasonable care.

---

  * Why eleven people were needed to watch the doors and take tickets during the last match of the night when fans were about to go home is anyone's guess.

  † Cornette says that he was once advised by a police officer in Little Rock, Arkansas, who was providing security, to wear a bullet-proof vest while at the venue.

At the same time, it was also not uncommon for promoters to try save a few bucks while providing pretty flimsy security. Jim Cornette tells the story of being attacked during a match in Gainesville, Georgia, while Cornette was outside the ring. The only thing separating the angry crowd from Cornette was a clothesline tied so loosely that people could step over the line. Not surprisingly, a drunk fan accosted Cornette, who responded by (legitimately) whacking the fan in the face with his tennis racquet.[41*]

The past history of incidents at wrestling events and the common practice of providing security to get the heels back to the dressing room safely suggests pretty strongly that the risk of an injury to a wrestler or a fan resulting from some sort of fan hostility toward a wrestler was foreseeable enough that a reasonable promoter would provide enough security (1) to keep the wrestlers reasonably safe while in the ring and while moving to and from the ring and (2) to keep the crowd reasonably safe by providing crowd control in the event that the crowd became unruly. Whether the appropriate number of security guards was four or fifteen or some other number is the sort of question we typically allow juries to decide based on the evidence presented. But with a crowd of 4,000 on hand, many of whom were predictably going to be riled up during the night, it sounds like Jim Crockett Promotions was trying to skimp on security by not paying for a law enforcement presence or at least a few more security guards. As such, a reasonable jury could definitely find that Jim Crockett Promotions had failed to exercise reasonable care by failing to provide adequate security. The West Virginia Supreme Court of Appeals agreed and reversed the lower court's decision to grant summary judgment to Jim Crockett Promotions.

Thus, it would be for a jury to determine whether Jim Crockett Promotions was negligent in not providing increased security that night in Beckley. If the jury found that Crockett was negligent, it would then be up to the jury to determine whether this negligence was the legal cause of Massey's injuries. For example, it would have been up to the jury to decide whether adequate security would have prevented the injuries Massey suffered. But Jim Crockett Promotions was potentially on the hook for allegedly skimping on the price of adequate security that night.

* * *

---

* There are numerous reported instances of Cornette using his tennis racquet in self-defense after being accosted by irate fans, some of which resulted in criminal charges being filed against Cornette.

Part 3: The Battery Claim Against Sweet Stan Lane and the Vicarious Liability Claim Against Jim Crockett Promotions

Massey also sued Sweet Stan Lane for battery. This was probably going to be a slam dunk claim for Massey. To recover for the tort of battery, the plaintiff must prove that the defendant acted with the intent to cause a harmful or offensive contact and that such a contact resulted. Lane intentionally punched Roy Massey in the face. That's a battery. The fact that Lane thought Massey had thrown something into the ring did not give him the legal right to pummel Massey. Lane suggested in his deposition that he struck Massey because he thought Massey was about to strike him first, so he was acting in self-defense.[42] There are two problems with this argument. The first is that Lane had grabbed Massey's arm when Lane approached Massey, which meant that even if Massey was about to try to hit Lane, Massey himself was acting in self-defense by that point. The second problem is that self-defense only works as a defense where the force used was not excessive. It's hard to see how the 6-foot, 245-pound Sweet Stan could have reasonably believed that he needed to punch the 5'6", 149-pound, 61-year-old Massey so hard that he broke five bones in Massey's face.* That seems excessive. So, Massey probably had Lane dead to rights on the battery claim.†

The reason why any of this matters is because Massey also alleged that Jim Crockett Promotions—which undoubtedly had deeper pockets than Sweet Stan Lane—should be held vicariously liable for Lane's battery of Massey. Vicarious liability is a form of liability in which an employer is held responsible for the wrongful acts of its employees. The employer is not liable because the employer did anything wrong. Instead, the employer is liable because one of its employees committed a wrongful act while in the scope of employment and the law deems it just to hold the employer responsible. Courts have offered several justifications for holding an employer liable for the torts of its employee, including the arguments that vicarious liability is proper since the employer has control over the employee and is profiting from that ability to control and the fact that vicarious liability makes it more likely a victim will ultimately be compensated since employers usually have insurance or at least deeper pockets than their employees.

---

* According to a brief filed in court, Massey had just gotten out of the hospital, where he had lost 30 pounds while being treated for black lung disease.

† Just a year earlier, wrestler Hacksaw Jim Duggan had similarly tried to claim self-defense after he punched a fan following a match. His self-defense argument failed for these same reasons. *Sills v. Mid-South Sports, Inc.*, 550 So. 2d 909, 912–13 (La. Ct. App. 1989).

Jim Crockett Promotions moved for summary judgment on the grounds that Lane was not acting within the scope of his employment when he attacked Massey. The trial court agreed. So, Massey appealed this decision to the West Virginia Supreme Court of Appeals.

* * *

Was Lane acting within the scope of employment when he punched out Roy Massey? For an act to be within the scope of employment, the employee's acts must (1) generally be of the kind he is employed to perform, (2) occur within the general time and location of the employee's job, and (3) be motivated, at least in part, by a purpose to serve the employer.[43] In other words, if Lane's act of punching Massey was too far removed from the kind of conduct he was employed to perform or if he was motivated solely by personal interests in punching Massey, his actions were not within the scope of employment and Jim Crockett Promotions could not be held vicariously liable.

In most workplaces, committing a battery is pretty clearly not within the scope of one's employment. But a professional wrestling event in the 1980s in the NWA was not like most workplaces. The West Virginia Supreme Court, either feigning ignorance of the nature of professional wrestling or betraying stunning actual ignorance, questioned whether it was part of Lane's job "to provoke and incite the spectators at the wrestling exhibition."[44] This was, of course, exactly what Lane's job as a heel entailed. It may not have been in Lane's job description to run into the stands and punch a fan, but it was unquestionably his job as a heel to provoke and incite the fans to the point of anger.

Courts are willing to find that a battery is within the scope of an individual's employment where violence can be expected due to the nature of the job. The classic example would be the bouncer who uses excessive force in removing an unruly patron; the force may have been excessive, but it is in the nature of a bouncer's job to sometimes use force. So, some violence is to be expected. And courts are sometimes willing to treat the use of force as being within the scope of employment where the force is triggered by an employment-related event, like where a manager reprimands an employee and then things turn physical.[45]* Given the threat of fan violence that heel wrestlers routinely faced at the time, it certainly wasn't out of the question to think that a heel might defend himself or retaliate after believing he had been attacked by a fan. For decades before, wrestlers used force to defend themselves when attacked by fans.[46]

---

* For an extreme version of this principle, see *LeBrane v. Lewis*, 292 So. 2d 216 (La. 1974) (holding that supervisor who stabbed subordinate on company premises in the course of a work-related dispute acted within the scope of employment).

3. Negligence and Battery

In fact, there were a few older decisions that explored this question of whether a professional wrestler's attack on a fan amounted to conduct within the scope of employment. In *Langness v. Ketonen*, heel wrestler Skagway Clements threw a "very spectacular" tantrum in the ring after being disqualified in a match against Myron Cox.[47] As part of the tantrum, Clements jumped up and down and kicked his feet out. The plaintiff and her husband left their third-row seats during the tantrum and proceeded to walk past the ring on their way to the exit, at which point the plaintiff was kicked in the face by Clements. There was disputed testimony as to whether Clements accidentally struck the plaintiff or whether Clements was responding after the plaintiff had taken off her shoe and struck Clements with it.[48] Either way, the court concluded, the jury could have found Clements was acting within the scope of employment as a heel:

> The jury could have found, from the evidence, that Clements was under instructions to put on a "tantrum" for the purpose of creating excitement and the "spectacular" display to which one witness referred. If, pursuant to such an instruction, Clements took it into his head to kick back towards spectators moving along the aisle, then that would be sufficient to support a finding that the assault was committed while he was acting within the course of his employment. It is not necessary to show that the employer specifically instructed his employee to commit an assault.[49]

A 1940 case from California actually has facts somewhat similar to those in *Massey*.[50] There, a wrestler named La Verne Baxter "suddenly and, apparently without provocation, jumped from the ring at the southwest corner thereof, and running toward appellant deliberately struck him over the head with a chair, inflicting painful injuries upon him."[51] According to the court, it was "clearly established" that the attack "had no connection whatsoever" with the wrestling event (although it's hard to understand why Baxter would have attacked a fan with a chair unless there was some connection).[52] Since there was no connection between the attack and the employment, the promoter could not be held vicariously liable.

In *Massey*, the trial court judge concluded that Jim Crockett Promotions could not be held vicariously liable because Sweet Stan Lane was not acting within the scope of his employment. According to the judge, Lane's attack was "actuated solely by his anger and was done in the spirit of malice and should be considered personal to him."[53] There is no doubt that Lane's attack was actuated by his anger. But his anger arguably arose from the performance of his job, a job that triggered real violence on the part of customers and workers alike often enough that it wasn't terribly surprising when it happened. In other words, this was not a purely personal beef that Lane had with Massey, having no connection to the match that night. It was a beef that was triggered directly by Lane's performance of his job. Moreover, the attack occurred at what was effectively Lane's workplace while he was effectively still on the clock. In short, there is a decent argument to be made that Lane was acting within the scope of his employment when he attacked Massey.

The West Virginia Supreme Court of Appeals may not have been "smart" to the realities of professional wrestling, but it picked up on this reality. The court correctly held (albeit without much explanation) that there was an issue to be resolved as to whether Lane was acting within the scope of his employment. Therefore, it denied Jim Crockett Promotions' motion for summary judgment on the vicarious liability claim.

* * *

Part 4: The Finish

I'd never gone to one of them before. My kids kept asking me and asking me, "Daddy, let's go over one time." I'm never going back to another one.
—Roy Massey, discussing the incident afterward.[54]

By overruling the trial court's decision to grant summary judgment in favor of Jim Crockett Promotions and the Midnight Express, the West Virginia Supreme Court was effectively placing the case back on track to go to trial. Over four years after the incident that night at the National Guard Armory, with trial rapidly approaching and Jim Crockett Promotions potentially facing a $6 million jury verdict, the parties agreed to a settlement. Massey ended up receiving $400,000.[55]

The settlement may have been facilitated by the realities behind the scenes. By the time of the settlement, media mogul Ted Turner had bought out Jim Crockett Promotions, and Jim Cornette and Sweet Stan Lane had left the promotion. Cornette was just a few months away from launching his own wrestling promotion, Smoky Mountain Wrestling, for which Lane would wrestle. As such, Cornette and Lane had no incentive to protect Jim Crockett Promotions (or Ted Turner) during any trial. Indeed, Cornette has since suggested on a wrestling podcast that he would have "stooged out" Jim Crockett Promotions for its handling of the event that night in Beckley had the case gone to trial.

* * *

Nearly 20 years after *Massey v. Jim Crockett Promotions, Inc.* settled, an event occurred at an NBA game that paralleled what took place in

Beckley that night. A fight broke out between members of the Detroit Pistons (the hometown babyfaces) and the Indiana Pacers (the visiting heels) that incensed the crowd. One member of the crowd was angered to the point that he threw a foreign object (in this case, a drink) at star player and noted professional basketball heel Ron Artest of the Pacers. Artest responded by going out into the crowd at the Palace in Auburn Hills, Michigan, and physically assaulting the wrong fan. Things got even more out hand at that point and more violence ensued.

The incident—dubbed "Malice at the Palace"—resulted in a lawsuit against Artest and his employer, the Indiana Pacers, among others.[56] It also resulted in widespread shock and horror among the public at large, which unlike professional wrestling fans, were unaccustomed to seeing violence spill out into the crowd. Roy Massey did not live to see the Malice at the Palace institute or the resulting litigation.* But for the other participants that night Beckley, the incident and the legal issues it raised should have been decidedly familiar.

---

* Massey passed away in 1998. https://twitter.com/thejimcornette/status/1082640189019836417.

Chapter 4

Antitrust and Interference with Contractual Relations

The Territory System v. Competition Law

> Every contract, combination in the form of trust or otherwise, or conspiracy, in restraint of trade or commerce among the several States, or with foreign nations, is declared to be illegal. Every person who shall make any contract or engage in any combination or conspiracy hereby declared to be illegal shall be deemed guilty of a felony....
> —Sherman Act, §1.

> Every person who shall monopolize, or attempt to monopolize, or combine or conspire with any other person or persons, to monopolize any part of the trade or commerce among the several States, or with foreign nations, shall be deemed guilty of a felony....
> —Sherman Act, §2.

> "It's like a Mafia," said Randy Savage, an ICW wrestler. "Wrestling is a monopoly. They (established promoters) get together in a room like this and divide up the country."
> —John Woestendiek, "Wrestling's 'Outcasts' Looking for Respect Riches," *Lexington Herald-Leader*, 30, March 3, 1981.

* * *

Part 1: A Brief History of Antitrust Law

The late 19th century in the United States was known as the Gilded Age, a time when vast economic growth revolutionized American society through industrial power and simultaneous population growth.[1] Much of the wealth creation during this time was concentrated in the hands of a relatively small number of corporations, thereby widening the wealth gap in the country. These corporations were able to accomplish this feat, in part, through the use of anti-competitive practices.

Competitors within a particular field would sometimes coordinate their efforts in an effort to limit competition within the field and increase prices.[2] This coordination would sometimes include agreements between competitors to set prices at a certain level and to allocate customer territories to particular competitors within the group.[3] Each member of this group (or "cartel") was still responsible for running its own business. But the idea, as described by one author, was "that if the contracting members adhere to the agreement, they will make more profits than they would in the absence of the agreement."[4] The members of these organizations would also sometimes agree to share resources as part of a pooling agreement in order to increase profits and limit outside competition.[5]

In an effort to put a stop to these and other forms of anti-competitive practices, Congress passed the Sherman Act in 1890.[6] Section 1 of the Act prohibits a business from entering into a contract, "combination," or conspiracy in restraint of trade. In the words of the Supreme Court, the Act prevents agreements that are "unreasonably restrictive of competitive conditions."[7] Such anti-competitive practices include agreements not to do business with one who does business with another competitor (called group boycotts); to fix employee wages at a set price so as to suppress employee wages (called wage-fixing schemes); and to divide a market between the members up into exclusive territories.[8] Section 2 of the Act prohibits attempts "to monopolize any part of the trade or commerce" among states, whether by an individual firm or through an agreement between firms.[9]

The Department of Justice (DOJ) has the authority to enforce the provisions of the Act. The federal Clayton Act gives private parties the authority to bring civil actions against parties who violate the Sherman Act. State attorneys general also have the authority to bring actions to enforce the provisions of the Act.[10]

Part 2: The National Wrestling Alliance and Antitrust Law

In the 1940s, there were wrestling promoters scattered across the country. Recognizing the benefit of sharing talent to maintain fan interest in a particular region, a group of midwestern promoters began working together. In time, these five midwestern promoters—Orville Brown

(Kansas City), Max Clayton (Omaha), P.L. "Pinky" George (Des Moines), Sam Muchnick (St. Louis), and Tony Stecher (Minneapolis)—banded together in 1948 to form the National Wrestling Alliance (NWA).

The group later agreed upon a plan of action that would serve as a how-to guide for members of the organization to develop and maintain the territory system that would remain in effect for roughly the next 40 years. As recorded in the minutes of an early meeting, several of the agreed-upon principles of the organization were blatantly illegal under federal antitrust law, either on their face or as applied by the members:

> 1. That this organization be a cooperative group in wrestling with each member to be free to run his existing territory as he sees fit without the interference of any other member of this group, and at no time be forced to pay any booking fee to any member of this group or to anyone else.
> 2. That all existing territories run by members of this group be respected and protected by the organization as a whole from any outside invasion of rights. Members of this group to do all in their power to help each with talent.
> 3. This organization to recognize only one heavyweight and one junior-heavyweight champion and champions of any kind recognized by this group shall at no time demand or get a fee for wrestling bouts acceding [sic] the usual 10%.....
> ....
> 9. This organization will act as its own governing body insofar as the conduct and actions of its wrestlers. If any wrestler does anything detrimental to the sport of wrestling, or detrimental to the interests of a promoter, he shall be suspended by that promoter immediately after he completes his bookings. That promoter shall immediately notify all of the members of the Alliance, and those members shall also bar this wrestler from their territories. The only way he may be reinstated as a wrestler in good standing with the organization is by clearing himself with the promoter whom he injured. When he does so and the promoter notifies the Alliance, this wrestler becomes eligible for future bookings. Notification of reinstatement should be made to the Secretary-Treasurer.[11]

The agreement between the members of the National Wrestling Alliance was exactly the sort of agreement that the Sherman Act was meant to prevent. Under the terms of the agreement, the promoters were declaring that the territory in a member operated "belonged" to that member and that no other member could run shows there. In antitrust terms, they had created what is known as a horizonal territorial agreement.

A *vertical* territorial agreement is an agreement whereby a seller agrees to sell its product downstream only to a distributor within a particular territory. For example, imagine that Company A manufactures television sets. Company A agrees to distribute its television sets only to Company B, and Company B agrees to only resell the sets within a particular state. So, Company B is the exclusive distributor of Company A's television sets within the state. There is nothing *per se* illegal about this type of vertical territorial agreement under the Sherman Act.[12] In this example, the distribution agreement makes it easier for Company A to manage the distribution of its product, and nothing in the agreement prevents other manufacturers of television sets from selling their own products within the state.

In contrast, *horizontal* restraints involve an agreement between competitors at the same level of the market. Think Apple and Microsoft or Ford and Chevrolet.[13] A horizontal territorial agreement (also known as a horizontal territorial allocation) is, in the words of the Supreme Court, "an agreement between competitors at the same level of the market structure to allocate territories in order to minimize competition." So, imagine if Ford and Chevrolet agreed that Florida "belonged" to Ford and that Texas "belonged" to Chevrolet. Because these kinds of agreements reduce or eliminate competition, they ultimately harm consumers due to the lack of freedom of choice concerning the goods or services offered and overall higher prices.[14] Such agreements "are naked restraints of trade with no purpose except stifling of competition" and "are *per se* violations of the Sherman Act."[15]

The agreement between the members of the NWA is a classic example of a horizontal territorial agreement. The members set up exclusive territories for the specific purpose of preventing competition on the part of non–Alliance promoters. The potential result was the establishment of a monopoly within a territory.

In addition, under the NWA's second agreed-upon principle, the promoters agreed (or "conspired" if you prefer) that not only were non-members prohibited from doing business in a member's territory, the members also would band together to protect another member from any such "invasion" by a non-member. In other words, the members of the NWA cartel would band together to help protect a member's monopoly by, for example, refusing to loan talent to outlaw promoters. The third principle articulated a wage-fixing scheme that capped the wages the champion could earn at 10 percent of the gate.

The agreement also laid the groundwork for the practice of blacklisting wrestlers who dared to cross promoters within the Alliance. Blacklisting is the practice of developing a list of individuals who are disapproved of and barred from employment. The Supreme Court had noted back in 1914 that blacklisting done for the purpose of restraining competition ran afoul of the Sherman Act.[16] On its face, the NWA's agreement did not expressly call for the blacklisting of wrestlers who chose to work for outlaw promoters who did not belong to the Alliance. But the agreement's sweeping language called for the suspension of a wrestler who did anything "detrimental to the interests of a promoter" within the Alliance. So, the language was certainly broad enough to apply to a wrestler who chose to work for an outlaw promoter. And the wrestler who engaged in such conduct would be suspended, not just within the promoter's territory, but within all of the other territories under the control of promoters within the Alliance. Regardless of the intent of the original agreement, the Alliance, in 1952, expressly agreed to a policy of blacklisting any wrestler who worked for an outlaw promoter.[17] Just a few years later, the Supreme Court would hold that a similar arrangement among members of the National Football League (the NFL) was illegal under the Sherman Act.*

* * *

By the early 1950s, membership in the NWA had grown to include nearly every major promoter across the country.[18] By 1956, there were 38 regional promotions under the NWA banner. According to Sam Muchnick, one of the organization's founding members, the NWA controlled wrestlers for 95 percent of regular arena wrestling shows and all televised shows, and the promoters' gross earnings were $25 million a year.[19]

The allegations contained in a lawsuit filed in the 1955 by wrestler/promoter Harold "Sonny" Myers against the NWA illustrate how the Alliance operated in practice. Myers operated a carnival in Iowa. As part of the carnival, Myers promoted wrestling matches. But wrestling in Iowa was under the control of NWA member Pinky George at the time. A dispute over whether Myers owed a booking fee to George for a carnival stop at the Pottawattamie County Fair in Avoca, Iowa, soon spiraled out of control and led to Myers filing suit against George.[20] According to Myers, George had informed Myers that George "had given notice to the wrestlers [Myers] had booked that they could not wrestle with [Myers] acting both as a promoter and a wrestler at the same exhibition; and if they did so he, George, would see that they never wrestled again for any member of the Alliance."[21] In other words, George said he was going to blacklist any wrestler who agreed to work for Myers.

George also allegedly told Myers that "the National Wresting Alliance gave me (George) the State of Iowa to book and promote and that he was the man who promotes in Iowa, and nobody else." Finally, George allegedly threatened Myers with physical harm, telling Myers that he

---

* The case, *Radovich v. NFL*, 352 U.S. 445 (1957), involved Bill Radovich, a former player for the Detroit Lions, who broke his contract with the Lions and signed with a team that was part of the rival All-America Conference. Radovich later sought to become a player-coach for a team in the Pacific Coast League, a league affiliated with the NFL. The NFL responded by telling the team that Radovich was blacklisted and that any team that employed him would suffer economic consequences.

4. Antitrust and Interference with Contractual Relations 57

"could never again promote any wrestling in the State of Iowa ... and for his insubordination he would see that appellee was hurt all over the country as a wrestler."[22]* The result of "this conspiracy and monopoly" on the part of the Alliance, according to Myers, was that it was "absolutely impossible for a person out of favor with any single promoter to have any freedom of contract or to earn a livelihood."[23]

Over the course of nearly nine years, Myers' suit worked its way up and down the federal court system before his case was finally dismissed.[24]† But by the time Myers's suit was just ramping up back in 1955, the U.S. Department of Justice had already begun its own investigation into the NWA's anti-competitive practices. DOJ lawyers began investigating the NWA in 1953 when a group of California promoters engaged in various anti-competitive practices, including threatening to blacklist wrestlers who agreed to wrestle for "outlaw" promotions, i.e., promotions that were not part of the NWA.[25] DOJ attorneys eventually expanded their investigation and learned about other anti-competitive practices on the part of NWA members across the country, such as paying wrestlers not to show up at events they had been hired to perform at by outlaw promoters.[26] Eventually, the Department acquired enough evidence to charge the members of the NWA with violations of federal antitrust law.

Facing potential legal liability, the exposure of the true nature of professional wrestling, and the forced dissolution of the Alliance, the NWA entered into a consent decree with DOJ in October 1956. Rather than contesting the charges against them, the members of the NWA promised to abandon their past illegal practices and abide by the law moving forward. Among other things, the members agreed to abandon the practices of designating territories as being under the exclusive control of promoters, restricting non-member promoters from promoting shows, and blacklisting wrestlers.[27]

* * *

In theory, the 1956 Consent Decree should have put a stop to the anti-competitive behavior of the NWA. But it clearly didn't. Just three

---

* This practice of deliberately injuring a performer during an event was known as "stretching" and was sometimes employed as a means of discouraging competition. According to the deposition testimony of former Olympic-wrestler-turned-professional-wrestler Bob Roop, the owners of the Florida territory would give would-be wrestlers "tryouts" against Roop and other wrestlers. The aspirants were required to sign a release, waiving their right to sue. Some of the individuals who tried out were wrestlers in competing organizations. The promoters instructed Roop to "stretch"—or cause actual physical pain to—these individuals, including in at least a couple of instances instructions to break the legs of these individuals. *Poffo v. Gulas et al.*, Civil Action NO. 79–147 (E.D. Ky [Lexington]), Deposition of Robert Roop, Feb. 19, 1980, at 22–26.

† More information about the trial in Myers' case appears in Chapter 1.

years after the consent decree, Baltimore promoter Edward Contos, Jr., brought a Sherman Act claim against the Capitol Wrestling Corporation, owned by Toots Mondt and Vince McMahon, Sr. The two sides had a falling out after Mondt and McMahon demanded a bigger cut from the shows Contos was putting on using talent supplied by Mondt and McMahon. According to Contos, the demand for more money by Mondt and McMahon was part of an attempt to squeeze Contos out of the business and establish a monopoly. What's more, according to Contos, when he attempted to obtain talent from other NWA promoters, they refused as per the longstanding practice of NWA members.[28]

Contos' suit failed after he was unable to prove an intent on the part of Mondt and McMahon to establish a monopoly or that the refusal of the other promoters to supply talent was part of a conspiracy. But in other situations, the monopolistic behavior of NWA members was too obvious to ignore.

Perhaps the most famous example of how the NWA continued its old practices even in the face of the consent decree is the so-called "Battle for Atlanta" in the 1970s. Following the death of NWA promoter Roy Gunkel in 1972, an intra–Alliance dispute erupted between Gunkel's widow, Ann, and promoter Lester Welch over the Georgia territory. The Alliance sided with Welch and refused to permit Gunkel to run shows in the state under the NWA banner. So, Gunkel started an outlaw promotion and engaged in some tough (and possibly illegal) competitive practices. These practices included persuading several local Georgia promoters to break their contracts with the NWA and start promoting her shows instead as well as convincing future media mogul Ted Turner to stop airing NWA shows on his television station and instead air Gunkel's.[29]

The NWA responded by running its standard playbook. The Alliance blacklisted or threatened to blacklist wrestlers who went to work for Gunkel; paid wrestlers under contract with Gunkel not to show up for advertised events; threatened wrestlers with the disclosure of embarrassing information; and pressured local coliseum owners not to rent their facilities to Gunkel.[30] Eventually, Gunkel lost the war.

* * *

The DOJ received multiple complaints alleging continued blacklisting and other anti-competitive practices on the part of NWA members following the 1956 consent decree.[31] But DOJ declined to bring further charges, citing limited funds.[32] Further involvement on the part of the government may not have been necessary to put a dent in the NWA, however, as wrestlers and promoters eventually began filing their own private lawsuits against the organization. Smaller promoters and blacklisted wrestlers increasingly brought their own lawsuits and alleged a host of familiar anti-competitive practices on the part of NWA members.[33]

Not all of these claims were successful. But they didn't need to be in order to severely weaken the NWA. Civil lawsuits may serve multiple goals. The most obvious is the goal of obtaining compensation for an injury. But civil suits may also serve a deterrent function. A successful civil suit may deter a defendant from engaging the same sort of wrongful behavior moving forward. It may also serve as a message to other potential defendants that they might want to stop engaging in the same forms of wrongful behavior lest they also be sued.

But even when a defendant prevails in a suit, the suit may serve a deterrent function. The NWA may have won some of the litigation it faced. But its members still had to endure the expense of hiring lawyers and going through the litigation process. In some cases, the members chose to settle and pay off plaintiffs rather than going through the expense and uncertainty of trial. But the more lawsuits one faces, the less profitable it becomes to continue to do business as usual.

And that's what happened with the NWA. There are numerous reasons why the old territory system in professional wrestling eventually died out. But one of them was almost certainly the civil litigation that the NWA's anti-competitive practices generated. The NWA's control over the wrestling business was in decline by the 1970s, and long-time NWA stalwart Sam Muchnick admitted that the decline was due, in no small part, to the expense of defending against so many civil suits.[34]

Part 3: The Tennessee Territory Wrestling Wars

While the NWA may have been in decline during the 1970s, it still retained considerable power within the Southeast. One of the most interesting examples of how the Alliance sometimes continued to operate in a manner that violated federal antitrust law and that amounted to various business torts are the wars that took place in the Tennessee territories during the 1970s.

In terms of geography and culture, there are three clear divisions within the State of Tennessee. There is Memphis in the west, Knoxville in the east, and Nashville in the middle. These divisions are officially referred to as the "Grand Divisions" and are reflected in the state flag with the inclusion of three stars, each representing a division. The wrestling territories in the state in the 1970s had their own divisions, which led to some wild behavior and a host of lawsuits alleging anticompetitive behavior and other forms of unfair business practices.

* * *

Jarrett v. Gulas

At one point, Nashville promoter Nick Gulas claimed to be the biggest promoter in professional wrestling.[35] Gulas got his start in the wrestling business back in 1938. He put on the first televised wrestling event ever in Nashville in 1952, and by 1975 he and his business partner Roy Welch were putting on shows in 48 cities in Tennessee and surrounding states.[36]

Gulas and Welch were long-time members of the NWA, and that membership helped the pair maintain exclusive control of their market. In fact, Welch was one of the NWA members named by the FBI as a co-conspirator and who had signed the 1956 consent decree. But, as was the case with other members of the NWA, the decree apparently did little to change the way Gulas and Welch ran their promotion. Gulas and Welch allegedly engaged in a variety of anti-competitive practices, including blacklisting wrestlers, threatening wrestlers who complained about blacklisting with "stretching," bribing coliseum managers, paying television stations not to air rival programming, and bribing members of the state athletic commission.[37] When, in 1974, a DOJ investigator concluded that there was sufficient evidence to charge NWA promoters with violation of the consent decree, the Gulas-Welch promotion in Tennessee was named as a potential defendant (although no official action was taken).[38] As one lawyer who obtained a relatively small settlement against Gulas, Welch, and other nearby promoters put it, "There was nothing going on that they didn't admit. Their attitude was 'We bought it [the territory] fair and square and if somebody doesn't want to go along with us, they don't for work for us. And if they don't work for us, they don't work.'"[39]

One of the key markets that Gulas and Welch controlled was the wrestling-crazy town of Memphis. In October 1976, the Saturday morning wrestling show in Memphis reached 135,000 households, almost as many as a Sunday night World Series game reached.[40] Saturday morning wrestling in Memphis had more viewers in the late 1970s than prime time shows like *All in the Family*.[41] And one of the main reasons why Memphis was the crown jewel of the Gulas/Welch promotion was booker Jerry Jarrett.

Jarrett got his start in the wrestling business selling programs and tickets as a kid for Gulas and Welch in Nashville in the 1950s. By the time he was 15, he was promoting wrestling events for the partnership in small towns in Middle Tennessee and Central Kentucky.[42] Jarrett went to work for Gulas and Welch after he finished college, learning the ropes by being

4. Antitrust and Interference with Contractual Relations 61

a referee and wrestler before ultimately becoming the booker—the matchmaker and person who writes the storylines—for the Memphis territory by the late 1960s.[43] Jarrett continued to promote shows in smaller towns for Gulas and Welch while the partners promoted shows in larger markets.

Drawing upon the popularity of the Memphis television programming, Jarrett eventually set up his own promotions in several cities, including Louisville. He cut Gulas and Welch in on the Louisville territory, but the group had to contend with the fact that the territory, which had fallen on hard times in recent years, still technically "belonged" to some other members of the NWA. These other promoters asserted their supposed ownership interest. Having learned a lesson from the DOJ consent decree, Jarrett says he responded by advising the promoter that "the law specifically did not allow for the ownership of towns." Nonetheless, in order to prevent a war within the NWA, Jarrett/Gulas/Welch gave these other promoters a share of the profits from Louisville.[44]

While the alliance between Jarrett and Gulas/Welch was seemingly reaping benefits for those involved, all was not well. In 1973, Jarrett was wrestling a match as part of a Memphis television taping when another wrestler, Mario Galento, attacked him. Of course, this sort of thing happens all the time in professional wrestling. But the difference this time was that the attack was real.* Jarrett has since stated that he believes Galento was put up to the attack by Welch, who may have believed that Jarrett was thinking about going into business for himself.[45]

The physical attack later gave way to legal warfare. Jarrett eventually acquired a 10 percent ownership interest in the entire Gulas/Welch operation. As Welch's health declined and he retired from the business, Jarrett says he paid Gulas $50,000 and signed a contract prepared by Gulas' lawyer for what Jarrett thought was a 50 percent ownership interest of the entire business.[46] As the story goes, it turned out that all he had bought was an option to buy into the business and that option had since expired. Jarrett, claiming betrayal, decided not to sue Gulas for fraud and instead decided to start his own promotion in direct competition with Gulas.[47] Thus began the Memphis Wrestling War of 1977.

* * *

Jarrett gave his notice to Gulas in February of 1977 and started his own promotion. Having served successfully as the booker in Memphis for a number of years, Jarrett was able to convince most of the big attractions in the territory to go with him and leave Gulas behind.[48] Jarrett also went

---

* Jarrett said he defended himself by plunging his finger into Galento's eye socket and pulling out Galento's eyeball.

to the TV station that broadcast Gulas' product in Memphis, WHBQ, in an effort to take Gulas' show off the air and replace it with Jarrett's new product. The station manager for WHBQ was apparently reluctant to cancel its contract with Gulas and enter into a new agreement with Jarrett. But for reasons that are not entirely clear, the station ultimately dropped Gulas' show but did not enter into a deal with Jarrett. Jarrett convinced Lance Russell, the program director and long-time wrestling announcer at WHBQ, to join him in his endeavor, and Jarrett was able to get a new TV deal with a different station, WMC.[49] Thus, Jarrett had a TV show to promote his product and Gulas did not.

Throughout the spring of 1977, Jarrett and Gulas put on competing live shows in Memphis. Gulas had a contract with Memphis' Mid–South Coliseum to rent the building on Monday nights to put on shows. But after Jarrett raided his roster, Gulas was unable to put on a show on April 7. Gulas' contract allowed him to rent the building on Mondays as long as he paid $1,000 a week, even if he did not put on a show. For his part, Jarrett also wanted to run shows at the venue on Monday nights or Sunday nights. Jarrett couldn't run his shows on Mondays because Gulas already had the Coliseum rented that night, even if he wasn't putting on any shows. And the Coliseum refused to allow Jarrett to book the building on Sundays, citing an unwritten policy of not renting the space on back-to-back nights for the same type of program.[50]

* * *

At this point, the two warring sides began exchanging lawsuits. Jarrett's lawyers threatened the Coliseum with an injunction requiring the Coliseum to rent its facilities to Jarrett. Harkening back to the DOJ consent decree, Jarrett's lawyers charged that the Coliseum's "favoritism" toward Gulas was "evidence of a general conspiracy to restrain freedom of trade and commerce and has monopolistic overtones."[51]

Jarrett also sued Gulas and members of the Tennessee Athletic Commission, alleging that the Commission and Gulas had engaged in a conspiracy in order to damage Jarrett's business. The suit claimed that Gulas had attempted to block Jarrett's efforts to put on shows in the Mid–South Coliseum and that Gulas and members of the Commission attempted to interfere with Jarrett's business by sabotaging production of Jarret's television shows and persuading wrestlers not to cooperate with him.[52] Or, as Jarrett's complaint put it, Gulas "used every trick, scheme or device to frustrate [Jarrett's] promoting wrestling within the city of Memphis and in Tennessee."[53]

For his part, Gulas eventually brought his own lawsuit against Jarrett, claiming $1.5 million in damages. Gulas alleged that three performers

4. Antitrust and Interference with Contractual Relations 63

(wrestlers Ron Garfield and Don Garfield and manager Las Vegas Louie) were under contract with him to perform in several towns during the week but that Jarrett paid the wrestlers $200 a piece per show not to show up.[54] Gulas sued the three performers for breach of contract and sought a restraining order preventing the three from violating their agreements with Gulas. But he also sued Jarrett and his partners for interfering with Gulas' contracts with the wrestlers and inducing the breaches of those contracts.[55]

* * *

While many of the earlier lawsuits involving the old territory system in wrestling involved alleged violations of federal antitrust law, there are other legal theories that potentially applied. One of the most common legal theories asserted in litigation between business competitors is a claim of tortious (or wrongful) interference with contractual or business relations. The basic idea of an interference claim is straightforward: two parties have a contract or business relationship and a third party knowingly and intentionally interferes with that relationship, resulting in economic harm to one of the original parties. The theory also applies to the situation where two parties are negotiating a contract and a third party interferes with that negotiation in order to prevent them from reaching a deal. To establish such a claim in Tennessee, the plaintiff must establish (1) the existence of a contract, (2) knowledge on the part of the defendant that the contract exists, (3) interference with that contract, (4) the defendant's improper motive (such as malice) or use of improper means (such as fraud or unfair competition), and (5) resulting economic harm to the plaintiff.[56]

This, for example, is what Gulas was alleging in his suit against Jarrett for paying wrestlers to no-show their bookings. Gulas had a contract with the three wrestlers for the wrestlers to work exclusively with Gulas for a six-month period. Either party was free to terminate the contract at any time, provided they gave 14 days' notice.[57] And Jarrett* interfered with that contractual relationship by allegedly paying the wrestlers not to perform. This, according to Gulas, resulted in economic harm in the form of potential ticket refunds and damage to his reputation that might hurt future business.

* * *

Gulas' case against Jarrett illustrates how the interference theory seeks to balance the competing societal interests in preserving the sanctity

---

* According to the complaint, it was wrestler Jerry "the King" Lawler, Jarrett's partner, who offered the $200 payment promise to the wrestlers.

of contracts and promoting competition. While the law protects a party to a contract from interference from an outside party, an exception exists where (1) the contract can be terminated for any reason and (2) the outside party is a competitor who brings about the termination of the contract by offering a better deal. This is sometimes known as the "competitor's privilege." As one court has explained, this rule is justified on the grounds that "competition, which though painful, fierce, frequently ruthless, sometimes Darwinian in its pitilessness, is the cornerstone of our highly successful economic system."[58] In short, we want to give parties the freedom to enter into the most efficient deal for their businesses, provided they don't use improper means (like fraud, threats of violence, etc.).

The same rule applies to a competitor's attempts to lure away a rival's employees. A competitor is free to offer a better deal to the employees of another employer as long as those employees are free to quit their jobs at any time for any reason. Most employees fall into that category, since few employees have employment contracts that last for a specific period of time or that place limits on an employee's ability to quit. Once again, the law wishes to encourage fair competition and economic efficiency. So, if you're offering a better deal to an employee than the employee's current employer is, and if that employee is free to quit at will, the law protects your behavior, provided you don't employ wrongful means as part of your efforts.

At first glance, it seems like this competitor's privilege might apply to Jarrett's actions and provided him with a defense. According to Gulas' complaint, Jarrett offered to hire the performers.[59]* And the performers were free to terminate the contract at any time, provided they gave Gulas two weeks' notice. So, it seems like maybe Jarrett was just offering the performers the kind of better deal that the law allows. But Jarrett also allegedly paid the performers to flat out breach their contracts by not showing up for scheduled events. Specifically paying a party not to perform a contract is the sort of restraint of trade that the Sherman Act was meant to prohibit. So, this wasn't really the sort of fair competition the competitor's privilege was meant to protect.

But Jarrett had another possible defense to Gulas' interference claim. There can be no unlawful breach of contract or interference with a contract if the contract is void because it violates public policy. If, for example, I pay someone to murder another person, and you convince that person not to commit the murder, I can't recover from the person who breached the murder contract. What's more, I can't recover from you for interfering

---

* The three performers did appear for Jarrett shortly after failing to appear for their scheduled shows with Gulas. *Memphis Commercial Appeal*, May 28, 1978, at 55.

with the performance of that contract. A murder contract would offend public policy and would be treated as being void by the courts.

Gulas' contract with the three wrestlers may not have been a murder contract, but it was still probably void as a matter of law because it violated public policy. The contract contained a non-compete clause. Once the contract ended, the three wrestlers were prohibited from performing "in *any* capacity, for *any* group or enterprise that has *anything* to do with professional wrestling within the states of Tennessee, Alabama, and Kentucky or *any* states in which Gulas Wrestling Enterprises Inc. may operate for a period of six months."[60] The law generally takes a dim view of non-compete agreements because they tend to limit the ability of workers to earn a livelihood. Courts will not enforce unless unless the employer is seeking to protect a legitimate interest and the restriction on employment is reasonable in terms of time, geography, and the activity restricted.

In terms of the legitimate interest the employer is seeking to protect, courts almost universally say that an employer lacks a legitimate purpose when the employer's sole purpose is to prevent competition.[61] If that is the employer's sole purpose, the non-compete agreement is void. But courts are more inclined to enforce such agreements where the employer is seeking to protect an interest in maintaining customer goodwill that the employer has invested time and money in developing. If the employer provides the worker with a loyal customer base that the worker may one deal "steal" when the worker leaves, and if the worker has unique or extraordinary talents, courts are more inclined to enforce a non-compete agreement. This was Gulas' best argument.

But a non-compete agreement also must be reasonable in terms of time, geography, and the activity restricted. While Gulas' non-compete agreement only prohibited wrestlers from working for six months after leaving, the agreement was sweeping in terms of its geographical limitation and the scope of the activities it prevented the wrestlers from engaging in. The agreement prohibited the wrestlers from working in *any* town— even in towns where Gulas didn't run shows—in Tennessee, Kentucky, or Alabama. This restriction also included towns (such as Louisville) that Jarrett was largely responsible for having developed. And the agreement was sweeping in terms of the activities it restricted; the non-compete agreement prohibited the performers from performing *in any capacity*, for *any* group or enterprise that has *anything* to do with professional wrestling.*

---

* Hilariously, Gulas would later refer to his non-compete agreement "as more in the nature of a gentleman's agreement" since he claims to have never actually enforced it and had been told that it was probably unenforceable anyway. *Poffo v. Gulas et al.*, Civil Action No. 79–147, Complaint (E.D. Ky [Lexington]), Aug. 22, 1979), Motion of Defendants Gulas and Renestro, Affidavit of Nick Gulas at 3.

IN THE CHANCERY COURT OF DAVIDSON COUNTY, TENNESSEE

GULAS WRESTLING ENTERPRISES,)
INCORPORATED,)
)
       Plaintiff,)
)
vs.   )   No. 78-791-I
)
LOUIE HIENMAN a/k/a LAS VEGAS LOUIE,)
RON GARFIELD a/k/a EARL WHITE,)
DON GARFIELD a/k/a DON GARFIELD)
KALT a/k/a DON FARGO, JARRETT)
ENTERPRISES, INCORPORATED;)
WELCH ENTERPRISES, INCORPORATED;)
JARRETT-WELCH WRESTLING COMPANY)
and their agents, officers and employees)
including but not limited to JERRY)
JARRETT and EDWARD A. WELCH a/k/a)
BUDDY FULLER and JERRY LAWLER,)
)
      Defendants.)

COMPLAINT

        This is an action for injunctive relief and liquidated damages. The plaintiff, Gulas Wrestling Enterprises, Incorporated, is a corporation organized under the laws of the State of Tennessee with its offices and principal place of business in the City of Nashville, Davidson County, Tennessee. The plaintiff corporation's principal business is the booking, promotion and management of professional wrestlers and professional wrestling events. Plaintiff corporation is engaged in this business in the State of Tennessee, Alabama, Kentucky and other states contiguous

---

Nick Gulas sues Las Vegas Louie, Ron Garfield, and Don Garfield (a.k.a. Don Fargo) for breaching their contracts, and sues Jerry Jarrett, Jerry Lawler, and Edward Welch (a.k.a. Buddy Fuller) for interfering with those contracts.

I _____ AGREE TO BE BOOKED AND WRESTLE EXCLUSIVELY FOR THE GULAS WRESTLING ENTERPRISES, INC., IN WHICH NICK GULAS IS PRESIDENT, FOR A PERIOD OF SIX MONTHS WITH AN OPTION TO RENEW THIS AGREEMENT PROVIDING THAT BOTH PARTIES AGREE TO THE ABOVE.

IF EITHER PARTY WISHES TO TERMINATE THIS AGREEMENT, FOR WHAT-EVER REASON, A NOTICE OF TERMINATION OF 14 DAYS MUST BE GIVEN.

I FURTHER AGREE THAT AFTER TERMINATION OF MY SERVICES FOR THE GULAS WRESTLING ENTERPRISES, INC., IN WHICH NICK GULAS IS PRESIDENT, I WILL NOT PERFORM, IN ANY CAPACITY, FOR ANY GROUP OR ENTERPRISE THAT HAS ANYTHING TO DO WITH PROFESSIONAL WRESTLING WITHIN THE STATES OF TENNESSEE, ALABAMA AND KENTUCKY OR ANY STATES IN WHICH GULAS WRESTLING ENTERPRISES INC., MAY OPERATE FOR A PERIOD OF SIX MONTHS.

Witness

Witness

4/12/78 D.K.

"A"

The non-compete agreement Gulas had his performers sign.

*   *   *

Ultimately, Nick Gulas' interference suit against Jerry Jarrett wasn't really about trying to recover money. In fact, Gulas voluntarily dismissed his legal action just a few months after filing it and obtaining an injunction prohibiting the three performers from breaching their contracts.[62] But the suit wasn't really about making the performers live up to their obligations and keeping Jarrett from trying to steal them away either.* Instead, Gulas was sending a message to Jarrett: stay away from my talent or I will sue you and make you hire a lawyer. (He was also sending a message to the wrestlers he had under contract: Don't break your contract with me or I will sue you and make you hire a lawyer.) Gulas didn't file his lawsuit for the purpose of obtaining compensation. He filed it for the purpose of deterrence.

* * *

Indeed, the entire Memphis war was just a series of wrongful interferences on the part of Gulas and Jarrett, often met with a lawsuit designed to accomplish some goal apart from compensation. Jarrett's initial successful efforts to persuade workers to leave Gulas and go with him was an interference that might have been protected by the competitor's privilege. His successful effort to persuade WHBQ to cancel its TV contract with Gulas was also an interference, which, depending on the nature of the station's contract with Gulas, may or may not have been wrongful. For his part, Gulas' alleged attempts to block Jarrett from putting on shows in the Mid-South Coliseum, sabotage production of Jarrett's television shows, and persuade wrestlers not to cooperate with him would be classic examples of wrongful interference.

Ultimately, what decided the outcome of the Memphis war was not the lawsuits the combatants filed against each other. It was the decision of the other members of the NWA not to choose sides in the conflict. The members chose not to expel or blackball either Gulas or Jarrett. Ironically, this syndicate, famed for its anti-competitive practices, decided to let the two men compete, using whatever wrongful conduct they wished.[63]

Here, Jarrett's ability to grab most of the wrestling talent and secure a television station to air his programming carried the day. By the summer of 1977, the Memphis war was effectively over. Jarrett's threatened legal action against the Mid-South Coliseum perhaps had its intended effect. The Coliseum relented and allowed Jarrett to run shows on Wednesdays, and Gulas experienced difficulty running his regular Monday shows.[64] By the beginning of June, Gulas had requested a release from his contact with the Coliseum, and Jarrett had signed a new contract to take over Gulas' Monday slot. Attendance at Gulas' shows had plummeted from around 11,000 customers at the beginning of March to a mere 484 by May 9.[65] Gulas had lost the Memphis War.

---

* It may not have been Gulas' intent to make the performers go back to work for him, but it might possibly have had that effect. Las Vegas Louie and Ron Garfield wound up going back to work for Gulas shortly after Gulas filed suit. But Don Garfield, a.k.a. Don Fargo, went on to work for Jarrett for the rest of the year.

IN THE CIRCUIT COURT FOR DAVIDSON COUNTY, TENNESSEE

JERRY JARRETT, EDWARD WELCH and)
GULAS WRESTLING ENTERPRISES, INC.,)
        Plaintiffs,)
)
vs.) No. E2953
)
NICK GULAS,)
        Defendant.)

COMPLAINT

Plaintiffs, Jerry Jarrett, Edward Welch and Gulas Wrestling Enterprises, Inc., would show unto the Court the following:

COUNT ONE

1. The Plaintiff, Jerry Jarrett, is a resident of Hendersonville, Sumner County, Tennessee. He is and has been engaged in the conducting and promoting of professional events for several years and owns thirty seven and one half percent of the common stock of Gulas Wrestling Enterprises, Inc.

2. The Plaintiff, Edward Welch, is a resident of Bolivar, Hardeman County, Tennessee. He is and has been engaged in the conducting and promoting of professional wrestling events for several years and owns thirty seven and one half percent of the common stock of Gulas Wrestling Enterprises, Inc.

3. The Plaintiff, Gulas Wrestling Enterprises, Inc. is incorporated and organized under the laws of the State of Tennessee having its principal place of business in Nashville, Tennessee. Said Corporation has been engaged in the conducting and promoting of professional events in the states of Tennessee, Alabama and Kentucky.

After the war between Jarrett and Gulas seemed to be over, hostilities flared again following Gulas' sale of his business to Jarrett and Edward Welch (Buddy Fuller).

WTVF

September 9, 1980

Mr. Tom Kerkeles
507 Benton Avenue
Nashville, Tennessee

Dear Mr. Kerkeles:

Following my telephone call from you last week I have had discussions with Harold Crump and Tom Ervin regarding the future of wrestling programs on WTVF.

We have been told by Mr. Nick Gulas that he has sold his company; therefore the contract he had signed with WTVF is no longer in effect.

Given the full situation, WTVF feels it must not become involved in the internal problems of a client organization and therefore we have decided to cancel the wrestling program effective immediately and remove such programming from our schedule.

We wish you and your associates the very best.

Sincerely,

Bill Jay

BJ:bb

474 James Robertson Parkway • Nashville, Tennessee 37219 • (615) 244-5000

EXHIBIT 2

Among Jarrett's allegations against Gulas was the charge that Gulas caused Nashville television station WTVF to cancel its contract to broadcast wrestling.

Gulas and Jarrett continued to do battle in Louisville in 1978, but Jarrett eventually prevailed there as well. Gulas continued to run shows in Nashville, Birmingham, and some small towns in Kentucky and Middle Tennessee, but his territory had shrunk dramatically.[66] Jarrett's territory included Memphis, Lexington, Louisville, and up into Evansville,

Indiana. Gulas retired a few years later, selling out (of all people) to Jarrett and his business partner Buddy Fuller.*

The Tennessee Stud v. The Knoxville Five

By 1979, there were three Grand Divisions in Tennessee wrestling: Jerry Jarrett's Continental Wrestling Association (CWA) promotion in Memphis and West Tennessee; what was left of Nick Gulas' NWA Mid–America promotion in Nashville and Middle Tennessee; and Ron Fuller's NWA Southeastern Championship Wrestling in Knoxville and East Tennessee.

Fuller (a.k.a. the Tennessee Stud) had acquired the Knoxville territory several years earlier. Former Olympic wrestler Bob Roop was serving as Fuller's booker at the time. Roop says he suspected Fuller was withholding money from ticket sales from live events. (Fuller vehemently denies this claim.) Roop, who had previously attempted to take over another territory from a different promoter, convinced three other performers—Bob Orton, Jr., Professor Boris Malenko, and Southeastern champion Ronnie Garvin— to walk out of the promotion and join with Kingsport, Tennessee, wrestler/promoter Ron Wright to form a new company—All Star Championship Wrestling—to compete against Fuller.[67] (The four wrestlers and promoter Wright would later become known as the Knoxville Five in wrestling lore.)

In early June 1979, the former Southeastern wrestlers failed to show up for scheduled Friday night matches in Knoxville.† They distributed

---

* Shockingly, this transaction did not go smoothly, and litigation ensued once again. Jarrett and Fuller alleged that Gulas had interfered with the company's contracts with other parties as a result of a dispute with Jarrett and Fuller over how Gulas would be paid. Among other acts, Gulas allegedly urged employees and other wrestlers to quit, caused the Nashville TV station that televised matches to cancel its contract with the company, and bad-mouthed Jarrett and Fuller to other companies with whom the pair did business. The suit alleged that Gulas' interference with the business had caused attendance to decline in Nashville, resulting in economic losses of $850,000. *Jerry Jarrett, Edward Welch, and Gulas Enterprises, Inc. v. Nick Gulas*, No. E-2953, Complaint (Davidson County Circuit Court Oct. 28, 1980); Adell Crowe, "Sabotage Alleged by Wrestling Suit," *The Tennessean*, Oct. 29, 1980, at 26. Gulas, of course, counter sued, alleging Jarrett and Fuller had conspired against him. *Jerry Jarrett, Edward Welch, and Gulas Enterprises, Inc. v. Nick Gulas*, No. E-2953, Countersuit (Davidson County Circuit Court, Nov. 10, 1980). The case settled before trial. *Jerry Jarrett, Edward Welch, and Gulas Enterprises, Inc. v. Nick Gulas*, No. E-2953, Order (Davidson County Circuit Court May 6, 1981). Sometime old rivals in the wrestling just can't let go of a feud. Jarrett and Fuller were represented in this litigation by lawyer Fred Thompson of Nashville, who would later go on to act in such films as *No Way Out*, *The Hunt for Red October*, and *Die Hard 2* before getting elected to the United States Senate in 1994. He later went on to portray a lawyer in the NBC show *Law and Order*.

† They actually did show up for the event, but they did so as spectators. They bought tickets for the event and watched in the audience because, they said, Fuller advertised that they would wrestle that night even though they had already given notice that they weren't going to perform. Thus, they claimed, they needed "to protect [their] professional reputations." "Write or Wrong," *The Knoxville News-Sentinel*, June 17, 1979, at 38 (Letters to the Editor).

handbills promoting their competing show in the Knoxville area on a Saturday night, which apparently caused some confusion as to whether the Southeastern promotion would run its regular Friday night show.[68] A letter to the editor claimed that fans who showed up with the offending handbill were not permitted to attend the Southeastern show on Friday.[69]

Fuller responded to the Knoxville Five's attempt to run opposition to his promotion by filing his own lawsuit against All Star Championship Wrestling and its outlaw wrestlers. Fuller alleged that the group had bought tickets to Southeastern Wrestling shows and behaved in "a disorderly and obnoxious" manner that drove away customers from Southeastern events.[70] In addition, he alleged that Wright and other All Star Wrestlers had made defamatory statements about him and Southeastern to venue owners as part of an attempt to cause the owners to stop doing business with Fuller and Southeastern.[71] Fuller also alleged that All Star Wrestling had deceptively used the trade name "Southeastern" in their promotions and essentially traded on the name of Fuller's company.[72] Therefore, according to the complaint, All Star Wrestling had slandered Fuller and tortiously interfered with Southeastern Championship Wrestling's business relationships with other parties.[73] Finally, Fuller later amended his complaint to allege that All Star had used Fuller's name in their advertisements by having All Star wrestlers challenge Fuller to matches. According to Fuller, this was done both to mislead the public into believing that Fuller would appear and to damage Fuller's reputation when he did not appear.[74]

Fuller's complaint requested that the court grant a restraining order enjoining the outlaw wrestlers from attending Southeastern matches; charged the defendants with tortiously interfering with Southeastern's business relationships and slandering Fuller; requested damages totaling $2.5 million; and requested that the court enjoin All Star Wrestling from using the trade name "Southeastern Champion" and the name "Ron Fuller" in their advertisements.[75]

The final outcome of the case was anti-climactic. In December 1979, the defendants voluntarily agreed not to "distract from or in any way impede any" Southeastern match.[76] The court dismissed Fuller's motion to enjoin All Star from using his name.[77] And for reasons not explained in the court record, somehow Fuller's interference and slander cases simply faded away without any resolution.

One possible reason why the case ended with a whimper instead of a bang is because Fuller had sold the Knoxville promotion while the matter was still pending.[78] Fuller decided that he didn't need the aggravation of the war in Knoxville. So, Fuller sold Southeastern before

4. Antitrust and Interference with Contractual Relations 73

the litigation was even concluded, leaving it to his successors to carry on the war.

* * *

Part 4: The Poffos v. Everybody

The end of Ron Fuller's litigation against the Knoxville Five didn't end the wrestling-related litigation in the area, however. Before Fuller left the area, the Poffo family—Angelo, Lanny, and Randy—had opened up a new front in the ongoing wrestling wars of 1979.

Angelo Poffo was the patriarch of the Poffo clan. Among Angelo's accomplishments was setting the world's record for sit-ups, completing 6,033 sit-ups in a little over four hours.* Angelo had been involved with professional wrestling for over two decades when his sons Lanny and Randy followed him into the business. "Leaping" Lanny Poffo would go on to attain success in the WWF in the 1980s and early 1990s. But it was his brother Randy—better known as the one and only "Macho Man" Randy Savage—who left the biggest mark on the sport among the Poffo family.

All three Poffos had worked for Nick Gulas in the preceding year. Lanny went off to the Pacific Northwest, but Angelo and Randy worked for Gulas until February of 1979. Lanny had a reputation at the time for being laid-back. Randy had a reputation for being crazy.[79] And Angelo, according to Bob Roop and Ronnie Garvin, had a reputation for going to work for a promoter and then establishing a rival promotion in opposition to the promoter.[80] Whether that supposed reputation was warranted or not, Angelo and Randy soon stopped working for Gulas, brought Lanny back east, and started a new promotion in Gulas' backyard.

The trio formed International Championship Wrestling (ICW) and began putting on shows in April 1979 around the Lexington, Kentucky, area as well as a few shows in middle Tennessee. Lexington was one of Jerry Jarrett's regular towns, and middle Tennessee and a few towns in Kentucky still remained part of Gulas' territory. So, the move put ICW in competition with Jarrett and Gulas. When the Knoxville Five broke off from Southeastern Championship Wrestling later that summer, the Poffos saw an opportunity to expand their reach. ICW and All Star Championship Wrestling started putting on shows together in and around Knoxville. So, not only had the Poffos antagonized Gulas and Jarrett, they had now made an enemy of Ron Fuller and Southeastern (as well as the subsequent

---

* Legend has it that the last 33 were done as an homage to Jesus Christ: one for each year of Jesus' life.

purchasers of Southeastern). And, since Gulas, Jarrett, and Fuller were all still affiliated with the NWA, the Poffos had theoretically made enemies of all of the other promoters within the NWA.

* * *

As the feud evolved over time, ICW claimed that Jarrett and the NWA engaged in various forms of anti-competitive behavior. For example, Jarrett's promotion was running shows once a month at Rupp Arena, the largest venue in Lexington, Kentucky. ICW was unable to schedule any events there because, according to the decision makers at Rupp, the Lexington market could not support two shows a month.* For their part, ICW wrestlers publicly charged that the Rupp officials were "taking money under the table" not to book ICW.[81] For the Poffos, the inability to book Rupp Arena was part and parcel of the NWA's monopolistic behavior. "It's like a Mafia," Randy Savage, was quoted as saying. "Wrestling is a monopoly. They (established promoters) get together in a room like this and divide up the country."[82] The Poffos also implied that Jarrett or others affiliated with him had engaged in more dramatic forms of anti-competitive behavior, including calling in a bomb threat at one show and threatening to kill the individual who built the wrestling rings for ICW.[83] ICW wrestlers engaged in other forms of self-help. In addition to attacking Rupp officials on TV, several wrestlers appeared at the venue to "welcome" Jarrett's performers. Words were exchanged, and one of the ICW wrestlers was arrested.[84]

Randy Savage and brother Lanny Poffo circa 1979. From the author's collection.

---

* The decision makers also stated publicly that "ICW is not the sort of organization we want to do business with." John Woestendiek, "Wrestling's 'Outcasts' Looking for Respect Riches," *Lexington Herald-Leader*, March 3, 1981, at 30.

DIST.	OFF.	DOCKET YR. NUMBER	FILING DATE MO. DAY YEAR	J	N/S	O	D PTF DEF	R 23	DEMAND NEAREST $1,000 $ 600 OTHER	JUDGE/MAG NUMBER	JURY DEM.	DOCKET YR. NUMBER
0643	5	79 147	08 22 79	3	410	1			INJUNCTION	4306 ~~4303~~	P	79 147

PLAINTIFFS

ANGELO POFFO, Ind.,
RANDY POFFO, Ind., &
LANNY POFFO, Ind., & d/b/a
INTERNATIONAL CHAMPIONSHIP
WRESTLING, INC.

Sherman Anti-Trust Act-T.15, USC, §§1&2
Conspiracy to monopolize the promotion &
conduct of professional wrestling
matches

DEFENDANTS

NICK GULAS, Ind.,
GEORGE GULAS, Ind., &
TOM RENESTO, Ind., &
 d/b/a NICK GULAS ENTERPRISES &
EDDY GRAHAM, d/b/a FLORIDA
 CHAMPIONSHIP WRESTLING &
JAMES E. BARNETT, d/b/a GEORGIA
 CHAMPIONSHIP WRESTLING &
ED FARHAT, d/b/a FARHAT
 ENTERPRISES (SHEIK) &
WILBUR SNYDER, Ind., &
RICHARD AFFLIS, aka DICK THE
 BRUISER, Ind., & WILBUR SNYDER &
 RICHARD AFFLIS, d/b/a CHAMPION-
 SHIP WRESTLING &
VERNE GAGNE &
JERRY JARRETT, IND., &
JERRY LAWLER, IND.
BUDDY FULLER, d/b/a SOUTHEASTERN
 WRESTLING, INC. &
ROBERT "BOB" GEIGEL, Ind. &
NATIONAL WRESTLING ALLIANCE, a
Corp   THE

ATTORNEYS

Plaintiffs' Attorney

Brian P. Gilfedder
109 North Mill Street
Lexington, KY 40507

Lyman Ingram
INGRAM & INGRAM
Baird-Brewer Building
Dyersburg, TN 38024
 (Buddy Fuller)

Defendants' Attorneys
Robert Measle and William Callion
FOWLER, MEASLE & BELL
Suite 4A, Citizens Bank Square
Lexington, KY 40507
(Local counsel for all defts.
 except defts. Renesto & Farhat)

Sue Ann Blakland
TROUTMAN, SANDERS, LOCKERMAN & ASHMORE
1400 Candler Building
127 Peachtree Street
Atlanta, Georgia 30303
 (Graham, Barnett, Gagne, Jarrett,
 Lawler, Geigel & Nat'l Wrestling
 Alliance)

Cecil Branstetter
BRANSTETTER, MOODY & KILGORE
200 Church Street
Nashville, TN. 37201
 (Nick and George Gulas)

Douglass Shortridge
One Indiana Square, Suite 1960
Indianapolis, Indiana 46204
 (Wilbur Snyder & Richard Afflis)

The docket sheet in the *Poffo v. Gulas* litigation. The sheet shows every step in the litigation, ending with the court's order dismissing the case in October 1982.

Not surprisingly, litigation also ensued. The Poffos filed a lawsuit in August 1979 in federal court in Lexington, Kentucky, alleging antitrust violations against members of the NWA.[85] The Poffos named over a dozen defendants, including most of the major promoters within the NWA at the time. Named as defendants were Nick Gulas, his son, George, and booker Tom Renesto; Jerry Jarrett and Jerry Lawler (who had an ownership interest in the CWA along with Jarrett); Buddy Fuller (of Southeastern); Eddie Graham (of Championship Wrestling from Florida); Jim Barnett (of Georgia Championship Wrestling); Ed Farhat (a.k.a. the Sheik) (of Big Time Wrestling in Detroit); Wilbur Snyder and Richard Afflis (a.k.a. Dick the Bruiser) (of Championship Wrestling in Indiana); Verne Gagne (of the American Wrestling Association in Minneapolis); and Bob Geigel (president of the NWA from Kansas City).

The Poffos alleged that these individuals had engaged in an unlawful conspiracy in violation of the Sherman Act. The broadly worded complaint alleged that the defendants had conspired to establish a monopoly in restraint of trade in the business of professional wrestling in Indiana, Kentucky, and Tennessee.[86] According to the complaint, the defendants had

    a. established and maintained horizontal and vertical territorial allocations;

    b. established territories in which designated promoters had exclusive authority to conduct business;

    c. used boycotts, economic sanctions, and physical threats and intimidations to maintain their exclusive territories;

    d. conspired to prevent the Poffos from obtaining the necessary licenses required by the Commonwealth of Kentucky to put on shows;

    e. agreed that only wrestlers under the control of the NWA could participate in events in the established territories, an agreement they enforced through boycotts, revocation of licenses, and salary-fixing;

    f. fixed ticket prices;

    g. conspired to control television broadcasts of matches;

    h. conspired to deny the use of public and private places of exhibition (e.g., Rupp Arena) of wrestling matches;

    i. exerted undue and improper influence over state and local public officials; and

    j. encouraged, directed, and perpetrated accts of physical violence.[87]

In their prayer for relief, the Poffos suit sought a total $2.4 million in damages.[88]

After a complaint is filed, a defendant is required to respond to each and every allegation and either admit or deny the allegations. Predictably, the defendants denied most of the Poffos' allegations. Nick Gulas went beyond the normal practice of simply admitting or denying the plaintiffs' allegations and instead attached an affidavit to his answer, in which he went into great detail about his dealings with the Poffos.

Gulas stated that the reason why Angelo and Randy left his

promotion is because Randy had threatened to kill Gulas' son, George.[89]*
Gulas denied ever having done anything to cause the Kentucky Athletic
Commission to deny the Poffos a license to put on shows.[90] In fact, Gulas
pointed out, he himself had been denied a license by the Commission the
year before at the time he was still doing battle with Jerry Jarrett. According to Gulas, Commissioner Frank Sgori had informed Gulas that before
a license would be issued, Gulas and Jarrett needed to agree to divide up
control of the wrestling market in Kentucky.[91] Gulas said he refused to do
so and ultimately brought suit against Sgori, resulting in Gulas' license in
Kentucky being renewed.[92] All of this demonstrated, Gulas argued, that he
lacked "any pull with the Kentucky Athletic Commission and could not
possibly have been instrumental in denial of any Kentucky licenses to the
plaintiffs Poffo."[93]

* * *

The parties began conducting depositions of the various players
shortly after the initial round of complaint and answers. The Poffos' lawyer called in the Poffos' confederates in the Knoxville War, Bob Roop and
Ronnie Garvin, to testify. Both men testified that other NWA promoters
had previously been concerned about Angelo Poffo coming into a territory
and then setting up a rival promotion. Roop described a supposed plan
on the part of promoters Jim Barnett and Eddie Graham to record and
selectively edit a video of Angelo losing a match to champion Harley Race
as a means of discrediting Angelo in case he decided to go into business
for himself and his sons.[94] Garvin testified that the Poffos had previously
expressed interest in 1977 in coming to Knoxville but that Southeastern's
owner, Ron Fuller, viewed them as being undesirable due to their supposed
habit of coming into a territory and then later setting up a rival promotion.[95] Garvin went so far as to claim that Barnett had encouraged Garvin
to injure Randy in a match back in 1976 and that Garvin had actually
attempted to do so.[96]†

Garvin also testified about supposed anti-competitive practices on
the part of various NWA promoters regarding the Poffos and All Star
Championship Wrestling. Garvin claimed that All Star had asked Barnett to loan the organization some talent from Georgia but Barnett had

---

* Gulas would later testify in a deposition that Randy Savage had actually been the heavyweight champion of his promotion at the time but that Gulas took the title off of Savage after he allegedly threatened George's life. *Poffo v. Gulas et al.*, Civil Action No. 79–147, Deposition Nick Gulas, at 21–22 (Dec. 16, 1981). An internet search of the lineage of the Mid-America Heavyweight Championship suggests that there was a phantom title change to Bobby Eaton right about the time Savage left the company.

† Both men testified to the practice of promoters using wrestlers to injure (or "stretch") other wrestlers who refused to cooperate or who were otherwise at odds with the promoter.

refused.[97] He also described supposed efforts on the part of Southeastern officials to pressure venues in Harlan, Kentucky, and other locations not to book All Star shows.[98]

The Poffos' lawyer also brought in other ICW wrestlers to testify about efforts on the part of Gulas to blacklist them. Wrestler Debbie Combs testified that Gulas told her that she would be fired if she went to work for the Poffos and that "the day [she] worked for the Poffos is the day [she] stopped being a girl wrestler."[99] Rip Rogers testified that he had worked for Gulas under a contract with a non-compete clause. When Rogers explored the possibility of going to work for Jerry Jarrett, Gulas informed Rogers that he would never work for the NWA again.[100]

In an interesting twist, perhaps the most damaging testimony came from one of the defendants. Ed Farhat (a.k.a. the Sheik or the Original Sheik) was named as a defendant in the Poffos' complaint. Farhat had run the Detroit-based Big Time Wrestling under the NWA banner for years and also ran shows in Cincinnati. But by the time of his deposition in 1981, Farhat was on the outs with the NWA, and Big Time Wrestling had gone out of business. And it was clear that Farhat had no great love for the remaining promoters in the NWA. He blamed the other members of the organization for promising to lend him talent when he asked for it, only for that talent to no-show the scheduled event, thereby damaging his promotion's reputation with the fans.[101] Farhat claimed to have been put on the NWA's "bad list" as a result of a working a show with wrestler Thunderbolt Patterson, who himself claimed to have been blacklisted by the NWA after siding with Ann Gunkel during the Battle for Atlanta and after filing a race discrimination claim against the organization. It was after all of this, Farhat claimed, that he was voted out of the NWA.[102] Farhat backed up the Poffos' claims during his deposition, stating that Nick Gulas had instructed Farhat not to lend the Poffos any of Farhat's talent after the Poffos started their own promotion.[103]

Several of the defendants were also deposed, but their testimony provided little insight into the NWA's alleged conspiracy against the Poffos. The fact that the Poffos had listed Nick Gulas as the first defendant in their complaint suggests that Gulas was initially the primary target of their ire. But by the time Jerry Jarrett was deposed in December 1981, the Poffos' main beef was with Jarrett. In addition to making various public accusations about Jarrett's supposed efforts to keep ICW from running shows in Kentucky, ICW performers would regularly appear on the ICW's weekly television show and mock, threaten, and generally criticize Jarrett's stable of performers. The bad blood between the two organizations at this point was intense. But the depositions of Jarrett and his business partner Jerry Lawler were uneventful. A subsequent deposition of promoter Jim Barnett

4. Antitrust and Interference with Contractual Relations

IN THE
UNITED STATES DISTRICT COURT
FOR THE EASTERN DISTRICT OF KENTUCKY
AT LEXINGTON

Eastern District of Kentucky
FILED
APR 9 1982
AT LEXINGTON
DAVIS T. McGARVEY
CLERK, U.S. DISTRICT COURT

ANGELO POFFO, et al,

    Plaintiffs,

-vs-

NICK GULAS, et al,

    Defendants.

No. 79-147
Civil

Deposition of: **EDDIE FARHAT**

Taken by: Counsel for Plaintiffs

Date: December 28, 1981

Purpose: For Discovery and All Other Purposes Provided by the Federal Rules of Civil Procedure

Before: Kimberly McClain Smith

Appearances:

MR. BRIAN P. GILFEDDER
Attorney at Law
Lexington, Kentucky

Counsel for Plaintiffs

MS. JUNE ANN KIRKLAND
Attorney at Law
Atlanta, Georgia

Counsel for Defendants

THELMA C. BURDICK and PHYLLIS ELLIOTT
(1931-1981)
REGISTERED PROFESSIONAL REPORTERS
102 SECURITY TRUST BLDG.
LEXINGTON, KENTUCKY 40507
(606) 254-1323

Ed Farhat (a.k.a. the Sheik or the Original Sheik), one of the defendants in the Poffo litigation, was deposed at the end of 1981.

80　Professional Wrestling and the Law

Q 18　Yes. When you first got in the wrestling business, that would have been about the early '50's?

A　Yeah, '58, I think it was. Twenty-nine years. Go back and I think it's '53.

Q 19　How did you learn to be a wrestler? Was it just by wrestling in matches?

A　Can I ask you a real good question? What does that got to do with me being here? Me, how did I become a wrestler?

Q 20　I need to check into your background.

A　For what?

Q 21　It has relevance to your testimony.

A　How I became a wrestler?

Q 22　Yes.

A　This gentleman taught me how to wrestle, Mr. Burt Ruby.

Q 23　Your experience in the wrestling business-

A　Yeah, Burt Ruby taught me how to wrestle. I wrestled for the YMCA's when I was younger.

Q 24　Did you wrestle strictly in the Detroit area at that time or did you move around the country?

A　No, I wrestled--the first part I wrestled in Detroit, then I moved around the country after I got experience.

BURDICK & ELLIOTT REPORTING, 102 SECURITY TRUST BLDG., LEXINGTON, KENTUCKY 40507

23

Despite being a defendant, he provided testimony that was generally favorable for the Poffos and critical of the NWA (and, in particular, defendant Jim Barnett).

4. Antitrust and Interference with Contractual Relations 81

for the Huntington and Parkersburg--

A   Well, Jim Barnett didn't tell you all the places we were partners in, that he didn't pay me, so if you want to get into that, I'll answer those for you. He didn't tell you the part that he didn't pay me, right?

Q 299   Let's go back to the question that I asked.

A   Yeah.

Q 300   Aside from the period of time, which I believe was two shows, where you and Mr. Barnett--

A   Yeah, we plugged in on his TV 17.

Q 301   You mentioned earlier that you had been on the television committee of the NWA, and I believe you mentioned that one of the things that that committee studied was the amount of violence used in tapes, and the problems that promoters have had in recent years with television stations objecting to violence on tapes. Have you used violence in your tapes at all or have you ever received a complaint from the television station about any type of violence in your tape?

A   I don't want to get into that, again.

Q 302   Have you ever used any gimmicks in your tapes?

A   What's a gimmick?

Q 303   Such as the--

Farhat didn't have a lawyer with him at the deposition. Things got combative when the lawyer for defendant Jim Barnett began asking questions of Farhat concerning the business.

A	What's the word gimmick? I don't understand what you're talking about. What's the word gimmick?

Q 304	Well, let me finish my question. Such as the tracing of an eye being gouged out?

A	I don't want to answer all of that, either.

Q 305	Or a snake being used with a wrestler in the ring?

A	I don't want to answer all that, it's ridiculous. Do we have to keep going through all this?

Q 306	Yes, for the record. As a wrestler--

A	I don't want to answer your questions. You're getting ridiculous.

Q 307	As a wrestler--

A	Are you listening to me?

Q 308	Are you--

A	I don't want to answer none of those things you're talking about. It's ridiculous. It has nothing to do--I don't care who you work for, what you do, because one of your clients is Jim Barnett, and you're talking just like Jim Barnett. You're checking my credibility. I don't care nothing about that. You come check my credibility, and you come to find out the truth about what's going on. They're trying to keep a man out of

Farhat got particularly annoyed when Barnett's lawyer began asking questions that might have required Farhat to break kayfabe.

4. Antitrust and Interference with Contractual Relations

the wrestling business, you know it, I know it, and they're doing the same thing to me, that's what we're here to talk about. Not whether they're bringing snakes into the ring or gimmicks. The word gimmick, you got from Jim Barnett.

Q 309   Mr. Farhat, I have to ask my questions for the record. You can refuse to answer my—

A   I refuse to answer them.

Q 310   —question as I ask it. I will still have to ask each of these questions.

A   Well, you better hurry up and get it done because they're all getting ridiculous.

Q 311   Then we'll have to leave it to the Court to determine whether or not—

A   Well, you bring me to Court then. You just tell them to bring me to Court. You bring Jim Barnett and those clients too, because I want to be there and talk to them, if they want to hear my voice.

Q 312   In wrestling are you a good guy or a bad guy?

A   It's none of your business or anybody else's business what I am.

Q 313   Does it have anything to do with how well a wrestler does as to whether it's characterized as a good guy or a bad guy?

Eventually, Farhat got so annoyed that he walked out of the deposition.

in February 1982, who had been accused of various bad acts by earlier witnesses, generated little of interest.

Part of the reason for this was the fact that by this point, the judge in the case had issued a ruling limiting the subject matter of depositions in the matter to two procedural issues: (1) whether a federal court in Kentucky had personal jurisdiction over the defendants and (2) whether the federal court in Lexington was the proper venue for the case.

Personal jurisdiction refers to the court's power over the parties in the lawsuit. The requirement of personal jurisdiction helps alleviate concerns about the unfairness of subjecting defendants to litigation in an inconvenient forum. In considering whether a court has personal jurisdiction over a non-resident defendant, the court will consider whether the defendant has sufficient "minimum contacts" to make it reasonable to require the defendant to respond to a lawsuit there. This is likely to be the case where the defendant has taken actions that were purposefully directed towards the forum state, such as doing business in the state, visiting the state, or bringing property into the state. The concept of *venue* focuses on whether the claim is filed in the appropriate specific court (in this case, the federal court in Lexington).

The various defendants had argued from the earliest stages of the litigation that the federal court in Lexington did not have personal jurisdiction over them and that Lexington was not the appropriate venue for the action. Several of the defendants (Graham, Barnett, Farhat, and Gagne) had previously submitted affidavits stating essentially that they had no contacts whatsoever with the Commonwealth of Kentucky. But it was not until over two years from the date the Poffos filed their complaint that the court appears to have focused on the issue. In January 1982, the court gave the Poffos' lawyer time to uncover sufficient evidence to establish that the court had personal jurisdiction over the defendants and that venue was proper.

On October 15, 1982, the court finally ruled on the defendants' motion to dismiss for lack of personal jurisdiction. The court found that that the plaintiffs had failed to establish that the defendants had the necessary "minimum contacts" with Kentucky to require them to appear in federal court in the state. As such, the court lacked personal jurisdiction over the defendants and entered an order dismissing the Poffos' case.[104]*

* * *

---

* The court's order strangely glosses over the fact that some of the defendants—most notably Jarrett and Lawler—had done considerable business in Kentucky and almost certainly had the minimum contacts necessary to justify hauling them into federal court in Kentucky.

The Poffos' case was dismissed on procedural grounds. The Poffos had been able to produce some evidence of anti-competitive behavior on the part of at least some of the defendants. But the fact that each of the witnesses who presented such evidence was employed by or doing business with the Poffos or had a grudge against the NWA might have called into question their credibility in front of a jury. But a jury never got to hear the case, and the full extent to which the members of the NWA actively worked to torpedo the Poffos' ICW promotion was never definitively resolved.

ICW performers continued to publicly attack Jarrett's promotion,* and the organization limped along through 1983 before closing up shop. In a bizarre twist, Jarrett and the Poffos later made peace, with the trio later joining Jarrett's CWA in 1984. Savage eventually made it to Rupp Arena, facing off against Jerry Lawler in front of a sold-out crowd.

* * *

Part 5: Vince McMahon, The Death of the Territory System, and Interference with Contractual Relations

For those familiar with the history of professional wrestling, the death of the old territory system and its collusive practices is well known. By the early 1980s, the system was on its last legs. And soon thereafter, a promoter from the Northeast would take the legs out once and for all.

In 1963, promoter Vincent J. McMahon, owner of the Capitol Wrestling Company, withdrew from the NWA over a dispute concerning the NWA world champion and renamed his company the World Wide Wrestling Federation (WWWF). McMahon would, of course, later shorten the name of the company to the more familiar World Wrestling Federation (WWF). The WWF would later rejoin the NWA, and McMahon continued to respect the territory system and stayed out of the NWA territories.

But his son, Vincent K. McMahon (or "Vince Jr.") did not have the same respect for the principles upon which the NWA was founded. When he took over the company from his father, Vince Jr. left the NWA again

---

* The most famous incident in the real-life involved an altercation between Savage and Bill Dundee (one of Jarrett's performers), which transpired right around the time the court dismissed the Poffos' claims. Depending on which version one believes (a) the two exchanged words, Dundee went to his car to get a gun, and Savage wrestled the gun away from Dundee and pistol-whipped him or (b) Savage and three other ICW wrestlers confronted Dundee, Savage sucker-punched Dundee, Dundee went to his car to get a gun, and Savage ran away.

and began running shows in the territories that had long belonged to other promoters. He no longer participated in the talent-sharing arrangement followed by the NWA and began signing away top talent from other promotions. The birth of cable television, VCRs, and pay-per-view events had changed the entertainment landscape, making entertainment less regional in nature. McMahon understood this new reality in a way that most other promoters did not.

Jerry Jarrett's Memphis operation broke off from the NWA in 1986. In an effort to stave off McMahon's assault, Jarrett temporarily joined forces with a couple of other holdout promotions (the American Wrestling Association and World Class Championship Wrestling), but the arrangement was short-lived and unsuccessful. By the late 1980s, the various promotions within the NWA began going out of business. Jim Crockett, who ran the Mid–Atlantic territory, bought out some of these promotions and was the last man standing in the NWA. But he couldn't survive McMahon's bare-knuckles (and possibly illegal) business approach.

In 1987, Crockett planned to put on his big pay-per-view event, Starrcade, on Thanksgiving. McMahon countered by creating a competing pay-per-view event, the Survivor Series, just for the purpose of competing with Starrcade. Crockett changed the starting time of Starrcade so as not to conflict with Survivor Series. But this wasn't good enough for McMahon. The WWF boss gave cable providers an ultimatum: if you run Starrcade, I won't let you run the WWF's huge Wrestlemania IV event in a few months. Faced with this threat, the cable companies caved and Starrcade was a huge flop.[105]

At this point, the astute reader might be asking, "wait, doesn't what Vince McMahon did amount to wrongful interference with Crockett's contracts with the cable operators?" If you're thinking that, you very well might be right. It seems obvious McMahon made his threat for the purpose of causing the cable operators to break their deals with Crockett so that McMahon could scoop up more customers for Survivor Series. He wasn't offering the sort of better deal that the law views as a permissible form of interference when he threatened cable providers; he appears to have been trying just to damage Crockett. And if, as it appears, Crockett had existing contracts with the cable operators and if neither party was free to terminate the contracts for whatever reason they wanted, McMahon's ultimatum would have probably been an unlawful form of interference in most states.*

---

* If, however, the cable operators were free to walk away from their deals at any time for any reason, McMahon's interference might have been protected as a legitimate form of competition (albeit, a no-holds-barred form).

The Starrcade debacle damaged Crockett's finances at a time when the company was already taking on water. The failure contributed to Crockett selling his company in 1988 to media mogul Ted Turner.* In other words, it's entirely possible that McMahon's possibly unlawful interference was the death blow in the war between the two foes. Turner rebranded Crockett's product as World Championship Wrestling (WCW) and did battle with McMahon and the WWF.†

WCW and the WWF/WWE engaged in their own war for over a decade, from which McMahon emerged victorious in 2001. McMahon eventually bought the wreckage of the company that had been WCW in March 2001. The third-place competitor in the business during this time, Extreme Championship Wrestling (ECW), had run its final live show a couple of months earlier before officially closing up shop in April 2001. Other companies would eventually form, but for a brief period of time, McMahon had something close to the monopoly over professional wrestling that the original members of the NWA had only dreamed of.

* * *

Conclusion

Flash forward 20 years. In January of 2022, Major League Wrestling (MLW) filed suit against the WWE, alleging that the WWE engaged in anti-competitive business practices toward MLW. The complaint alleged tortious interference with MLW's business relationships and violations of the Sherman Act. According to the complaint, the WWE

- pressured Tubi, a streaming service owned by Fox, to terminate its agreement with the MLW to air MLW content by threatening to withhold WWE content from Fox;
- refused to hire performers who had worked for MLW;
- attempted to induce MLW performers to breach their exclusive contracts with MLW and sign with WWE; and
- interfered with MLW's broadcasting agreement with VICE TV.[106]

Later court filings alleged other forms of anti-competitive practices on the part of WWE with respect to other wrestling organizations. These included encouraging Madison Square Garden to cancel an event jointly

---

* For more information on the fall of Crockett's operation, see *Shaun Assael & Mike Mooneyham, Sex, Lies, and Headlocks* 75–80 (2002).

† The war that eventually developed between Turner and McMahon involved its own set of competitive business practices, some of which are discussed in Chapter 7.

offered by Ring of Honor and New Japan Pro-Wrestling, scheduled for the same weekend as WWE's showcase event, Wrestlemania.[107] WWE also allegedly blocked All Elite Wrestling (AEW) from putting on shows at the Heritage Bank Center in Cincinnati, Ohio.[108]

In other words, the WWE allegedly engaged in the exact same tactics that the original NWA members had pioneered some 70 years earlier and that its members allegedly employed until the organization's demise. The more things change in professional wrestling, the more they stay the same.

Postscript: The Right of Publicity

NWA Southeastern Wrestling, Inc. v.
All Star Championship Wrestling, Inc. (1979)

As part of his lawsuit against the outlaw All Star Championship Wrestling organization, Ron Fuller alleged that the group had exploited the market value of Fuller's name and invaded Fuller's privacy by using his name in their advertisements. Specifically, several of All Star's newspaper ads promoted a so-called "Chicken Challenge" at their events. All Star advertised that wrestler Bob Orton, Jr., would face Fuller in a match "if Fuller shows up."[109]* In response, Fuller sought an injunction prohibiting All-Star from using Fuller's name in their promotions and damages for the unauthorized use of his name.[110]

* * *

In the late 1890s, young Abigail Roberson was subjected to "scoffs and jeers" by passersby in Monroe County, New York. She was humiliated to the point that she was treated by a physician and confined to her bed. The reason? Without Roberson's consent, the Franklin Mills Flour Company had used Roberson's likeness in an advertisement for its product. The ads were posted in stores, warehouses, saloons, and other public places to the point that people recognized Roberson and apparently mocked her. According to Roberson, she suffered severe distress as a result.[111]

Roberson sued, claiming that the company had violated her "right of privacy." Roberson's claim faced one significant obstacle: the law did not recognize any such right at the time. A few years earlier, a couple of

---

* Also on the card for one of those shows was an event in which "Ginger," a 750-pound bear, would challenge "all comers." The ad explained that "[a] beautiful trophy will be presented to the fan who proves to be the best bear wrestler."

lawyers* had written a law review article in which they argued that the law *should* recognize such a right.[112] But at the time, New York did not recognize such a right. As a result, Roberson's claim failed.[113] The New York legislature responded to the *Roberson* case by enacting the first statute to recognize a right to privacy. The statute prohibits the use of a living person's name, portrait or picture for advertising or trade purposes without prior written consent and provides a remedy to one whose rights under the statute were violated.[114]

* * *

Several years later in Georgia, artist Paolo Pavesich noticed his picture in an advertisement appearing in the *Atlanta Constitution* newspaper. The New England Mutual Life Insurance Company placed an ad for life insurance in the paper featuring photographs of two men alongside each other. One was a picture of Pavesich. The other was a picture "of an ill-dressed and sickly looking person."[115] The ad encouraged readers to purchase life insurance. Above Pavesich's picture were the words, "Do it now. The man who did." Above the picture of the ill-dressed and sickly looking person were the words, "Do it while you can. The man who didn't." Pavesich had not consented to this use of his likeness, nor did he even own life insurance with New England Mutual. And even though the ad actually placed Pavesich in a positive light (as "the man who did"), Pavesich sued the company for $25,000 in a Georgia state court.[116]

Pavesich ultimately had more luck with his claim than Abigail Roberson had earlier in New York. The Georgia Supreme Court concluded that every individual enjoyed a right of privacy. Therefore, "[t]he publication of a picture of a person, without his consent, as a part of an advertisement, for the purpose of exploiting the publisher's business, is a violation of the right of privacy of the person whose picture is reproduced, and entitles him to recover, without proof of special damage."[117]

* * *

These early 20th century decisions and statutes helped establish the tort law theory of invasion of privacy. There are several different versions of this theory, but the kind at issue in Pavesich's case protects against "the appropriation of another's name and likeness ... without consent and for the financial gain of the appropriator."[118] The right at issue is sometimes referred to as the right of publicity. Unlike the other types of invasion of privacy claims, which protect an individual from emotional and mental harms, the primary goal of the right of publicity claim is to protect

---

* One of the lawyers was Louis D. Brandeis, who would go on to serve on the United States Supreme Court.

an individual's proprietary interest in his or her likeness.[119] In essence, the theory prevents an individual or company from making a buck off of another person's name or likeness without that person's consent.*

* * *

This was the claim that Fuller asserted against All Star Championship Wrestling. According to Fuller, the promotion was using Fuller's name, without his consent, for financial gain. The fact that the outlaw group had (in Fuller's eyes) stabbed him in the back and was still in possession of the Southeastern Championship Belt (see Chapter 2) undoubtedly only made the use of his name to promote their shows that much more galling.

Courts in Tennessee had considered this type of claim before. Prior to Elvis Presley's death in 1977, Elvis had assigned the right to exploit the use of his name and likeness to Boxcar Enterprises in exchange for royalties. Following Elvis' death, the Memphis Development Foundation, a Tennessee non-profit corporation, announced plans to erect a statue in honor of the King in Memphis. In order to generate donations for the project, the Foundation sent those who donated $25 or more an eight-inch pewter replica of the proposed statue.

The specific legal question in the case was whether Elvis' right of publicity survived his death. If so, Boxcar had the right to prevent the Foundation from making use of Elvis' name and likeness for financial gain.[120] If not, the Foundation was free to appropriate his name and likeness for financial gain. The courts held that Elvis' right of publicity did not survive his death.† But the courts that considered the case had no doubt that had Elvis himself asserted the claim, he would have prevailed. As the United States Court of Appeals for the Sixth Circuit noted, "[t]he famous have an exclusive legal right during life to control and profit from the commercial use of their name and personality."[121] Elvis himself "had what has been recognized in Tennessee as a valuable proprietary right, a kind of property right in his name and image, and he had an exclusive right to market it, to assign it, or to benefit from its use commercially."[122]

* * *

---

* Some states recognize a right of publicity that extends beyond one's name or likeness and includes other aspects of an individual's identity. Thus, for example, *Tonight Show* host Johnny Carson was able to state a claim against the Here's Johnny Portable Toilets company for having misappropriated Carson's signature phrase, "Here's Johnny." See *Carson v. Here's Johnny Portable Toilets, Inc.*, 698 F.2d 631 (6th Cir. 1983). In another case, actress Bette Midler successfully asserted a claim against Ford Motor for using a Bette Midler soundalike in one of its advertisements. See *Midler v. Ford Motor Co.*, 849 F.2d 460 (9th Cir. 1988).

† The Tennessee legislature later enacted a statute that effectively overruled this decision and provided that the right of publicity did survive one's death, thus giving Elvis' estate greater control over the use of his name and likeness. See *Tenn. Code. Ann.* § 47-25-1101 et seq.

4. Antitrust and Interference with Contractual Relations   91

In theory, Fuller had a decent claim here. Fuller was well known in the area, and his name had value. So, he had the exclusive right to benefit from the commercial use of that name. And All Star Championship Wrestling was pretty clearly using his name, without his consent, to draw customers. Unfortunately for Fuller, the judge assigned to his case was unsympathetic to Fuller's complaint about All Star's "Chicken Challenge."*

According to the judge, "[b]y engaging in the professional wrestling business, by his previous habits, and by the customs of trade and uses in the professional wrestling business," Fuller had "waived his right to privacy so far as it relates to the use of his name in challenge situations."[123] There is a long history in the wrestling business of performers calling out performers in other promotions. Shane Douglas made a name for himself in (and drew ratings for) Extreme Championship Wrestling (ECW) by regularly insulting and challenging Ric Flair of WCW in the 1990s. Eric Bischoff of WCW famously challenged Vince McMahon of the WWF to appear on a WCW pay-per-view event to fight. The court's opinion in Fuller's cases explained that "[i]t is an accepted manner of usage in the trade to issue challenges from one wrestler to another." According to the court, that was all that All Star had done here.

This raises an interesting legal point. If one consents to another's use of their name or likeness for commercial purposes, they have no claim that their right of privacy or right of publicity has been violated. Presumably, this is what the court was suggesting in Fuller's case. Fuller may not have ever told All Star that the company could use his name in advertising, but by participating in the world of professional wrestling, he was impliedly consenting to the normal practices within the business. One of those practices, according to the court, was to drop the name of another wrestler when issuing a challenge.

But there is a strong argument that the court's approach was flawed. In support of its conclusion, the court cited the Tennessee case of *Martin v. Senators, Inc.*[124] There, an employee of the Senators Club, a nightspot that members of the public could pay to join, gave the defendant permission to use her photograph in a "bulletin" for club members. Senators Club then ran an advertisement in the *Knoxville News-Sentinel* that used the same photograph. According to the Tennessee Supreme Court, the fact that the employee had expressly consented to the publication of her photo in the

---

* All Star Wrestling and its confederate, International Championship Wrestling, employed a similar tactic against Nick Gulas. One advertisement announced that Randy "Macho Man" Savage would offer $5,000 to face Gulas' son, George, in a "Baby Bottle Challenge" "if George shows up?????" ICW Poffo Universe, https://icwpoffouniverse.webs.com/091879%20icw%20ad%20springfield%20tennessee.jpg.

IN THE CHANCERY COURT FOR KNOX COUNTY, TENNESSEE AT KNOXVILLE

NWA SOUTHEASTERN WRESTLING, INC.,)
and RONALD WELCH a/k/a RON FULLER,)
)
        Plaintiffs,   )
)
vs.   )   No. 67652
)
ALL STAR CHAMPIONSHIP WRESTLING, INC.,)
RONNIE GARVIN, BOB ORTON, JR.,   )   12:05 P.M.
BOB ROOP and RON WRIGHT,   )
)   FILED
        Defendants.   )   OCT 2 1979
                                        M. DAVID CATE, C. & M.

                    COMPLAINT
                        I

        Plaintiff NWA Southeastern Wrestling, Inc., (hereinafter "Southeastern Wrestling") is a Tennessee corporation, having its principal office and place of business in Knox County, Tennessee, and is engaged in the business of promoting and conducting professional wrestling matches open to the public throughout East Tennessee and Southeastern Kentucky. Plaintiff Ronald Welch a/k/a Ron Fuller (hereinafter "Ron Fuller") is a citizen and resident of Knox County, Tennessee.

                        II

        Defendant All Star Championship Wrestling, Inc., (hereinafter "All Star") is a Tennessee corporation and is engaged in the business of promoting, conducting and exhibiting professional wrestling matches in Tennessee, including Knox County, and whose agent for service of process is Luther R. Wright, 901 Bloomingdale Pike, Kingsport, Tennessee 37660. Defendants Ronnie Garvin, Bob Orton, Jr., and Bob

The first filing in Southeastern Wrestling Association's lawsuit against four of the Knoxville Five (minus Boris Malenko, who was in the process of retiring at this point).

bulletin, which was available to members of the public who belonged to the club, also meant that she had impliedly consented to publication of her photo in a public newspaper.[125]

There are at least two things that are arguably wrong with the court's reliance on the *Senators* case in Fuller's situation. The first is the fact that the *Senators* decision is probably just plain wrong. Consent to the use of one's picture in a publication limited to a group of people is, as a matter of common sense, not the same thing as consenting to have the picture used in advertisement that is distributed all over town for the sole economic benefit of the publisher.

4. Antitrust and Interference with Contractual Relations   93

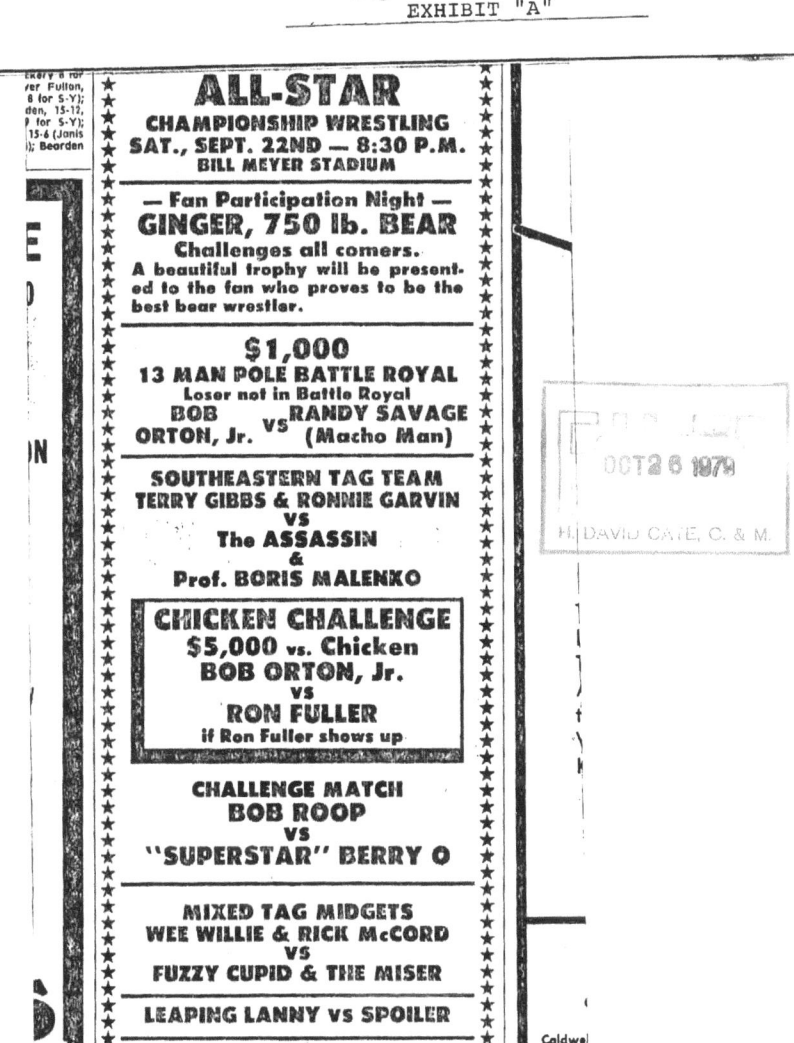

The Chicken Challenge ad that Ron Fuller found objectionable.

The second problem with the court's decision is that it ignored the context in which All Star used Fuller's name. It would have been one thing if one member of All Star challenged another member of that organization to a match, or if one of the wrestlers in Fuller's group challenged another of Fuller's wrestlers. This is the sort of use of one's name that every wrestler consents to. That is not just a custom of the business, it is the essence of the business itself. But Fuller was in competition with All Star, and Fuller's competitor was arguably seeking to profit from Fuller's name in its advertisements. From time to time, a wrestler in one promotion might reference another wrestler in a different promotion. But that's a far cry from trying to lure customers to spend their money in the hopes that a performer from another promotion will show up to accept a challenge. And the fact that All Star was also using the trade name "Southeastern" in its advertisements, thereby seeking to profit off the name of Fuller's company, only made the situation worse. It's hard to conclude that Fuller consented in any meaningful way to All Star's use of his name in advertising for "the Chicken Challenge."

* * *

Fuller's lawyers filed a motion asking the court to reconsider its decision but eventually voluntarily dismissed the suit.[126] Fuller's run of bad luck in the Knox County courthouse had ended for the moment. But his lawsuit over the Chicken Challenge remains an interesting footnote in the legal history of professional wrestling.

Chapter 5

Labor and Employment Law

"The Contractor is a freelance performer who values his/her independence and freedom to engage in other business activities, not have a 9 to 5 job and prefers to operate as an independent contractor."
—Contract between TNA Entertainment, LLC and wrestler Matt Hardy (March 1, 2015).

"Defendant WWE exercises virtually complete dominion and control over its wrestlers and their performances...."
—*Levy v. World Wresting Entertainment, Inc.*, Plaintiffs' Memorandum in Opposition to Defendant's Motion to Dismiss, No. 3:08cv1289 (PCD) (D. Conn. November 26, 2008).

* * *

One reason why wrestling promoters in the territory days were able to engage in the practice of blacklisting wrestlers discussed in Chapter 4 is because of the imbalance of power between promoters and wrestlers. Promoters were organized and worked together to increase their profits. The wrestlers lacked any similar kind of organization that could counter-balance the strength of the promoters. In other words, the wrestlers lacked a union.

But it wasn't just the lack of a union that weakened the position of wrestlers relative to management. While wrestlers may have worked exclusively for a promoter, they were not employees. Instead, they were classified as independent contractors. The distinction is legally significant. The fact that wrestlers were classified as independent contractors instead of employees meant that they were not entitled to the full protection of the various state and federal laws that protect employees in the workplace.

Both of these situations continue into the present day. There is no labor union devoted to protecting the right of wrestlers, and the biggest wrestling promotion in the world, WWE, classifies its in-ring performers as independent contractors instead of employees. This chapter explores how labor and employment laws have largely worked to the disadvantage of professional wrestlers and examines how the law in this area may evolve in the future.

* * *

Part 1: The Origins of the Independent Contractor Classification

The modern relationship between a performer and a promoter has its origins in the old territory system. Back in the territory days, the relationship between promoter and wrestler was fairly informal. Much like today's driver for a ride-sharing company like Uber or Lyft, the typical wrestler in the territory days was not locked into a long-term contract. A promoter might hire a wrestler in advance to work a series of shows, but wrestlers were not typically signed to long-term contracts. This gave performers at least some flexibility to move on to another promoter when it was financially more advantageous to do so. Sometimes a state athletic commission might require a written contract for a night's performance, but sometimes a handshake deal between promoter and wrestler was all that transpired. Like Uber drivers, wrestlers weren't typically paid a weekly or monthly salary. Instead, like Uber drivers, wrestlers in the territory days might get a guaranteed minimum (say $25) for their night's performance, with the rest of the compensation depending on "the gate," or how many tickets the promoter sold for the night. (Unlike Uber drivers, however, there wasn't always a set rate or percentage from the gate that the performer was entitled to. Sometimes, it was simply up to the discretion of the promoter.)

While the relationship between promoter and performer could be informal, there was one feature of the relationship that limited the freedom and flexibility that wrestlers enjoyed. Regardless of the formal details of the arrangement between a performer and a promoter, it was understood that while working for the promoter in a territory, a wrestler wouldn't work for another promoter.* So, unlike the Uber driver who can also work for Lyft or DoorDash, a wrestler could not work one night for, say, promoter Eddie Graham in Florida and the next night for, say, Jim Barnett in Georgia unless the two promoters agreed to permit such an arrangement. The typical wrestler worked for one promoter and one promoter only until it was time to move on to a new territory.

---

* There were exceptions, André the Giant being the most notable.

In the territory days, the understanding—whether in writing or not—was that a wrestler was not the promoter's employee. The wrestler was an independent contractor.[1] Independence is the hallmark of an independent contractor.[2] As explained by one court, an independent contractor generally has the freedom to "work in his own way."[3] In contrast, an employee is subject to the control of the employer. The wrestler in the territory days had some characteristics of an independent contractor. For example, a wrestler had independence in the sense that a wrestler was generally free to pack up stakes and move on to a new gig whenever the wrestler wanted. But other aspects of the relationship between promoter and performer—such as the fact that a wrestler couldn't work for another promoter—are more typical of an employer-employee relationship. Regardless, for purposes of the business, promoters classified performers as independent contractors. This classification has carried forward into the modern WWE, well after the death of the territory system. Today's standard WWE contract expressly defines performers as independent contractors and not employees.

* * *

Part 2: The Legal Significance of the Classification

The issue of whether a professional wrestler is an employee of a promoter or an independent contractor has arisen in legal cases since at least the 1940s.[4] The distinction between an employee and an independent contractor matters for purposes of labor and employment law. Federal labor law is based on the assumption that there is inequality of bargaining between employers and employees and that this inequality works to the disadvantage of employees. This inequality of bargaining power, it is presumed, generally results in lower wages and worse working conditions for employees. As the logic goes, the most effective way for employees to level the playing field and attain better wages and working conditions is to organize so that they may bargain with employers over the terms and conditions of their employment and provide other forms of mutual aid or protection.[5]

In order to help fulfill these goals, § 7 of the National Labor Relations Act (the NLRA) states the right of employees "to self-organization, to form, join, or assist labor organizations, to bargain collectively through representatives of their own choosing, and to engage in other concerted activities for the purpose of collective bargaining or other mutual aid or protection."[6] In short, the NLRA protects the right of employees to form unions so that they have a better chance of obtaining higher wages and improved working conditions by banding together to bargain with the employer. As a result, employers are prohibited from firing or otherwise disciplining employees for attempting to organize a union, threatening employees with adverse consequences if they participate in union activities, or taking other actions that "interfere with, restrain, or coerce employees in the exercise of [their] rights" under the NLRA.[7]

Importantly, the rights afforded by the NLRA—including the right to unionize—are only afforded to employees, not independent contractors. The NLRA expressly excludes independent contractors from its coverage.[8] So, if a group of workers sought to unionize, and it was determined that they were independent contractors, the National Labor Relations Board (NLRB)—the federal agency that oversees the NLRA—would not certify any union that they formed.

The question of whether professional wrestlers are independent contractors or employees has come up in the union context before. Back in 1953, the California Supreme Court decided *Rubin v. American Sportsmen Television Equity Society*, a labor dispute involving professional wrestlers. The case involved a labor organization consisting of at least some professional wrestlers that had not yet been certified by the NLRB. The organization demanded that a group of wrestling promoters use only wrestlers who were members of the labor organization in the promoters' televised events. The promoters refused, so the labor organization began picketing the promoters' events. The promoters responded by seeking an injunction preventing the picketing on the part of the labor organization, in part, on the grounds that the wrestlers were independent contractors and, therefore, that federal law did not give them the right to picket.[9]

The parties submitted conflicting affidavits on the question of whether the wrestlers were employees or independent contractors. As discussed in more detail below, the key distinction between employees and independent contractors is control. The more control the employer has over the manner in which the worker performs a job, the more likely the worker is to be classified as an employee. The less control the employer has, the more likely the worker is to be an independent contractor. The promoters submitted an affidavit from eleven wrestlers that contained the almost certainly false and perjured claim that the promoters "exercised no control over the wrestlers' methods of performance or results to be obtained in the wrestling matches."[10] Based on the evidence presented, the trial court issued the injunction based on the tentative conclusion that the wrestlers were independent contractors rather than employees.[11] The California Supreme Court affirmed the decision on appeal.

The question in *Rubin* over whether the wrestlers were employees of the promoter or merely independent contractors was never fully litigated. So, the decision has limited precedential value. But it remains the leading case on the question of the employment status of professional wrestlers. If the holding from *Rubin* applies to, say, the wrestlers under contract to WWE, those wrestlers, as independent contractors, lack the same rights as employees under the NLRA.

* * *

The question of whether wrestlers are employees or independent contractors isn't limited to the ability of wrestlers to form a union. There are a host of other state and federal laws that govern the workplace. Most of these laws extend protection only to employees:

- **Workplace safety**: The Occupational Safety and Health Act (OSHA) requires an employer to "furnish to each of his *employees* employment and a place of employment which are free from recognized hazards that are causing or are likely to cause death or serious physical harm to his employees."[12]
- **Wage and hour**: The Fair Labor Standards Act (FLSA) requires an employer to "pay to each of his *employees*" a minimum wage and prohibits an employer from requiring "any of his *employees*" from working more than 40 hours in a work week.[13]
- **Leave time**: The Family and Medical Leave Act (FMLA) requires an employer to provide "an eligible *employee*" up to 12 weeks of unpaid leave where the employee has a serious medical condition.[14] The FMLA also provides for up to 12 weeks of unpaid leave for mothers and fathers following childbirth and to provide care for a family member with a serious medical condition. Over a dozen states require employers to provide *paid* parental and caregiving leave to employees (but not independent contractors).
- **Workers' compensation**: Workers' compensation programs for injuries on the job are administered at the state level. But the typical statute only covers employees, not independent contractors.[15] Employers are required to purchase workers' compensation insurance for their employees, and like all forms of insurance, rates increase as more employees are injured on the job and seek benefits. So, classifying a worker as an independent contractor instead of an employee cuts down on an employer's expenditures.
- **Unemployment insurance**: State unemployment benefits are also generally limited to employees. Employers are required to pay a special tax in order to fund a state's unemployment insurance program. And like workers' compensation, the more employees

who file for benefits after losing their jobs with an employer, the higher the tax to the employer is. So, again, it works to an employer's advantage to classify a worker as an independent contractor in terms of unemployment insurance costs.
- **Discrimination**: All of the major federal statutes prohibiting employment discrimination—Title VII, the Age Discrimination in Employment Act, etc.—protect employees from discrimination but not independent contractors.
- **Retaliation**: Most of the various statutes governing the workplace prohibit an employer from retaliating against an employee who assert their rights under the statutes. So, for example, an employer cannot fire an employee who has filed for workers' compensation benefits or complained about unlawful discrimination. But, once again, this protection from retaliation extends only to employees, not independent contractors.

All of these laws have application to the relationship between promoter and wrestler. But perhaps the most relevant are the laws related to leave time and workers' compensation. When it comes to injuries, the NFL Players Association (NFLPA) notes that professional football has a 100 percent injury rate.[16] The same is true for professional wrestling. To be a wrestler is to live with pain. Former wrestler Scott Levy (a.k.a. Raven) once advised, "If you want to be a wrestler, you have to be a big guy, and you have to perform in pain. If you choose to do neither, pick another profession."[17] Injuries range from nagging aches and pains to career-ending paralysis. As author David Shoemaker puts it, "[e]very night on the road ends with ice bags or painkillers or just plain old *pain*, the unrelenting kind, the 'you sit down in your rental car and electric voltage shoots up your spine' kind of pain."[18] The outcomes of matches may be pre-determined and there are sometimes "injuries" that are part of a plot line, but professional wrestling takes a very real toll on the body.

NFL players experience similar pain during the NFL season. By law, players are eligible to receive workers' compensation benefits for their injuries.[19] For example, Hall of Fame wide receiver Michael Irvin collected nearly $250,000 in workers' compensation for injuries accumulated during his career.[20] In contrast, WWE performers are entitled to nothing under state workers' compensation plans as a result of being classified as independent contractors.*

---

* Beginning somewhere around 1999, World Championship Wrestling (WCW) provided workers' compensation insurance for its performers, despite classifying them as independent contractors. *See Eudy v. Universal Wrestling Corp.*, 611 S.E.2d 770, 774 (Ga. Ct. App. 2005); *Hart v. District of Columbia Dept. of Emp. Servs.*, 843 A.2d 746, 748 (D.C. Ct. App. 2004). WCW was eventually bought out by Vince McMahon and WWE.

NFL players have an offseason they can use to let their bodies heal. Professional wrestlers do not. If wrestlers were classified as employees, they would have the right under the FMLA to take up to 12 weeks off (unpaid) in the event of a serious medical condition. And an employer is prohibited from firing or otherwise discriminating against an employee who takes such leave. In contrast, at least in the not-too-distant past, WWE contracts expressly provided that the company could fire an employee who was unable to work for more than six weeks due to injury.[21] WWE contracts with its performers also make clear that the performers are not employees and that the company has the contractual right to fire its performers *for any reason*, provided the promotion provides 90 days' notice.[22]

While the FMLA is a federal statute, some states have their own state leave statutes that provide for *paid* leave time in the event of a serious medical condition. Connecticut, where WWE is incorporated, is one such state. Under Connecticut's Paid Leave Act, employees are entitled to up to 12 weeks of paid leave (at a reduced rate) in the event of a serious medical condition.[23] But, again, independent contractors do not enjoy the same right.

The accumulation of injuries and damage to the human body through years of continuous work (and the use of painkillers to treat the pain and the use of anabolic steroids to increase muscle mass) has long-term effects. The number of wrestlers who have died early deaths is jaw-dropping.[24] For example, a 2014 study found that the mortality rate of professional wrestlers was up to 2.9 times greater than that of men in the general population.[25] Another 2014 study found that the mortality rates for some age groups of wrestlers were more than five times higher than the general population. The same study found that the mortality rate among professional wrestlers was also significantly higher than it was other professional athletes.[26]

* * *

Another consequence of classifying wrestlers as independent contractors instead of employees is that promotions are not required to provide health insurance to performers. Under the Affordable Care Act, most employers are required to provide health insurance to their full-time employees (but not their independent contractors). WWE pays for medical expenses incurred as result of in-ring injuries.[27] But WWE contracts advise performers—sometimes in all caps and bold font—that medical insurance is the responsibility of the performer.[28]

WWE does sponsor a wellness program for its performers. Among other things, the program includes cardiovascular testing, substance abuse testing, brain function testing, and referral to health care providers.[29] WWE routinely touts its wellness program when questioned about the health and safety of its workers. But for all of its benefits, WWE's program falls short of the benefits provided by actual employer-provided health insurance. For example, imagine an office employee who is diagnosed with cancer or whose family member is diagnosed with cancer. That employee would have employer-provided health insurance that would cover at least some of the costs of treating the condition. A WWE performer in the same situation would not.

* * *

Being classified as an independent contractor has other financial impacts on workers. Under the Federal Insurance Contributions Act (FICA), employee wages are taxed at a rate of 7.65 percent in order to fund federal Social Security, Medicare, and Medicaid programs. Employers withhold these taxes from employees' paychecks. Independent contractors are taxed at the higher rate of 15.3 percent and must handle payment themselves.

Federal law does not require employers to provide retirement plans for their employees. However, a number of states (including Connecticut, where WWE is based) require employers to offer retirement savings plans if they do not already voluntarily do so.[30] But as is the case with all of the laws described above, the mandate only applies to employees, not independent contractors.

* * *

Finally, the question of independent contractor status is also relevant for purposes of tort suits that seek to hold an employer liable for the wrongs committed by an employee. Recall the lawsuit from Chapter 3 involving Sweet Stan Lane of the Midnight Express beating up poor, unfortunate Roy Massey. In addition to suing Lane, Massey sought to hold Jim Crockett Promotions vicariously liable for Lane's battery of Massey. As discussed in that chapter, Massey could only hold Crockett vicariously liable if Lane was acting within the scope of employment at the time. But there is another requirement of vicarious liability. Before an employer can be held liable for the torts of a worker, that worker must be an employee of the employer, not an independent contractor. So, obviously, it is the best interests of wrestling promoters that wrestlers are classified as independent contractors instead of employees.

In the *Massey* case, the West Virginia Supreme Court of Appeals offhandedly referred to Lane as an employee.[31] But that may not have been accurate. As discussed above, promoters have long classified their wrestlers as independent contractors. In the brief he filed with the West Virginia Supreme Court of Appeals, Massey's lawyer seemed to anticipate a possible argument on this point by Jim Crockett Promotions' attorneys. At several points, the brief notes the control Jim Crockett Promotions had over the wrestlers, for example, pointing out that Crockett controlled the use of the name "Midnight Express" and had the right to tell the wrestlers to perform under a different stage name.[32] So, Massey's lawyer wanted to make the point clear that the Lane was really an employee, no matter how Crockett classified him. Crockett's lawyers do not appear to have contested this characterization of the wrestlers as employees, but it was potentially a decisive issue in the case.

* * *

Part 3: *Levy v. World Wrestling Entertainment, Inc.*

To be clear, for plenty of people, the benefits of being classified as an independent contractor—even when that classification is debatable—outweigh the downsides. Being an employee means being subject to the employer's right to control when and how the employee does the job. In the modern gig economy, there are plenty of workers who prefer the freedom of being an independent contractor.

But there are also plenty of workers who should, by rights, be classified as employees and enjoy the legal protections afforded to employees but who are instead misclassified as independent contractors. The misclassification of workers as independent contractors is fairly common in the U.S. Several studies suggest that between 10 and 20 percent of workers are misclassified as independent contractors.[33] Misclassification occurs most commonly in industries where employers have an economic incentive to misclassify.[34] For example, a *Harvard Business Review* article suggests that about one-third of construction workers in the South—workers who are frequently injured on the job and would benefit from worker's compensation—are misclassified by their employers as independent contractors.[35]

* * *

There have been a handful of lawsuits against WWE within the past two decades charging that the company misclassified its performers as independent contractors instead of employees. For example, in 2008, former WWE wrestlers Raven (Scott Levy), Chris Kanyon (Christopher Klucsarits), and "Above Average" Mike Sanders (Michael Sanders) sued WWE, alleging that the organization had misclassified them as independent contractors and failed to make the required withholdings from their paychecks.³⁶ In their complaint filed in federal court in Connecticut, the wrestlers laid out their position as to the control that WWE exercised over performers:

> 4. At all times relevant herein, defendant WWE has exercised total control over all aspects of the wrestlers' employment, including as follows:
> - defendant determines the wrestlers' physical training regimen;
> - defendant determines the wrestlers' skill training regimen;
> - defendant determines the location where the wrestlers perform;
> - defendant determines the time the wrestlers perform;
> - defendant determines who the wrestlers compete with and against, the duration of each match, and the outcome of each match;
> - defendant has the right to require that the wrestlers wrestle in a team and has the right to choose the co-workers for such a team;
> - defendant determines the costumes and hairstyles that the wrestlers' wear and has the right to require the use of company costumes and performance props;
> - defendant determines the wrestlers' stage persona and the specific traits of that persona, and further determines the mannerisms that the wrestlers use while performing and what signature moves and props the wrestlers use and when they may use them;
> - defendant requires the wrestlers to adhere to certain story lines, including the specific dialogue of the requisite pre- and post-match boasting and badmouthing of the wrestlers' opponent(s);
> - defendant has the right to use the wrestlers' likeness or image in perpetuity;
> - defendant has the right to negotiate and enter into any agreements for the exploitation of intellectual property based on the wrestlers' personae for merchandising, commercial tie-ins, publishing, personal appearances, performances in non-wrestling events, and endorsements;
> - defendant has the right to require the wrestlers to submit to drug screening;
> - defendant unilaterally determines how the wrestlers are compensated.
>
> 5. At all times relevant herein, plaintiffs and the other wrestlers hired by defendant WWE provide and provided services which is and was an integral part of defendant's business enterprise. The "Booking Contract" explicitly forbids plaintiffs and the other wrestlers from having separate or distinct occupation or business.

The wrestlers' suit failed for a variety of reasons before the case ever reached trial. So, the plaintiffs' allegations were never put the test, and the court never actually considered the central question of whether the performers were employees or independent contractors.³⁷

In 2016, over 50 former wrestlers brought suit in federal court in Connecticut, alleging a variety of legal claims against WWE.* Among the legal theories the wrestlers asserted was the claim that WWE had misclassified them as independent contractors, thereby depriving them of the protections afforded to employees under federal law. The wrestlers' complaint contained many of the same allegations as the 2008 lawsuit in terms of the control WWE exercised over its performers and how they performed their jobs.[38] The suit also alleged various ways in which WWE retained control over its performers, including by damaging the future career prospects of wrestlers who questioned WWE's control by assigning them ridiculous gimmicks or having them "job" (or lose) repeatedly.[39]

Once again, the case was dismissed before the court ever considered the merits of the claim.[40] As a result, there is no published decision in which a modern court has directly considered the question of whether WWE wrestlers are employees or independent contractors.

* * *

Part 4: Misclassification?

So, are WWE employees or independent contractors? As mentioned, the standard WWE contract that performers have signed in recent decades expressly provides that the performers are independent contractors and not employees.† But the fact that the parties contractually defined a worker as an independent contractor does not conclusively resolve the issue.

Traditionally, courts and agencies considered a host of different factors to determine a worker's status. Some courts consider five factors. Others consider six or seven. The IRS used to consider 20 factors but now considers only three.[41] But, regardless of the approach, the most important factor in any of these tests focuses on the concept of employer control, specifically whether the employer has the right to control and direct the worker in the performance of the work and the manner in which the work is to be done. In other words, if the employer has the right to control *how* the worker does the job, the worker is most likely an employee. If, instead, the employer hires the worker to perform a job but leaves the details as to how the job will be

---

* These claims are covered in Chapter 9.

† Interestingly, WWE had claimed in a previous sexual harassment lawsuit that one of its performers was actually an employee and not an independent contractor. The reasons are somewhat complex, but the short version is that if the wrestler were deemed an employee, her emotional injuries would be covered by workers' compensation and, therefore, she could not bring a separate lawsuit. The workers' compensation costs would have been less than the payout in a lawsuit. So, it worked to WWE's advantage in that instance to have the wrestler, Nicole Bass, classified as an employee. *Bass v. World Wrestling Federation Entertainment, Inc.*, 129 F. Supp. 2d 491 (E.D.N.Y. 2001).

accomplished to the worker, the worker is most likely an independent contractor. As stated by one court, an independent contractor is "one who contracts to perform a certain work for another according to his own means and methods, free from control of his employer in all details connected with the performance of the work except as to its product or result."[42] In other words, an employer tells an independent contractor to get a particular job done. But *how* the job actually gets done is up to the contractor. In contrast, an employer has the right to tell an employee exactly how to do the job.

Courts and government agencies also consider a variety of other factors in helping to make the determination. The following factors tend to suggest that a worker is an employee rather than an independent contractor:

- the agreement between the parties anticipates close supervision of the individual's work;
- the worker's opportunity for entrepreneurial gain or loss;
- work that does not require the services of one who is highly educated or skilled;
- the employer supplies the instrumentalities, tools, and the place of work for the person doing the work;
- payment on an hourly or monthly basis instead of payment by the job;
- employment over an extended period of time with regular hours;
- full time employment by one employer;
- employment in a specific area;
- the fact that the work is part of the regular business of the employer (as opposed to being a special project);
- custom within the industry; and
- the parties' understanding that there is an employer-employee relationship.[43]

The question of whether any worker is an employee or an independent contractor is fact specific. In the case of wrestling, for example, there is a significant difference between a WWE Superstar and a guy who occasionally works indie shows in a church basement. But applying these and similar factors, courts in the 20th century reached sometimes different conclusions as to whether wrestlers were employees or independent contractors.

*Langness v. Ketonen**

A wrestler injured a fan at a match in Tacoma, Washington, in 1950. The fan sought to hold the promoter vicariously liable for the wrestler's wrongful conduct, so the fan needed to establish that the wrestler was an employee

---

* This case is also discussed in Chapter 3.

of the promoter and not an independent contractor. The court considered several factors but focused most heavily on the custom within the wrestling industry as to the promoter's right to control the actions of the wrestlers in the ring. In perhaps the first recorded breach of kayfabe in the courtroom, a retired wrestler/referee/promoter testified that promoters had "complete control of a wrestling exhibition" and gave directions as to how and what to do in the ring.[44] In short, promoters had the right to control and direct wrestlers in the performance of their work and in the manner in which the work was to be done. This made them employees according to the court.

1969 IRS Revenue Ruling

A 1969 Revenue Ruling from the Internal Revenue Service (IRS) concluded that a group of professional wrestlers were independent contractors for purposes of the withholding of federal income tax from their paychecks.[45] The decision is noteworthy, in part, because it was decided under what is now the obvious fiction that professional wrestling was a legitimate sporting contest. The ruling notes that the wrestlers were "engaged on a contract basis for each match" they wrestled and that the contracts were in writing "on forms required by the State athletic commission and the rules and made a part of each contract." One of the terms of the contract was that if a wrestler "fouls his opponent during the contest in which he is engaged, whether intentionally or unintentionally, he will not be entitled to receive the compensation contracted for" except for the reimbursement of expenses incurred by the wrestler to perform.*

The IRS noted certain factors that cut in favor of a finding of independent contractor status, such as the fact that the wrestlers were engaged in a distinct occupation or business of their own, were engaged only for a short period of time, and were paid by the job. But perhaps most importantly, the IRS pointed to the now-obvious fiction that the promoter had "no right to exercise direction or control over the details of the work performed by the wrestler other than to see that he does not break the rules of the State athletic commission, which are embodied in the contract or the other terms specifically set forth therein." Thus, the promoter supposedly had, at best, only a limited right to control the manner in which the wrestlers performed in a match.

Silvia v. Woodhouse

A 1969 case from Massachusetts involved another situation in which a fan was injured while attending a match. The fan was injured when one

---

* If this term of the contract was ever actually taken literally, it would have meant that no heel wrestler would have ever had a right to be paid.

wrestler punched another wrestler who was trying to get back into the ring, causing the wrestler to fall to the ground and onto the plaintiff.[46] The plaintiff sought to hold the promotion, Santos Wrestling Enterprises, Inc., vicariously liable for the negligence of the wrestlers in injuring the plaintiff. This would, of course, require a finding that the wrestlers were employees of Santos, which would probably have required a finding that Santos retained the right to control the manner in which the wrestlers performed. Once again, the court's ruling on this issue was based on the fiction that Santos did not have the right to control the performance of the wrestlers. "There was no evidence to prove that Santos was more than the matchmaker for the wrestlers or that it gave any instructions to them beyond those relating to the time limit of the bouts.* The wrestlers, therefore, were independent contractors."[47]

White v. Frenkel

A 1993 case from Louisiana came out the other way when evidence concerning the realities of the relationship between promoters and wrestlers was presented to the court. The case involved John E. Frenkel, III, a.k.a. "Hollywood" John Tatum, a wrestler who worked for Mid–South Wrestling. Tatum was driving from a match in Alexandria, Louisiana, earlier in the night when he attempted to pass two tractor trailers, resulting in a collision with an oncoming vehicle that killed the other driver and injured Tatum's sleeping passenger.† Tatum's passenger and the widow of the dead driver sued Tatum for negligence and also sought to hold Mid–South vicariously liable for Tatum's negligence.[48]

The trial judge found that Tatum was an employee of Mid–South for purposes of vicarious liability, and the Louisiana Court of Appeal affirmed. On appeal, the court pointed to several facts that supported the conclusion that Mid–South retained the right to control the work of Tatum. Tatum "was told where to go, when to be there and exactly what to do when he got there." His passenger testified that Mid–South determined who would win and who would lose. Tatum couldn't refuse to wrestle without risking being fined or fired, and he couldn't work for any other promoter. Interestingly, by 1993, "Cowboy" Bill Watts, the owner of Mid–South, felt comfortable enough to disclose some of the secrets of the business. Watts explained that he alone determined who was a

---

* Santos did concede that he would sometimes ask a "superior" wrestler to "take it easy" on an opponent.

† Tatum was criminally charged with negligent homicide. Jerry Humphries, "Pro Wrestler Charged with Negligent Homicide," *The Town Talk* (Alexandria, LA), Nov. 26, 1986, at 8.

top-card wrestler, that Tatum's pay didn't depend on whether he won or lost and was solely within Watts' discretion, and that Watts retained the right to fine wrestlers any amount he chose. Tatum testified that he did not share any of the proceeds from the sale of merchandise and that "he had to do exactly as Mid-South told him or he would be fired." In short, both Tatum and Watts testified that "Mid–South had total control over who [Tatum] wrestled, where he wrestled, when he wrestled, how much he was paid and that he could be (and in fact was) fired at the will of Mid–South without liability for breach of contract."[49] This made Tatum an employee (and also helped make Mid–South vicariously liable for Tatum's negligence).

* * *

With the exception of *White*, each of these cases was decided in the kayfabe era. So, since some of the details concerning the true nature of the business were not fully disclosed, courts (and the IRS) were generally making their decisions on the basis of incomplete or faulty information. But the conflicting results in the decisions are actually typical of the law in this area. It can be tough to predict how a court will rule on the question of whether a worker is an employee or an independent contractor on the basis of the multi-factor tests that courts employ.[50]

For example, different courts have reached different conclusions as to whether drivers who work for ride-share companies like Uber and Lyft qualify as employees or independent contractors.[51] An Uber or Lyft driver is generally free to work whatever hours the driver wants. Drivers also provide their own cars and car insurance and do not get paid a salary. These are hallmarks of an independent contractor. But the companies also exert control over how the drivers do their jobs. In support of the argument that drivers are actually employees, courts have pointed to the fact that Uber and Lyft have (at least in the past) prohibited drivers from talking on the phone, required drivers to "dress professionally," required drivers to send the customer who has ordered a ride a text message when the driver is 1–2 minutes away from the pickup location, and placed limits on a driver's choice of radio stations.[52]

* * *

So, is the modern WWE performer an employee or an independent contractor? As is the case with Uber and Lyft drivers, the answer is complicated. As mentioned, the most important factor in the analysis is whether the employer has the right to control how the worker does the job. But it's not entirely clear how that factor should play out in the world of professional wrestling. "It's both," former wrestler and current trainer

Dr. Tom Prichard* said when asked who has control over what happens in the ring.[53] Prichard explains that the booker for the promotion provides the "vision" for the match. The booker has the final word on who wins a match, how the match will end (known as "the finish" in the business), and how the match will advance the overall angle or storyline that is in place. All of that suggests that the booker, who works on behalf of the employer, has the right to control the performance of the job. But, depending on the promoter and the situation, the performers might have a fair amount of control over the *details* of what happens in the ring. Historically, many wrestlers would "call" a match on the fly in the ring. In other words, they would communicate with each other about what would happen next in a match, leading up to the ultimate finish provided by the booker. This gave the wrestlers themselves significant control over how the wrestlers did their jobs in the ring. Even today, where wrestlers more frequently pre-plan the details of their matches, the wrestlers are often exercising at least some degree of control over the details of the matches, subject to some instruction from the booker and subject to the booker's right to control the overall script.[54] So, does the promoter have the right to control what takes place during a match or does the wrestler? To some extent, it's both.

The modern wrestler working on the independent or indie circuit is an example of a worker who would probably be classified as an independent contractor. These are performers who are not signed to a long-term, exclusive contract with a promoter and are instead free to work when and for whom they choose. This is the sort of freedom that it is typical of an independent contractor. But even the indie wrestler is still subject to some control on the part of a promoter in terms of who wins and loses a match, what the finish is, etc.

But WWE exerts far more control over its roster than the typical independent promoter does. For example, WWE determines who a performer will wrestle, when and where they wrestle, and where they will appear on the card. WWE also can and does decide what a performer's persona or gimmick should be. Importantly, the promotion also has significant control over what the performer says in one of the most important parts of the job: the interview (or promo).

When it comes to a promo, the closest analogy for a WWE performer is to a stage or screen actor. The producer retains the ultimate right of control as to "the script," the look of the performance, etc. There are usually lines from a script that actors must deliver. But how the actors deliver those

---

* Prichard wrestled in various territories across the country from the late 1970s into the mid 1990s. He performed in the WWF for several years before going on to become a trainer for the company for several years. He now runs a wrestling school in Tennessee with Glenn Jacobs, a.k.a. the wrestler Kane, a.k.a. the Mayor of Knox County, Tennessee.

5. Labor and Employment Law 111

lines is, to some extent, up to the actors. A director, acting as the producer's agent, might try influence the way an actor delivers a line or insist that the actor deliver the line in a certain way. But, as a matter of custom, actors generally have wide latitude as to how they perform their jobs. Perhaps not surprisingly, there is some dispute as to under what circumstances actors should be classified as employees or independent contractors.[55]

It is difficult for any performer in the modern WWE to succeed without having talent on the mic. Back in the territory days, performers may have been given some key points to mention in their interviews, but the substance of the interviews and how it was delivered was largely up to the performers. Some wrestlers were good workers in the ring but lousy on the mic or vice versa. Over time, interviews have become increasingly scripted. More trusted workers get more leeway to improvise during a promo. But in general, WWE performers cannot free associate their way through a promo; they have to stick to a script. So, the modern WWE retains considerable control over how the performers do this part of their jobs.

Courts consider other factors aside from the right to control, some of which might arguably cut both ways in the case of the typical WWE performer. For example, an independent contractor generally provides their own tools and place to work. WWE obviously provides the ring where the performers perform, but a publicly available 2010 contract indicates that wrestlers were required to provide their own costumes and gear (in other words, their "tools").[56] But most of the factors that courts consider cut in favor of employee status in the case of modern WWE wrestlers. For example, one factor courts often consider is whether the worker is employed over an extended period of time. Today, the typical WWE wrestler has a contract that extends for months or years, which would cut in favor of employee status. Another consideration is whether the worker is paid on a regular basis (by the hour, by the week, or by the month) as opposed to being paid by the job. The typical WWE contract provides wrestlers with a guaranteed yearly salary, a fact that cuts strongly in favor of employee status. Independent contractors set their own hours and decide who they work with.[57] In contrast, WWE tells its performers when and where they need to show and who they will wrestle.

But the factor that cuts most strongly in favor of employee status in the case of WWE is the fact that wrestlers work full time for the promotion. Today, the standard WWE contract prohibits a wrestler from working for another organization. One of the hallmarks of an independent contractor is that the contractor is truly "independent" and is not locked down to one employer. That definitely does not describe a modern WWE performer or a performer in the old territory system.

For a while, WWE also limited the ability of its performers to earn money from third-party platforms, such as Cameo and Twitch. So, not only could WWE performers not earn extra money by occasionally taking a one-off wrestling gig for another promoter, but they could also not earn money on the side by recording messages for fans. Eventually, WWE relented and now permits its performers to earn supplemental income from these kinds of third-party platforms. But the control that WWE seeks to assert over its performers' ability to make money on the side further supports the idea that WWE seeks to retain the control that is typical of an employer-employee relationship.

* * *

In 2018, the California Supreme Court adopted a new, simpler test for determining employee vs. independent contractor status in a case involving California's wage and hour law, which regulates such things as overtime pay and minimum wages.[58] The decision to adopt a new test was driven by at least two concerns. One was the reality that the use of multi-factor tests didn't provide employers and workers with clear guidance as to how the worker should be classified. So, it was tough to determine how a worker should be classified. This meant that many disputes on this question had to be resolved through the time-consuming and expensive process of litigation.[59] The second was the concern over the ability of employers to structure their agreements with workers in a way that enabled them to avoid the reach of state and federal workplace law.[60] There are certainly plenty of workers in the gig economy who value the freedom of being an independent contractor over the greater protection the law affords to employees. But according to the court, absent evidence that a worker independently made this choice, employers should not be allowed to avoid their obligations with respect to minimum wages, safety, and other workplace matters that the law imposes upon them.

Based on these kinds of concerns, the California Supreme Court adopted what is known as the "ABC Test" (cleverly named for the fact that there are three parts to the test: Parts A, B, and C). Numerous states employ the same or a similar test. Importantly, Connecticut—where WWE is located and whose law, according to WWE contracts, will apply in the event of a dispute—is one of those states that applies the test in at least some circumstances.[61]

If and when a new lawsuit against WWE is filed alleging that WWE has misclassified its wrestlers as independent contractors, it's difficult to see how WWE's wrestlers could be classified as anything other than employees under this test. The ABC test starts with the presumption that a worker is an employee, and it's then up to the employer to prove otherwise. Under this test, a worker will be classified as an employee unless *all three* of the following requirements are met:

"(A) The worker is free from the control and direction of the hiring entity in connection with the performance of the work, both under the contract for the performance of the work and in fact."

This part of the test focuses on the same control idea that courts have historically relied upon. The California Supreme Court has explained that "a business need not control the *precise* manner or details of the work in order to be found to have maintained the necessary control" to classify a worker as an employee.[62] Note that under this part of the test, the fact that a contract specifies that the worker is an independent contractor does not necessarily mean that the worker really is an independent contractor. The test is ultimately one of control, not how the parties classify the relationship.

Most of the allegations in the 2008 suit brought by wrestler Raven and others—that WWE has the right to control the costumes and hairstyles that the wrestlers wear, the stage persona they adopt, the dialogue they speak in interviews, as well as other details of the work they perform—remain undeniably true. So, while there might be an argument that the wrestlers retain *some* control over the details of the matches themselves or the characters they portray,* they don't appear "to be *free* from the control and direction" of WWE in the performance of their work under Part A of the ABC test.

"(B) The worker performs work that is outside the usual course of the hiring entity's business."

The California Supreme Court has explained that Part (B) of the test looks to whether the worker is "in the same business as the hiring entity, or if they performed a different type of service." The intent of this factor is to protect "individuals ... who would ordinarily be viewed by others as working in the hiring entity's business and not as working, instead, in the worker's own independent business."[63] As an example, if a retail store hires an outside plumber to fix a leak, the plumber would be performing work outside the usual course of the retail store's business. So, the plumber is most likely an independent contractor. In contrast, if a clothing manufacturer hires a seamstress to make dresses using patterns supplied by the manufacturer, the seamstress' work would be within the usual course of the manufacturer's business and is probably an employee.[64]

---

* But the WWE contract also provides that a wrestler's ring name, character, gestures, routines, etc., belong to WWE. *See* Contract between WWE and Chavo Guerrero, Jr. (April 5, 2010), http://ia802906.us.archive.org/32/items/gov.uscourts.ctd.113085/gov.uscourts.ctd.113085.1.5.pdf.

A WWE wrestler is like a seamstress hired by a clothing manufacturer to make clothes; both do work that is within the usual course of the employer's business. WWE's business is "sports entertainment" (or professional wrestling). So, the wrestlers perform work that is part of the usual course of WWE's business. WWE cannot satisfy this part of the test.

Finally there is

"(C) The worker is customarily engaged in an independently established trade, occupation, or business of the same nature as that involved in the work performed."

Under this part of the test, if a worker has an existing business operation that involves the same general type of work performed by the employer, the worker is most likely an independent contractor.* WWE expressly prohibits its wrestlers from wrestling for another organization. In other words, WWE wrestlers are not permitted to engage in "business of the same nature as that involved in the work performed" for the WWE. So, WWE cannot satisfy this part of the test.

* * *

Under the ABC test, WWE would have to prevail on each part of the test in order to classify its performers as independent contractors. It probably can't prevail on any of them.

* * *

Part 5: The Future

So, if the modern WWE performer is really an employee and not an independent contractor, and if this misclassification generally works to the detriment of performers, why has nothing changed? Why don't current wrestlers challenge the misclassification in court or seek to form a union in order to bring about change? The most obvious answer is fear of retaliation.

Numerous studies reveal that the biggest reason why workers do not file complaints concerning unlawful employment practices is the fear of employer retaliation.[65] Employees (but not independent contractors) are protected from employer retaliation under nearly every federal statute governing the workplace. Employers are obviously prohibited from

---

* California's legislature eventually approved a measure that adopted this ABC test. Under pressure from companies like Lyft and Uber, the new law created exceptions app-based rideshare and delivery platforms as well as some other exceptions. So, these workers are still classified as independent contractors.

engaging in retaliation that results in a firing, demotion, etc. Most employers who have full-time legal representation (like WWE) are smart enough to not immediately fire an employee who raises concerns about working conditions or files a lawsuit, thereby making the retaliatory nature of the action obvious. But employers have a host of other ways of making the lives of their workers more unpleasant in retaliation for conduct the employer is unhappy about. For example, employers have been known to reassign employees to less desirable (but technically equivalent) jobs, engage in excessive documentation of supposed poor performance, and threaten those whom the employer suspects of thinking about filing a lawsuit. This is why most of the major federal statutes governing the workplace also prohibit an employer from engaging in any form of retaliation that might deter a reasonable employee from asserting the employee's rights, even if the retaliation falls short of an actual firing.[66]

Those same kinds of concerns are present in the case of WWE. Union-side lawyer Lucas Middlebrook observes that the fear of retaliation "could be the single biggest obstacle to unionization in the professional wrestling industry."[67] The stories about Vince McMahon allegedly punishing performers for various perceived offenses by giving them humiliating gimmicks are the stuff of legend (whether true or not).[68] It would also be a fairly simple matter for WWE to force a popular wrestler into doing jobs (or losing) to lesser opponents in order to damage the wrestler's future career opportunities in retaliation for the performer having challenged WWE's practices in court. When an employer takes such actions, the employer is not only getting revenge on the offending employee but is also sending a message to other workers that a similar fate awaits them if they likewise cross the employer. So, these are actions that might well dissuade a reasonable employee from taking such action and, therefore, should be illegal. But employees can be forgiven for not wanting to rely on the possibility of recovering money in a lawsuit if they end up facing these kinds of retaliatory actions.

One situation in which some courts have been reluctant to find that an employer's retaliatory actions are illegal is where an employer merely *threatens* to take action against an employee who engages in some form of protected conduct. These courts have concluded that mere threats of discipline or firing are not enough to dissuade a reasonable employee from asserting their rights.[69] It's worth noting, however, that the National Labor Relations Act explicitly makes it unlawful for an employer to threaten to take action against employees for engaging in union activities.[70] So, while it might not be unlawful for an employer to threaten an employee with termination or discipline if the employee, say, files a race discrimination complaint against the employer, it would be illegal if the employer threatened to fire an employee who was talking with co-workers about the possibility of organizing a union.*

* * *

Ultimately, it will probably require either a performer insisting on their legal rights as an employee or a group of employees attempting to unionize in order for WWE performers to be correctly classified as employees. Of course, doing so might potentially subject that performer to retaliation, even if doing so would be illegal. But as Middlebrook notes, the more people who publicly voice support for these rights, the less likely retaliation is to succeed.[71] And there are at least some reasons to believe that the threat of retaliation might not be as likely to have quite the same deterrent effect as it would in the past.

As discussed in Chapter 4, back when the National Wrestling Alliance (NWA) was at full force, the members of the Alliance had the power to damage any other promoter or wrestler who crossed the organization. The threat of firing and then blacklisting a wrestler who did something a promoter didn't like was real. In his book *Chokehold*, former wrestler Jim Wilson detailed what he believes was the retaliation that followed when he failed to comply with demands for sexual favors from an NWA promoter. According to Wilson, not only was he routinely booked to lose matches afterward, but he was also blacklisted by the members of the NWA and unable to find a job in the business.[72] It would be remarkable if active performers during that time didn't routinely bite their tongues about unlawful employer conduct for fear of retaliation.

The reason the NWA was able to scare wrestlers into submission was because (depending on the decade in question) the wrestlers had no other meaningful employment options in the business. For a while at least, the NWA's anti-competitive practices effectively limited competition to rogue "outlaw" promoters, who couldn't pay as much as NWA promoters and

---

* A clear example of this sort of prohibited employer interference with the ability of workers to organize involves an alleged incident WWE/WWF owner Vince McMahon and wrestler/announcer/future governor Jesse "the Body" Ventura. Back in 1986, Ventura was an announcer for the WWF. The company was getting ready to put on its huge pay-per-view event WrestleMania II when Ventura spoke to the wrestlers in the locker room and tried to convince them of the need to form a union. According to Ventura, McMahon found out about Ventura's speech and "basically threatened to fire" Ventura if he ever brought up unionization again. Javier Ojst, "Wrestling Union—Failed Attempts and a History of Blackballing by WWE," *Pro Wrestling Stories*, Jan. 10, 2023, https://prowrestlingstories.com/pro-wrestling-stories/wrestling-union/. According to Ventura, he later learned that it was Hulk Hogan who had informed McMahon about Ventura's speech. Stephen Sonneveld, "Why WWE, Pro Wrestlers Should Form a Professional Wrestling Union," *Bleacher Report*, March 19, 2012, https://bleacherreport.com/articles/1110575-wwe-news-wrestlings-risks-warrant-a-labor-unions-rewards.

whose promotions looked decidedly bush league in comparison. This resulted in a significant disparity of power between promoter and performer.

Retaliation is more likely to occur where there is this sort of power disparity between employer and employee. The greater the disparity, the more likely employer retaliation is. When WWE's only real competition, World Championship Wrestling, folded in 2001, Vince McMahon and WWE had a virtual monopoly for a while. Competitors soon emerged (TNA, Ring of Honor, Global Force Wrestling, etc.), but none was ever more than a distant second in terms of television ratings or profits. It was not until All Elite Wrestling (AEW) was established in 2019 that WWE faced competition that threatened WWE's standing as the dominant player in the industry. Between 2019 and 2021, AEW's regular Wednesday night television program Dynamite defeated WWE's NXT program in a majority of head-to-head contests.[73] AEW is still clearly Pepsi to WWE's Coke. The ratings for WWE's main show, Raw, far surpass those of AEW's Dynamite. But when workers have more employment options, the disparity in power narrows. So, as long as viable alternatives for workers exist, perhaps the fear of retaliation on the part of WWE will not carry quite the same weight it once did.

* * *

Or perhaps the old distinctions between employee and independent contractor are simply not as relevant as they once were in some fields, and it is time for employment law to take notice of this fact. Historically, employment law has only recognized two kinds of workers. One is either an employee or an independent contractor. There is no in-between. But the modern gig economy and the fallout from the pandemic illustrate the shortcomings of this narrow conception of the workforce. The pandemic caused many workers to re-evaluate their relationships with their jobs and their employers. Laid off from work or forced to work from home, many workers soon realized that they didn't necessarily need to endure their old, unpleasant working conditions and that they enjoyed the freedom of working from home. One of the takeaways from the pandemic was that workers value flexibility and freedom. At the same time, they still want some of the traditional security that comes along with a standard 9–5 office job, such as health insurance and retirement plans. So, many workers seek to find the sweet spot between the freedom afforded to independent contractors and the security afforded to employees.

AEW's success actually highlights the evolving nature of the employment relationship in a post–COVID world. The average AEW performer might be paid less than the average WWE performer. But the company gives its performers much greater flexibility than their WWE counterparts in terms of their ability to work from other promotions on off nights and in terms of the number of hours they work.[74] AEW performers don't work nearly as many shows as WWE performers, thus giving them the chance to recuperate in between shows or take on other gigs if they so choose. And while AEW president Tony Khan has downplayed the likelihood of offering health insurance to all of its performers, the company has a practice of hiring some of its performers as employees who do other jobs within the company aside from wrestling so that they are eligible for health insurance. According to Khan, a "large percentage" of the AEW roster are covered by the company's insurance plan.[75]

Labor and employment law scholars have noted several possibilities for moving this area of employment law into a direction that better reflects the realities of the modern workforce. For example, Professor Orly Lobel has suggested that there are some statutory rights, like the right to be free from workplace discrimination and retaliation, that should extend to all workers, regardless of whether they are employees or independent contractors.[76]

Another possibility would be for courts or legislatures to recognize a third or intermediate category of workers for certain jobs. In addition to employees and independent contractors, Canada recognizes the category of "dependent contractor." A dependent contractor is a worker who does not qualify as an employee due to the employer's lack of control but is still nonetheless dependent upon the employer to such an extent that the worker should be afforded more rights than an independent contractor. Where a contractor is economically dependent on the employer due to the fact that the contractor works exclusively or almost exclusively for the employer, the contractor should be classified as a dependent contractor. Arguably, this classification could apply to AEW or WWE wrestlers. Courts could then recognize that the dependent contractor is entitled to certain rights, like the right to advance notice of termination of the relationship, the right to organize that exists under the NLRA, or the right to a reasonably safe work environment.[77]

* * *

Part 6: Conclusion

The business of professional wrestling has changed dramatically since the days when performers would drive from town to town within a territory and move from territory to territory, without much in the way of job security, hoping all along that the promoter wouldn't shortchange them too much when it came time to count the ticket sales. The business has changed and the relationship between promoter and performer has evolved over time. But the law has failed to keep pace with these realities in terms of how it extends legal protection to workers. The same is arguably true for other kinds of employment relationships. But as the unfairness of the current approach in some workplaces becomes increasingly obvious, it is possible that the law in the area may start to evolve.

CHAPTER 6

Sex Discrimination, Constitutional Law, and Lady Wrestlers

Rose Hesseltine, Gerry Hunter, Silvia Calzadilla, Ethel Whitehead, Betty Niccoli, and Titi Paris v. Sexist Attitudes

> "If women are to have equal rights with men, and that certainly is the trend, why should they not have the right to wrestle as well as rivet?"
> —Decatur Herald and Review, May 26, 1955.[1]

The WWE made history in 2019 with its Wrestlemania 35 event. For the first time in the company's history, the main event featured women. Three women, to be precise: Becky Lynch, Ronda Rousey, and Charlotte Flair. Today, women's matches often occupy prominent slots on professional wrestling cards.

The current state of affairs was a long time in the making. As was the case with men, the origins of women's wrestling can be traced back to traveling carnivals. The sport started out with more-or-less legitimate athletic competitions before gradually evolving into pure entertainment by the 1930s. But "lady wrestlers," as they were called, sometimes faced significant barriers. Some were cultural. The idea of women wrestling was seen by some as a threat to good morals, "calculated to degrade human nature to its most bestial depths."[2]

Other barriers were more formal in nature. Women were often not permitted on the same card as men, and some state athletic commissions prohibited women's wrestling altogether.[3] As was the case with professional baseball, the onset of World War II resulted in something of a shortage of male talent within the wrestling business. As a result, the popularity

6. Sex Discrimination, Constitutional Law, and Lady Wrestlers

of women's wrestling grew during this timeframe. But even after the war, there remained states that barred women from obtaining a license to wrestle. As this chapter describes, it took years of courtroom battles to help lay the groundwork for modern women to enjoy the status in the wrestling world they enjoy today.

Part 1: Sex Discrimination, Constitutional Law, and Lady Wrestlers in the 1950s

If there is an agreed-upon date as to when the civil rights movement began, it is May 17, 1954. This is the day the United States Supreme Court released its landmark decision in *Brown v. Board of Education*. *Brown* famously held that the segregation of public education based solely on race violates the Equal Protection Clause of the Fourteenth Amendment to the United States Constitution.[4] For years, the courts—including the Supreme Court itself—had narrowly interpreted the federal Constitution in a manner that provided few legal rights for black citizens. *Brown v. Board of Education* marked a colossal shift in the law and helped spawn new court decisions and new laws that paved the way for more equal treatment under the law for African Americans.

The decision also offered a glimmer of hope for those who believed that women were entitled to equal protection under the law. Since the inception of the country, the law had treated women as having limited rights. For example, from the time of the adoption of the Constitution and well into the 19th century, the law took the position "that a woman had no legal existence separate from her husband, who was regarded as her head and representative in the social state."[5] As a result, a married woman was legally incapable of entering into a contract without her husband's consent.[6] A 1950 *Stanford Law Review* article cataloged a host of laws that were still on the books at the time that treated men and women differently, ranging from laws banning women from serving on juries[7] to requiring women to wait longer than men to remarry[8] to prohibiting women from being employed in certain supposedly dangerous fields, such as mining or handling intoxicating liquors.[9]

As interpreted by the United States Supreme Court during this timeframe, the federal Constitution did little to protect women from arbitrary and damaging classifications on the basis of sex. For example, in 1872, the Court held that it was constitutional for the State of Illinois to deny a woman a license to practice law on the grounds that she was a woman. Justice Joseph P. Bradley wrote a concurring opinion in which he went a step further, explaining that Illinois' exclusion of women from the practice of law was justified because "God designed the sexes to occupy different spheres of action, and that it belonged to men to make, apply, and execute the laws."[10] According to Bradley, "[t]he natural and proper timidity and delicacy which belongs to the female sex evidently unfits it for many of the occupations of civil life."[11]

The Court was willing to uphold the constitutionality of other sex-based classifications on based on the "delicate" nature of the female sex. For example, in a 1924 case, the Court considered whether a New York statute that prohibited the employment of women between the hours of 10 p.m. and 6 a.m. violated the Fourteenth Amendment. As far as the Court was concerned, as long as the New York legislature had a reasonable basis for drawing this distinction between men and women, it was not the Court's job to second guess that decision. And in this case, according to the Court, the legislature "had before it a mass of information" suggesting that "night work is substantially and especially detrimental to the health of women," given their more "delicate" nature.[12] Thus, the statute was constitutional.

* * *

Hesseltine v. State Athletic Commission

The Supreme Court's decision in *Brown v. Board of Education* signaled new possibilities for proponents of equal rights for women. If legal classifications on the basis of race that disadvantaged African Americans could violate the federal Constitution, surely there was a similar argument to be made about classifications that adversely impacted women. One of the first people to put that theory to the test was Rose Hesseltine.

Described by the *Chicago Tribune* as "a diminutive redhead who likes to wrestle," Rose Hesseltine wrestled under the name Rose Roman.[13] When she applied for a wrestling license with the Illinois State Athletic Commission in 1954, she had reportedly already performed in 32 states.[14] But the Commission denied her application, citing its Rule Number 182, which prohibited women from participating in professional wrestling exhibitions in Illinois.[15]* Hesseltine challenged the Commission's denial in Cook County Circuit Court just a few months after *Brown* was decided.

---

* Illinois was not alone at the time in having a state athletic commission that refused to issue licenses to women wrestlers. For example, the state athletic commission in Pennsylvania adopted a similar rule. A bill was introduced in the Pennsylvania state legislature in 1955 to prohibit the commission from doing so, but the bill failed to garner a majority. "House Rejects Plan for Women's Wrestling Bouts," *Allentown Morning Call*, March 29, 1955, at 23. The Republican caucus lined up against the measure on the grounds that while the bill permitted women to wrestle, the bill failed to specifically prohibit women from wrestling men. The Republican House whip commented, "I don't think that would be moral and I don't think the church groups would like it." Thomas P. Snyder, "Wrestling Bill Loses in House," *Pittsburgh Sun-Telegraph*, March 29, 1955, at 17.

An Illinois assistant attorney general defended the Commission's rule on the need to protect "the fragility of women."[16] The Circuit Court concluded that Rule Number 182 "constituted an invalid usurpation by the Commission of a legislative function" and struck the rule down.[17] Hesseltine called it "a great day for women wrestlers" because "150 other women wrestlers in the United States can now wrestle in Illinois."[18] However, the Commission appealed the decision to the Illinois Supreme Court.*

In *Brown v. Board of Education*, the Supreme Court applied a form of judicial review that became known as "strict scrutiny." When state law draws distinctions on the base of race or national origin, a court will strictly scrutinize the constitutionality of the state law and will declare the law unconstitutional unless the state can demonstrate that it (1) had a compelling interest in drawing the distinction (in other words, it had a *really* strong reason for treating people differently on the basis of race) and (2) used the least restrictive means available to accomplish the state's interest (in other words, there was no other way to accomplish the state's compelling goals). While *Brown* established that legal distinctions drawn on the basis of race were presumptively unconstitutional, the Court hadn't considered what form of judicial review should apply in the case of sex-based distinctions like that of the Illinois State Athletic Commission's Rule Number 182 in light of *Brown*. So, theoretically, Hesseltine's case provided the Illinois Supreme Court with the opportunity to consider the constitutionality of the rule in a manner consistent with *Brown*.

The court chose not to do so, however. Instead, it took the easy way out. Rather than confronting "the serious constitutional questions" raised by the Commission's decision to prohibit women from engaging in professional wrestling, the court instead focused on a narrower issue: did the state statute that authorized the Commission to grant licenses grant the Commission the authority to enact Rule Number 182?

The relevant section of the statute authorized the Commission to develop "reasonable rules and regulations, to establish the qualifications" of applicants who wished to hold wrestling and boxing exhibitions and to issue such licensees to such applicants.[19] Stated more plainly, the

---

* The decision also led to a Republican member of the state legislature, Louis "Uncle Louie" Janczak, to introduce legislation specifically outlawing women's wrestling. "Bill Would Bar Women's Mat Matches," *Chicago Tribune*, Feb. 3, 1955, at 62. While it does not appear the bill was passed, Janczak's act prompted Ada Ash, a professional wrestler (who also wrestled alligators), to challenge Janczak to a wrestling match. "I got an extra pair of tights. Let him get in the ring with me," Ash was quoted as saying. "I can't wrestle another lady in Chicago, but I can wrestle an alligator. And I could get a job doing a strip tease in 50 joints in town tonight and Janczak wouldn't say a word, let alone introduce a bill!" Lewis Williams, "This Lady Wrestles Alligators and Challenges Legislator," *Chicago Tribune*, June 1, 1955, at 44.

Commission was authorized by statute to develop rules for the issuing of a license to one who wished to *hold* a wrestling or boxing event, not *participate* in such an event. So, the section of the statute the Commission claimed authority under only gave the Commission the authority to develop licensing rules for wrestling promoters, not the wrestlers themselves. According to the Illinois Supreme Court, this section "obviously cannot be construed to grant authority for the adoption of a rule prohibiting women from participating in wrestling exhibitions." And the statute as a whole did not hint in any way that women were not qualified to receive wrestling licenses So, in the court's view, Rule Number 182 was "an arbitrary assumption of power by the commission" that exceeded the scope of its authority.[20]

The court's decision was brief, consisting of only five paragraphs. And it failed to address the vastly more meaningful question as to whether, as a matter of constitutional law, a state could permit a man to engage in a wrestling or boxing exhibition but prohibit a women from doing so. But the decision nonetheless allowed Hesseltine and other "lady wrestlers" to earn a living performing in Chicago and other Illinois towns.*

* * *

State v. Hunter

Prior to Hesseltine's legal action, a woman who applied for a license to wrestle in Illinois would be denied the license. In Oregon, a woman who tried to wrestle professionally could be arrested. This is what happened to wrestlers Gerry Hunter and Gene Stewart when they tried to hold a match in Oregon City, Oregon, in October 1955.

For reasons that are not entirely clear, the issue of women's professional wrestling was a hot one in Oregon beginning somewhere around 1940. Local athletic commissions in Oregon at the time decided whether to grant a license to one wishing to be a professional wrestler. Some local commissions granted licenses to women and others did not, thus generating controversies at the local level.[21] So, for example, when acclaimed wrestler Clara Mortensen was scheduled to wrestle a match in Portland in 1940, the local athletic association barred her from doing so.[22]

In 1955, the issue heated up again. In January, a local judge in Oregon City had ruled that Oregon law did not prohibit women from taking part in a wrestling exhibition.[23] This apparently prompted Earl Hill, a Republican member of the Oregon legislature, to announce that he would introduce a bill prohibiting women's wrestling on the grounds that it was

---

* Hesseltine continued to wrestle into the early 1960s. Videos of some of her matches are available online.

degrading.²⁴ Similar laws already existed in a few states, including California, Washington, and Idaho.²⁵ A legislative supporter of the bill argued that the measure was necessary to protect public morals because women's wrestling events "attracted children who were subjected to the bawdy remarks of the audiences."²⁶ The Oregon legislature passed the measure, which ultimately provided that "[n]o person other than a person of the male sex shall participate in or be licensed to participate in any wrestling competition or wrestling exhibition."²⁷ The governor signed the measure in May. The law itself provided that "an emergency is declared to exist" and that the measure was necessary "for the immediate preservation of the public peace, health, and safety." As a result of the supposed emergency, the Act became effective immediately upon passage.²⁸ Oregon's attorney general dismissed concerns regarding the constitutionality of the measure.²⁹

The new law meant that female wrestlers who had previously been able to earn money by wrestling in the state were no longer able to do so. One such wrestler was "Blonde Bombshell" Gerry Hunter.* Hunter wrestled fairly regularly around Oregon during the early 1950s, most often in the Oregon City area. When a scheduled match was cancelled following the governor's signature, Hunter did not take the state's action lightly. Hunter and another wrestler (who listed themselves as "promoters") published a "notice to the public" in a local Oregon paper in which they announced the cancellation of a planned match, took the governor of Oregon to task for signing the measure, and questioned the motivations of those responsible for the new law:

> It is stated that the passing of this Bill 566 was for Safety and Health. But we can't say whose health. Most of the girl wrestlers out of work are World War II vets with Honorable Discharges. So the state couldn't be worried about their health.....
>
> P.S. During the War, Gerry Hunter, local wrestling champion, pulled on a Green Chain† for several years at the Booth Kelly Lumber Mill at Wendling, Oregon. Why then did the state not worry about her health at that time? Or was it because pulling lumber didn't affect the wrestling activities of those who are so eager to see the girls stop wrestling?³⁰

Despite the ban on women's wrestling, Hunter and Stewart went ahead with a match on May 25, knowing in advance that they would be arrested. The police did indeed arrest the two shortly after the match began and charged with them with the crime of "participating in wrestling

---

* In most news stories and advertisements at the time, Hunter is listed as "Gerry" but is listed as "Jerry" in the complaint.

† The term refers to sorting lumber.

> **NOTICE TO THE PUBLIC . . .**
>
> Since our good Governor signed Bill 566 banning women wrestling in Oregon, there will be no girls wrestling at the Cascade Club until further notice. Our attorneys are investigating the emergency clause that was on the same bill. It is stated that the passing of this Bill 566 was for Safety and Health. But we can't say whose health. Most of the girl wrestlers out of work are War War II vets with Honorable Discharges. So the state couldn't be worried about their health. But we will find out for ourselves and for you, the people, who wanted them out of the way. Fortunately the girls are offered work and exile in the Dominion of Canada, where they can wrestle 6 nights a week and thus earn a livelihood in the profession they have trained so hard to learn. We also learned there are several other countries which allow these same privileges to the ladies, where Oregon doesn't. We will keep the public posted as to results.
>
> Signed:
> YOGI HUSSANE,
> GERRY HUNTER,
> Promoters.
>
> P.S.: During the War, Gerry Hunter, local wrestling champion, pulled on a Green Chain for several years at the Booth Kelly Lumber Mill at Wendling, Oregon. Why then did the state not worry about her health at that time? Or was it because pulling lumber didn't affect the wrestling activities of those who are so eager to see the girls stop wrestling?

competition and exhibition" in violation of the provisions of the newly signed law. Specifically, the criminal complaint charged that Hunter "being a person not of the male sex, to wit: of the female sex, did then and there unlawfully and willfully participate in a wrestling competition and wrestling competition and wrestling exhibition, said act of defendant being contrary to the statute in such cases made and provided, and against the peace and dignity of the State of Oregon."[31]

Hunter's arrest served as a test case to challenge the constitutionality of the criminal statute. Like the plaintiffs in *Brown v. Board of Education* had done previously, Hunter alleged that the statute denied women wrestlers equal protection under the law in violation of the Fourteenth Amendment through its differing treatment of men and women.[32] But while *Brown* made clear that race-based classifications were subject to strict judicial scrutiny, the United States Supreme Court had historically been much more forgiving of sex-based classifications like that in Hunter's case. For example, in 1948—just a few years before *Brown v. Board* was decided—the Court decided *Goesaert v. Cleary*, a decision that upheld a state law that prohibited a woman from being licensed as a bartender unless the bar

Left: The "public notice" that wrestlers Gerry Hunter and Yogi Hussane took out, complaining about the ban on women's wrestling. Hussane and Hunter frequently appeared on the same card and even sometimes wrestled as partners in mixed tag-team matches.

was owned by her husband or father. According to the Court, the Constitution "does not preclude the States from drawing a sharp line between the sexes." If it chose to, a state "could, beyond question, forbid all women from working behind a bar."[33] So, Hunter faced a significant obstacle when challenging Oregon's sex-based classification: Supreme Court precedent was not on her side.

The Oregon Supreme Court brushed aside Hunter's claim. The State of Oregon didn't need to show that it had a compelling reason for the distinction between men and women that it drew. All it needed to do to justify the law, the court said, was show that the distinction the statute drew was "reasonable and natural."[34] And it was reasonable and natural for the Oregon legislature to conclude that banning women from professional wrestling was "in the interests of the public health, safety, morals, and welfare" (although the court didn't offer any explanation as to why that might be the case).[35] The court actually pointed out that Oregon had its own judicial decision involving women and saloons. Back in 1907, the court had previously upheld the constitutionality of a statute that prohibited women from entering and remaining in saloons.[36] If it was constitutionally permissible to prohibit women from entering bars, certainly it was permissible to keep them from entering the wrestling ring.

The remainder of the court's decision serves as either a woefully bad attempt at humor or a remarkable time capsule, encapsulating prevailing views on the subject of women's equality at the time. Beyond the supposed concern for the public's welfare, the Oregon Supreme Court thought it obvious that the Oregon legislature (which was "predominately masculine" according to the court) "intended that there should be at least one island on the sea of life reserved for man that would be impregnable to the assault of woman."[37]

> Women had already invaded practically every activity formerly considered suitable and appropriate for men only. In the field of sports she had taken up, among other games, baseball, basketball, golf, bowling, hockey, long distance swimming, and racing, in all of which she had become more or less proficient, and in some had excelled. In the business and industrial fields as an employee or as an executive, in the professions, in politics, as well as in almost every other line of human endeavor, she had matched her wits and prowess with those of mere man, and, we are frank to concede, in many instances had outdone him. In these circumstances, is it any wonder that the legislative assembly took advantage of the police power of the state in its decision to halt this ever-increasing feminine encroachment upon what for ages had been considered strictly as manly arts and privileges? Was the Act an unjust and unconstitutional discrimination against woman? Have her civil or political rights been unconstitutionally denied her? Under the circumstances, we think not.[38]

Hunter's career as a wrestler in Oregon had been squashed. In a 2023 interview, Hunter's son explained why his mother got into the business originally: "She did it for the money. It was just a job."[39] Hunter would occasionally wrestle outside of Oregon following the decision and would sometimes appear as a referee for men's events in Oregon (which wasn't prohibited under Oregon's statute).[40] But the decision put an end to her wrestling career in Oregon (as it did other women wrestlers).

* * *

Part 2: The Fight Continues in the 1960s

Courts continued to uphold the constitutionality of state laws that treated men and women differently on important matters into the 1960s. For example, in 1961, the United States Supreme Court declared that a Florida statute exempting women, but not men, from jury service did not violate the Fourteenth Amendment.[41] According to the Court, the state's classification was reasonable in light of the fact that "woman is still regarded as the center of home and family life" and should be relieved of the obligation of jury duty.[42]

But while the courts lagged behind, Congress moved forward. In 1963, Congress passed the Equal Pay Act, which prohibited sex-based wage discrimination. In 1964, President Lyndon Johnson signed into law the Civil Rights Act of 1964. Title VII of the Act prohibited private employers from discriminating on the basis of race, color, religion, national origin, and sex.*

But an applicant for a wrestling license still had to contend with the New York State Athletic Commission. Since the 1920s, a New York statute gave the Commission sweeping authority to regulate wrestling and boxing in the state. The Commission had "the sole direction, management, control and jurisdiction" over licenses to hold wrestling exhibitions as well as over licenses to the participants in such exhibitions. The Commission was directed to issue a license if, in the Commission's judgment, the "character and general fitness of an applicant ... are such that the participation of such applicant will be consistent with the public interest, convenience or necessity and with the best interest of ... wrestling generally."[43]

---

* Ironically, the prohibition on sex discrimination in the workplace was added by a member of Congress who was an opponent of civil rights. The congressman added the measure as a last-ditch attempt to defeat the bill, thinking it might cause colleagues who were on the fence to vote against the measure. Robert C. Bird, "More Than a Congressional Joke: A Fresh Look at the Legislative History of Sex Discrimination of the 1964 Civil Rights Act," 3 *Wm. & Mary J. Women & L.* 137, 150–53 (1997).

6. Sex Discrimination, Constitutional Law, and Lady Wrestlers

The Commission made full use of the powers granted to it by the New York legislature. In 1934, a woman applied for a license to be a manager for her brother, a featherweight boxer.[44] In response, the Commission announced that "no license be issued to any females in the future."[45] In 1952, the Commission announced that it would not issue licenses to female wrestlers.[46] Eventually, the Commission adopted a formal rule declaring that "[n]o women may compete in any wrestling or boxing contest or exhibition and no women may be licensed as a boxer, wrestler, manager or second."[47]

Matter of Whitehead v Krulewitch

In September 1964—just two months after President Lyndon Johnson signed Title VII into law—the Commission received a request from the promotion operated by famed champion Mildred Burke to permit women to wrestle in New York.[48] In November, Ethel Whitehead of Buffalo applied for and was denied a license to wrestle. The Commission's letter of denial was short and to the point: "New York State laws do not permit women to wrestle." But, the Commission helpfully noted, if the laws ever changed, the Commission would be happy to accept an application from Whitehead.[49]

Whitehead did not take the decision lying down. In February 1965, she brought suit, alleging that the Commission had violated her civil rights by denying her a license on the basis of her sex. Whitehead sought an order directing the Commission to issue her license. By this point, the Commission had been advised by a lawyer in the New York Attorney General's Office that its ban was probably unlawful.[50] Nonetheless, the Commission dug in and fought Whitehead in court.

The complaint Whitehead's lawyer filed wasn't a model of clarity. It merely alleged that the Commission's decision to deny Whitehead a license was a violation of her civil rights, without referencing the Fourteenth Amendment or any other possible source of those rights. Past decisions strongly indicated that a court would not apply the strict form of judicial scrutiny used in race discrimination cases and would instead only require that the sex-based differential treatment was reasonable and had a rational basis. So, the complaint alleged that the Commission's decision was "arbitrary and capricious," a legal term of art used when a government agency allegedly acted in an unreasonable manner when carrying out the responsibilities delegated to it by a legislature.

In their brief to the court (signed by New York's Attorney General), the commissioners almost seemed to go out of their way to confirm their decision really was arbitrary and capricious. By modern standards, the brief is stunning in its chauvinism. The commissioners offered what they viewed as several plausible reasons why it would be reasonable for the Commission to deny a wrestling license to a woman. Nearly all of them drew upon longstanding stereotypes regarding the roles of men and women in society.

For example, the commissioners stated as fact (without offering any actual support for) the notion that women were more susceptible to physical injury than men as a justification for the ban. The commissioners also included the following gem:

(1) Pitting one man against another in tests of physical strength and skills is atavistic, and "hallowed" by tradition. As long as Man remains uncivilized in any degree, such spectacles remain almost as necessary as food and drink. With women, the answer is obvious.

In other words, there is an almost primal need to watch men beat each other up. But that's not the case with women.

The commissioners found support for their argument in *Goesaert v. Cleary*, the United States Supreme Court decision from 18 years earlier involving a state ban on women bartenders. There, Justice Felix Frankfurter wrote that while the ban

The New York State Athletic Commission was kind enough to return Ethel Whitehead's application fee for a wrestling license.

may have been based on old-fashioned notions of femininity, "the Constitution does not require legislatures to reflect sociological insight, or shifting social standards."[51] In other words, it was perfectly fine for a state legislature to draw sex-based distinctions on the basis of outdated views. This was particularly true in matters such as the regulation of liquor sales, over which the states had long exercised control. Citing this decision, the commissioners argued that the ban on women's wrestling was reasonable in light of the fact that "[t]he last vestiges of old-fashioned decency and the 'mother' or 'lady' image in the public eye are vanishing just because of attempted moves such as in the instant case."

Finally, the commissioners supported their decisions by offering a charming analogy between prostitutes and women wrestlers: "The argument that the prohibition against women wrestlers deprives them of 'their only source of living' is just as valid when applied to prostitutes, as well as others barred by statutes from pursuing their natural bent for earning their keep." Of course, both men and women were prohibited "from pursuing their natural bent" and earning a living by being a prostitute, but only women were prohibited from being professional wrestlers.

Whitehead faced a tough road on appeal. Not only did she have to overcome some decidedly unfavorable prior judicial precedent, as the party appealing the lower court decision, she had to overcome the natural tendency of appellate courts to defer to the decision of the original judge in this case. Not surprisingly, she couldn't surmount these obstacles. The Appellate Division of the New York Supreme Court affirmed the lower court's decision of the Commission without even authoring a formal opinion.[52] Once again, old-fashioned notions of the proper role of women had scored a pinfall over the right of women to earn a living inside the wrestling ring.

Calzadilla v. Dooley

Wrestler Silvia Calzadilla* was the next to take on the Commission. In 1967, Calzadilla applied to the New York State Athletic Association for a license to wrestle. Her application was denied on the grounds that under Commission rules, "[n]o women may compete in any wrestling or boxing contest or exhibition and no women may be licensed as a boxer, wrestler, manager or second."[53] Calzadilla challenged the decision in court.

Calzadilla's lawyers came prepared. While the Commission's actual objection to licensing women may have been that wrestling was not ladylike, publicly the Commission expressed other reservations. One was the

---

*Calzadilla wrestled under the name Silvia (or Sylvia) Torres.

fear that women's wrestling would somehow provoke riots. Another was health related. "[S]uppose a woman is four months' pregnant and decides she needs the money and takes a wrestling match," said a spokesperson for the Commission. "She could lose the baby and we'd be responsible." Another health concern? The fear (supposedly cited by doctors) that wrestling might result in breast cancer.*[54]

To address these concerns, Calzadilla's lawyers gathered letters from promoters and state athletic commissioners in other states where women's wrestling was legal, each of whom said women's wrestling had not led to riots. Local law enforcement officials said the same in their letters.† Calzadilla's lawyers also pointed out that there were no statistics or other evidence establishing any correlation between wrestling and cancer (in either men or women) or that trauma to a woman's breast was any more likely to lead to cancer than to a man.[55] In support of this position, Calzadilla's lawyers included a letter from the chief of breast surgery at a Buffalo hospital, who reported that "there is no evidence to show that there is any greater likelihood of women getting cancer of the breast from wrestling than men."[56]

Calzadilla's lawyers argued that the justifications offered by the Commission for denying Calzadilla a license were "frivolous," "arbitrary," and "capricious."[57] This sort of strong language was actually necessary to their case, because under existing law, the Commission simply needed to establish that its justification for drawing a distinction on the basis of sex was reasonable. Calzadilla's lawyers conceded that where a sex-based distinction was "fair, just, and sensible," there was no constitutional basis to object. However, where, as here, the classification was based on "an artificial premise"—like the non-existent connection between women's wrestling and riots or breast cancer—the classification is unconstitutional.[58]

In response, the Commission largely ignored these arguments. Instead, the Commission simply relied on past precedent. The Commission had denied Ethel Whitehead's application for a license only a few years before, and the same court had upheld the Commission's action. Thus, there was nothing to talk about.[59]

Calzadilla scored an initial win in court. The Commission made a motion to dismiss Calzadilla's claim before any evidence was gathered. The trial court dismissed the Commission's motion. But on appeal, the Commission had more luck.

The appellate court noted that the New York legislature had delegated

---

* There is a long history of this sort of paternalism in the sports world. For example, from 1928 to 1960, the Olympics did not include an 800 meter run for women for fear that women were too frail to withstand the rigors of such a race.

† In fact, one law enforcement official said that women wrestlers "have a soothing effect on both the male and female spectators."

sweeping authority to the Commission to regulate wrestling matches in the state. As the court noted, the relevant statute designated the Commission as having "the sole control, authority and jurisdiction over all licenses" to hold and participate in wrestling or boxing matches. The statute instructed the Commission that it could grant a license to any applicant who, in the Commission's judgment, possessed the "financial responsibility, experience, character and general fitness" such that the participation of the applicant would be "consistent with the public interest, convenience or necessity and with the best interests of boxing or wrestling generally and in conformity with the purposes of this act." While this standard was somewhat vague,* the same "consistent with the public interest, convenience or necessity" language had withstood challenges in court before. So, in the appellate court's view, it wasn't as if the Commission had gone rogue or was making licensing decisions without any sort of standard to guide it.

What's more, the court explained, one needed to take the somewhat shady histories of wrestling and boxing into account when assessing the Commission's decisions. One of the purposes of the statute granting the

Silvia Calzadilla (Torres) files her appeal.

---

* For example, what does it mean to say that one possesses the "character and general fitness" to be a professional wrestler? If past history was any guide, this was a pretty low standard.

Commission its authority was to help clean up these sports, which had "in the past been infested with undesirable elements."⁶⁰ Based on all of this, the court concluded that the Commission's decisions were entitled to "a great deal of latitude and discretion" and its rules should be enforced unless "clearly arbitrary."⁶¹

Further stacking the odds against Calzadilla was the fact that nearly all of the prior judicial decisions involving sex-based classifications like those at issue in Calzadilla's case had adopted a relaxed form of judicial review. As long as the classification was reasonable—and here the word "reasonable" was defined quite broadly—the classification passed constitutional muster. So, a court actually started with the presumption that there was some *"reasonably conceivable* set of facts" that would justify a sex-based classification.⁶²

Under this relaxed standard of review, the appellate court had little trouble concluding that the Commission's blanket rule denying all women the ability to wrestle was reasonable.⁶³ The court failed to explain exactly why the rule was reasonable. In light of the fact that Calzadilla had pretty clearly established that letting women wrestle was not going to result in an increase in the number of riots or incidents of breast cancer, the possible justifications for the rule were fairly limited. The court noted the possibility that

28

EXHIBIT #2 ANNEXED TO PETITION.

LETTER DATED APRIL 10, 1967.

ROSWELL PARK MEMORIAL INSTITUTE
Buffalo, New York 14203

April 10, 1967

State of New York
Department of Health
Hollis S. Ingraham, M. D.
Commissioner

George E. Moore, M.D., Ph.D.
Director

Mr. James W. Vogel
Lutwack, Feldman & Burke
287 Washington Street
Buffalo, New York 14203

Dear Mr. Vogel:

I received your letter of April 6, 1967, requesting information about cancer of the breast in connection with lady wrestlers.

It is my opinion that there is no evidence to show that there is any greater likelihood of women getting cancer of the breast from wrestling than men. Also, I do not believe that wrestling is apt to cause cancer of the breast in women.

Sincerely yours,

THOMAS L. DAO (ljc)
THOMAS L. DAO, M.D., *Chief
Department of Breast Surgery
Research Professor of Physiology*

TLD/ljc

One of Calzadilla's medical experts opines that wrestling does not put women at any greater risk of breast cancer.

6. Sex Discrimination, Constitutional Law, and Lady Wrestlers

the true justification for the rules was "founded on a mid–Victorian concept which females have long since abandoned and which has no place in this enlightened last third of the Twentieth Century."[64] But the court quickly brushed the argument aside. Quoting an earlier decision from the United States Supreme Court, the court stated that "[t]he Constitution does not require things which are different in fact or opinion to be treated in law as though they were the same."[65]

The court granted the Commission's motion to dismiss Calzadilla's claim. Lady wrestling was still outlawed in New York.

* * *

Part 3: Betty Niccoli, Titi Paris, and the Women's Liberation Movement v. The New York State Athletic Commission

In 1970, Betty Niccoli was, in the words of an Associated Press story, "a buxom 26-year-old miss from Kansas City whose measurements are 5-foot-1, 130 pounds and 36–29–38."[66] Niccoli was a veteran of the women's wrestling scene who had wrestled all across the Midwest, Texas, and California. But, of course, she had never wrestled in New York. "It's a matter of dollars and cents," Niccoli explained as to why she wanted to wrestle in the Empire State. "[I]t would kick up my income $7,000 a year if I could perform in New York."[67]

In October 1970, Niccoli launched a public relations assault on the New York State Athletic Commission. Attractive and well-spoken, Niccoli was the perfect person to bring attention to the rights of women wrestlers. Newspapers across the country reported that Niccoli had filed an application with the Commission and hired a lawyer. (The media speculated that her efforts were being sponsored by "those associated with the women's liberation movement," speculation that Niccoli dismissed.) "I can wrestle in all but five states," Niccoli was quoted as saying. "And why they don't let women wrestle in these states defies reason. They give all sorts of excuses but they don't hold water."[68] Niccoli flew out to New York in November for a hearing.

And then … it's not entirely clear what happened. For some reason, the minutes from Commission meetings between December 12, 1969, and March 27, 1973, are missing from state records.[69] While there were a spate of news stories leading up to the Commission's scheduled November 1970 hearing, the media quickly lost interest in the case. So, there is no way to be certain as to what transpired following Niccoli's hearing.

According to Niccoli, she did appear before the Commission, where she was reportedly told that she didn't look like a wrestler and was asked why she wanted to fight men. Niccoli said that she was told at the end of the hearing that the Commission would give her a license.[70] But it seems clear that Niccoli did not receive a license, nor does it appear that she ever filed suit.

* * *

Titi Paris was another wrestler during this time who sought to break New York's gender barrier. Paris (whose real name was Fatiha Djaileb but who also wrestled as Chi-Chi Paris, Princess Chi-Chi, and other names) had wrestled for years and had now settled in Brooklyn with her husband and child. Given her family responsibilities, it wasn't easy for her to travel around the country to wrestle, so she wanted to be able to perform close to home.[71] According to Paris, she sought a wrestling license from the Commission in November 1971. Later that month, she received a letter from Commission Chairman Edwin B. Dooley informing her that the Commission's rules prevented it from issuing her a license. Around this time, the Brooklyn resident also sent letters to at least two members of the U.S. House of Representatives and the National Organization of Women (NOW) in an attempt to enlist the organization's help.[72]

While Paris was unsuccessful in attaining a license, she can probably lay claim to participating in the first women's professional wrestling match in the state (or at least the first that was publicly reported on). In 1972, author Rosalyn Drexler, a former professional wrestler, published a novel about a female wrestler entitled *To Smithereens*.* As part of the promotion for the book, the publisher set up a party at Gil Clancy's Telstar Gym that featured a match between Paris and Cora Combs on March 8. A sympathetic *New York Post* story about the event featured numerous quotes from both women mocking Chairman Dooley and the Commission's ban. Paris also described her unsuccessful attempts to obtain a license.[73] So, not only did Paris help make history by competing in the (illegal) match, she also brought more attention to the Commission's ban.*

* * *

By this point, it had to have been clear to the Commission that it was on the wrong side of the women's equality movement. For example, around this time, state and federal courts started to reevaluate their pre-existing approaches to state-sponsored sex-based distinctions involving the sale of

---

* Interestingly, while Combs was critical of the Commission's rule and its chauvinism, she acknowledged "there's some things a man's superior to a woman in. Like running the country. Women just aren't ready for that."

alcohol.[74] One of these decisions came down just a few months before Niccoli filed her application for a wrestling license. As mentioned, back in 1948, the Supreme Court had little trouble concluding that a state law that prevented women from serving liquor as bartenders was constitutional under the Equal Protection Clause. But in June 1970, a New York federal court found that the refusal of an ale house to serve alcohol to women was unconstitutional in *Seidenberg v. McSorleys' Old Ale House, Inc.*[75]*

The *Seidenberg* decision should have been an ominous one for the New York State Athletic Commission. For one, the court made clear that it didn't feel particularly bound by the Supreme Court's earlier decision permitting states to ban women bartenders in light of changing times. "Social mores have not stood still since" the defendant in that case successfully argued that "moral and social" problems might arise from permitting women to serve as bartenders, the court noted.[76]

What's more, the court didn't seem particularly inclined to defer to the justifications the defendant offered for the sex-based distinction it drew. Theoretically, all the defendant needed to do was show some reasonable basis for deciding that men, but not women, should be able to drink at the bar. But the court concluded that each basis the defendant was offered was unreasonable. The court rejected the idea suggested by the Oregon Supreme Court years earlier that the desire to establish a safe haven for men where they could "retreat from womanhood" justified excluding women.[77] The court also noted that "the vast majority of bars and taverns do cater to both sexes"[78] (just as the vast majority of states allowed both men's and women's wrestling matches).† The court concluded its opinions with an observation about changing times that should have sent shivers down the collective spines of the members of the State Athletic Commission:

> Outdated images of bars as dens of coarseness and iniquity and of women as peculiarly delicate and impressionable creatures in need of protection from the rough and tumble of unvarnished humanity will no longer justify sexual separatism. At least to this extent woman's "emancipation" is recognized.[79]

If this decision from close to home wasn't enough to get the Commission's attention, the United States Supreme Court's decision in *Reed v. Reed*

---

* In order for there to be a violation of the Constitution, there must be state (or government) action. The Constitution prohibits the government, not private actors, from infringing on constitutional rights. The defendant in *Seidenberg* was a private organization. But the court nonetheless found state action due, in part, to the fact that the organization operated pursuant to a liquor license granted by the New York State Liquor Authority, which, like the State Athletic Commission, had broad authority when it came to issuing licenses.

† The defendant also made the spectacularly bad argument that "it is unreasonable to impose upon it by judicial mandate the modifications in its sanitary facilities that would be required if it is directed to cater to women as well as men."

in November 1971 definitely should have. In *Reed*, a minor had died without a will. The child's parents had separated prior to the child's death, and both parents sought to be appointed administrator of the child's estate. An Idaho statute provided that as between persons equally qualified to administer estates, males must be preferred to females. The Idaho legislature decided to favor men in this situation because ... well, just because. The best justification the legislature could offer was that the distinction in favor of men eliminated the need for a court to hold a hearing as to which parent was better qualified to serve as the administrator.[80] However, the Supreme Court held that the statute violated the Equal Protection Clause of the Fourteenth Amendment.[81] Under the relaxed standard of judicial review that applied in the case of sex-based classifications, a defendant merely had to offer a reasonable justification for the distinction. But, according to the Court, Idaho's decision was the sort of arbitrary classification that could not withstand even minimal scrutiny.[82]

By the end of 1971, it was clear that courts were increasingly moving to the point where they would no longer stand idly by and uphold legal rules that disadvantaged women.

* * *

Changes were also happening in Congress and state legislatures. The U.S. House of Representatives passed the Equal Rights Amendment in October of 1971. The Senate followed suit on March 22, 1972. Only a month earlier, the Senate had passed Title IX, which prohibits sex discrimination in any education program that receives federal financial assistance and which revolutionized women's amateur athletics. In May 1972, the New York State Assembly took direct aim at the Commission's ban on women's wrestling by approving a measure to legalize women's wrestling in the state. The bill was introduced by Assemblyman Vander L. Beatty of Brooklyn, who explained that one of his constituents "is a wrestler who wrote me and said she can wrestle in Massachusetts, but not in Brooklyn."[83] That Brooklyn wrestler was almost certainly Titi Paris, who had previously sent a letter to Rep. Shirley Chisholm, who forwarded the letter to Beatty.[84] Although the measure died in committee in the state Senate, the walls appeared to be closing in on the Commission.[85] On May 18, 1972, the New York legislature ratified the Equal Rights Amendment.

* * *

Finally, on June 5, 1972, the New York State Athletic Commission reversed its rule prohibiting women from wrestling. Citing "the trend toward women's participation in various things," Chairman Edwin B. Dooley announced that the Commission had "amended its rules to permit the licensing of women wrestlers to compete in New York with persons of the same sex."[86] Chairman Dooley expressed the view that the writing had basically been on the wall when the New York legislature ratified the Equal Rights Amendment just a few weeks earlier.[87] But a spokesperson for the Commission also recognized the role that prior legal challenges had on the Commission, attributing the reversal to the fact that female applicants "had been bothering and bothering us, so we finally decided to give it a try."[88] The lady wrestlers had won.

Part IV: Conclusion

On July 1, 1972, the Fabulous Moolah and Vicki Williams performed at Madison Square Garden on front of a crowd of over 19,000.* This event is generally considered the first-ever women's professional wrestling event in the state. At the time, Moolah was the biggest powerbroker in the world of women's wrestling, running a stable of women wrestlers whom she loaned out to promoters. She had worked with Vince McMahon, Sr., who controlled wrestling in New York, for over a decade, so it was natural that when Madison Square Garden became an option for women that Moolah would get the first job there.

Moolah would take credit for lifting the ban in her autobiography.[89] Moolah provides a laughable account of a supposed conversation she had with Vince McMahon, Sr., in which the two of them decided to try to get the ban lifted.† It's true that Moolah spoke out publicly about the ban in New York during this general time period.[90] And it's also possible that McMahon may have worked behind the scenes to get the ban lifted. (It's hard to know since the Commission's records during this time no longer exist.) But nothing indicates that Moolah ever filed for a license or took the Commission to court.

While Moolah and Williams may have been the first women to engage in a licensed wrestling exhibition in the state, much of the credit for their ability to do so lies with the efforts of other women. By "bothering and bothering" the courts and commissioners for years, these women helped wear down the New York State Athletic Commission into overturning its ban.

In the short term, the victory was perhaps more meaningful on a symbolic level than it was on a practical level. Because Moolah and

---

* The main event that night featured Pedro Morales defeating George "the Animal" Steele.

† "With you leading the way, Moolah," McMahon supposedly said, "I know we can do it." Moolah also suggests that her appearance in a February 1969 episode of the *Mike Douglas Show* led the Commission to reverse its ban (in June 1972).

McMahon had a stranglehold on women's wrestling in the state, only women who worked for Moolah were able to truly benefit from the ban in New York being lifted. For example, Titi Paris would complain mightily to anyone whom she thought would listen in the months and years that followed about her inability to get booked in New York due to the monopoly that Moolah and McMahon enjoyed.[91] Betty Niccoli remained miffed for decades at being denied the chance to be the first to wrestle at Madison Square Garden. "I fought this to be the first one in there," said Niccoli years later. "I never even got a foot in the door," said Niccoli.[92]*

But the efforts of Niccoli, Paris, and those who challenged the bans in place in New York and other states played a meaningful role in the fight for gender equality in the sports and entertainment world. Their efforts also bore practical fruit. In 1973, Vera Katz took office in the Oregon legislature. During her first term, she introduced legislation to repeal the 1955 ban on women's wrestling in the state. A 2023 article in *The Oregonian* recounts Katz explaining the symbolic significance of her bill:

> "This is not an important bill, in that it does not affect the lives of many persons," Katz told a Centennial High School student in a 1973 letter among her papers archived at Portland State University. "This is an important bill, in that the principle of equality, under the law, is not yet a reality for citizens regardless of their sex."[93]

Katz invited Gerry Hunter, one of the people whose life was affected by the 1955 law, to testify before the legislature concerning Katz's bill. The bill eventually passed in 1975, thus permitting women in Oregon to earn money through professional wrestling if they chose to. Women like Hunter helped nudge the principle of equality under the law, regardless of sex, closer to reality.

* * *

In 1976, the United States Supreme Court held in *Craig v. Boren* that the lower level of judicial scrutiny that merely required a state to offer a rational basis for a sex-based classifications would no longer apply. Instead, states that sought to treat men and women differently on the basis of sex would now have to satisfy a more rigorous standard of review.[94] Over time, the Court refined this intermediate standard of review to the point that in order for a defendant to justify a sex-based distinction, a defendant must offer an "exceedingly persuasive" justification for the distinction.[95] The days when states could rely on "'archaic and overbroad' generalizations" about women to justify differential treatment and receive blanket protection from the courts were over.

---

* Nonetheless, according to a 2023 interview with her husband (wrestler Akio Sato), she remained quite proud of the role she played in helping to bring about the end to the ban.

* * *

On June 23, 1972, President Richard Nixon signed Title IX into law. The law became effective on July 1, 1972—the same day Moolah and Williams appeared in Madison Square Garden for the first time. The law had a revolutionary effect on women's athletics, including wrestling. Women's wrestling became an Olympic event for the first time ever in 2004. Today, over 50,000 girls participate in high school wrestling programs, and there are dozens of colleges and universities that have women's wrestling programs.

Postscript: Sexual Harassment

Grant v. World Wrestling Entertainment, Civil Action No. 3:24-cv-90 (S.D.N.Y. 2024)

Betty Niccoli and those who came before her were victims of sex discrimination in the wrestling business. But another form of sex discrimination continued to exist years after the sex barrier in Madison Square Garden was broken in 1972. This form of discrimination—sexual harassment—would capture the attention of wrestling fans and the general public several times beginning in the 1990s and up to the present day.

The term "sexual harassment" first entered the public consciousness in 1991 when law professor Anita Hill testified before the United States Senate Judiciary Committee that Supreme Court nominee Clarence Thomas had engaged in sexual misconduct in the workplace. But the term first appeared in legal literature in 1979 when law professor Catherine MacKinnon published her book *Sexual Harassment of Working Women*. MacKinnon identified two forms of sexual harassment: (1) *quid pro quo* harassment, "in which sexual compliance is exchanged, or proposed to be exchanged, for an employment opportunity" (for example, "sleep with me or you're fired")[96] and (2) "hostile work environment" harassment, where sexualized conduct is so severe or pervasive that it "simply makes the workplace environment unbearable."[97] In either situation, MacKinnon argued, such conduct amounted to unlawful employment discrimination in violation of Title VII of the Civil Rights Act of 1964, which prohibits "discrimination ... because of ... sex." MacKinnon's work strongly influenced the courts, and soon sexual harassment claims became a fixture of employment discrimination law. Estimates as to the prevalence of sexual harassment in the workplace today vary, but according to one source, 40% of women and 16% of men report having been sexually harassed at work.[98]

Wrestling promoters had allegedly engaged in various forms of sexual harassment long before judges and lawyers began using the term regularly. There are numerous tales from the 1940s through the 1980s of promoters promising aspiring wrestlers professional success in exchange for sexual favors (or threatening to derail their careers if they refused to comply with the promoter's sexual demands). But it was not until shortly after the Clarence Thomas/Anita Hill controversy that the general public learned of the possibility of sexual harassment taking place in the wrestling business. And in 2022 and 2024, the public would again learn of some deeply disturbing allegations of sexual harassment taking place at the highest levels of the WWE hierarchy.

* * *

In early 1992, scandal hit the WWF. Several news outlets began reporting that sexual harassment was rampant within the WWF. But it was the nature of the harassment that was the real headline-grabber. The accusers were all men who had allegedly been harassed by high-ranking men within the WWF. The most shocking allegation came from Tom Cole, a young man who claimed to have been harassed when he had been a "ring boy," a teenager who helped set up and take down the wrestling ring.[99] Cole alleged that Mel Phillips, a WWF ring announcer who oversaw the ring set up, engaged in sexually inappropriate behavior toward Cole when Cole was still a teen. In addition, Phillips' boss, Terry Garvin, also propositioned Cole. When Cole refused the advances of these men, he found himself out of a job.[100] Cole's allegations resulted in several other individuals coming forward with their own tales of sexual harassment in the WWF. One was a former announcer. Two were wrestlers. But they all told essentially the same story: higher-ups within the organization had pressured them to have sex with the implied (and sometime express) threat that there would be consequences for their careers if they refused.

In a March 1992 episode of the television show *Donahue*, host Phil Donahue provided a forum for the accusers and the WWF's Vince McMahon. Former WWF announcer Murray Hodgson claimed that he refused the sexual advances of McMahon's right-hand man, Pat Patterson, and was fired as a result. Former WWF wrestler Barry Orton (a.k.a. Barry O) stated that he had been subjected to unwanted sexual advances by WWF official Terry Garvin years earlier during a car trip before he joined the WWF. Next up was former wrestler Tom Hankins, who told a story about Patterson conditioning a job offer on Hankins' willingness to have sex with him.

On the surface, the accusations of Hodgson and Hankins involved classic examples of *quid pro quo* harassment. Higher-ups within the WWF were conditioning future employment opportunities on submission to

6. Sex Discrimination, Constitutional Law, and Lady Wrestlers 143

demands for sexual favors. However, Orton did not claim to have suffered any adverse consequences as a result of rebuffing Garvin's sexual advances. Instead, what Orton was describing was something along the lines of the "hostile work environment" form of sexual harassment in which sexualized conduct makes the workplace unbearable.

While there may have been factual questions as to what actually transpired in all of these interactions, the accusers were all describing conduct that was potentially unlawful under Title VII had it involved a male supervisor and a female subordinate. If, for example, a heterosexual male supervisor's proposal of sex in exchange for a female employee's submission to the male supervisor's advances constituted discrimination because of sex in violation of Title VII, logically, the result should be the same where a homosexual male supervisor proposed the same exchange to a male employee. But in 1992, it was still an open question whether same-sex sexual harassment was unlawful under Title VII. Indeed, there were several judicial decisions around this time that took the position that same-sex sexual harassment was simply not illegal under Title VII.[101]

It would be another six years before the Supreme Court resolved the issue. In *Oncale v. Sundowner Offshore Services, Inc.*, the Court held that same-sex sexual harassment violated Title VII.[102] The Court had little trouble concluding that sexual harassment of the kind alleged by Cole and Hodgson amounted to unlawful sex discrimination. In addition, the Court concluded that same-sex harassment that resulted in an objectively hostile work environment also violated Title VII.

In response to the scandal, McMahon disavowed any knowledge of harassment on the part of Patterson and Garvin and noted that both men had resigned from the company. From both a public relations and legal standpoint, this was a wise decision for McMahon. In order to avoid liability where a supervisor's harassment results in a hostile work environment, the employer must show that it reasonably tried to prevent and promptly correct the harassing behavior.[103] If McMahon admitted to having known about any harassment on the part of Patterson and Garvin and failed to do anything about it, he would have potentially been opening the door to further claims due to his failure to prevent harassment. And from a legal matter, McMahon's decision to fire Patterson and Garvin demonstrated his supposed efforts to promptly correct the harassing behavior once it was brought to his attention.*

But Cole's allegations in particular potentially presented the WWF with a more problematic situation. Cole claimed to have been pressured to have sex by Phillips and Garvin and then to have lost his job as a result

---

* McMahon would eventually rehire Patterson.

of his refusal to comply. Under Title VII, where a supervisor's harassment results in a tangible job action—like losing one's job or being denied a job—the employer is automatically liable. The fact that the employer had an internal complaint procedure in place or fired the offending supervisor is not a defense for the employer.[104] So, if Cole's allegations were true, the WWF was on the hook as a legal matter, never mind the terrible publicity that was taking place.

Cole was seeking to collect $750,000 from the WWF, and he had a good case. McMahon caught a break, however. During settlement negotiations with McMahon and his lawyer, the naïve Cole blurted out that all he wanted was his old job back. Cole's lawyer then inexplicably left Cole alone in the room with McMahon, who bonded with Cole by telling him that he, too, had been molested as a teenager. When Cole's lawyer came back into the room, the two sides had reached a settlement: Cole would get his job back and the WWF would pay him $55,000.[105] With Cole now back in the WWF fold, the scandal quickly died down. McMahon and the WWF had dodged a bullet.

* * *

McMahon and the WWF managed to survive the sex scandals of the early 1990s. Rather than retreating to the more family-friendly fare that been the company's trademark during the 1980s, the WWF instead launched what became known as the "Attitude Era," a period in the WWF's history that pushed—and sometimes blew right past—notions of good taste and acceptable television. Key to the success of the Attitude Era was the WWF's decision to prominently feature women in its programming. Some of the female "Divas" (for example, Lita and Ivory) were solid wrestlers. Others were on TV largely to titillate. Bikini contests and bra-and-panties matches became standard fare during this era.

In this era of hyper-sexualization and objectification of the WWF's female performers, it was hardly surprising that sexual harassment backstage allegedly flourished. The world of professional wrestling had long been a boy's club, with humor and practical jokes ranging from the merely gross to the truly disgusting. And according to two female performers, the behavior sometimes led to a hostile work environment. Nicole Bass was a bodybuilder turned wrestler. In 1999, she sued the WWF, alleging that she had been subjected to a hostile work environment on the basis of sex. According to Bass, she and other female performers were subjected to "repeated and unwelcome sexual advances and intrusions" by male members of the WWF.[106] This included several men "accidentally" entering the women's locker room while the women were changing or showering.[107]

Bass' allegations were echoed by another, more successful wrestler:

6. Sex Discrimination, Constitutional Law, and Lady Wrestlers 145

Rena Mero (a.k.a. Sable).* Mero filed her own sexual harassment against the WWF around the time of Bass' suit. In addition to alleging that men would walk into the women's locker room "as if by accident," Mero alleged that

> men would cut holes in the walls to watch the women dressing; extras were hired as WWF regulars to expose their breasts; big nipple contests were engaged in; [and] men regularly bragged about their sexual encounters without regard to the women present.[108]

As a result, Mero alleged, she had been subjected to a hostile work environment.

Only a year earlier, the Supreme Court in its *Oncale* decision had emphasized that Title VII did not impose "a general civility code for the American workplace." In a passage in the opinion that almost seemed like it had been written with the world of professional wrestling in mind, the Court explained that the issue of whether a workplace was objectively hostile must be considered in light of the particular workplace in question:

> A professional football player's working environment is not severely or pervasively abusive, for example, if the coach smacks him on the buttocks as he heads onto the field—even if the same behavior would reasonably be experienced as abusive by the coach's secretary (male or female) back at the office. The real social impact of workplace behavior often depends on a constellation of surrounding circumstances, expectations, and relationships which are not fully captured by a simple recitation of the words used or the physical acts performed. Common sense, and an appropriate sensitivity to social context, will enable courts and juries to distinguish between simple teasing or roughhousing among members of the same sex, and conduct which a reasonable person in the plaintiff's position would find severely hostile or abusive.[109]

In other words, what might obviously amount to harassment in a Microsoft boardroom might not rise to the level of an objectively hostile work environment in the WWF locker room.

Title VII's prohibition sexual harassment was an uneasy fit in the world of professional wrestling of the time. Teasing, roughhousing, and worse were commonplace, regardless of the sex of the perpetrator and victim. It would take something fairly extreme to rise to the level of actionable harassment within that world. Mero settled her suit shortly after filing it.[110] Bass' suit made it to trial in 2002, but a jury ruled against her in less than five hours.[111] The WWF had withstood another sex scandal.†

---

* Bass had actually served as Mero's "bodyguard" during her brief time in the WWF.

† Just a few months earlier while returning on a flight from the U.K., a number of WWF performers engaged in various forms of drunken debauchery, including alleged sexual harassment of a flight attendant.

* * *

Evidence of more extreme conduct taking place within the WWE would eventually come to light. In June 2022, the *Wall Street Journal* reported that the WWE board of directors was investigating a $3 million settlement with a former employee with whom McMahon had allegedly had an affair.[112] The settlement included a non-disclosure agreement (NDA) that prohibited the former employee from discussing her relationship with McMahon. The *Journal* also referenced other NDAs McMahon had entered into with other women associated with the WWE that related to sexual improprieties on the part of McMahon and WWE's head of talent relations John Laurinaitis.

A few weeks later, the *Journal* followed up with details on these other settlements, including the fact that McMahon had paid several women more than $12 million over the course of 16 years to settle various potential claims of improper sexual conduct.[113] One of the settlements involved a former wrestler who alleged a case of *quid pro quo* harassment; according to the wrestler, McMahon coerced her into performing oral sex on him and "then demoted her and, ultimately, declined to renew her contract in 2005 after she resisted further sexual encounters."[114] In another instance, McMahon allegedly sent unsolicited nude photos of himself to a WWE contractor and sexually harassed her on the job, thus potentially resulting in a hostile work environment.* As part of their settlements, the individuals were required to sign NDAs.

While WWE had faced sexual harassment allegations before, these were different. For one, the charges of misconduct involved McMahon himself. For another, societal attitudes regarding workplace harassment in 2022 differed dramatically than attitudes in 1992 or even 2002. The #MeToo movement, which exploded in 2017 following numerous allegations of sexual harassment by famed Hollywood producer Harvey Weinstein, raised new levels of awareness regarding the frequency of harassment in the workplace. Not only did more women feel empowered to reveal their own past encounters with harassment, the public at large became more educated concerning the severity of the problem. As the law regarding sexual harassment evolved over the decades, employers increasingly took steps to shield themselves from liability by adopting training and internal reporting procedures designed to address instances of workplace harassment.

For its part, professional wrestling was no longer the boys' club/

---

* It is worth noting that Title VII only protects employees from employment discrimination, not independent contractors. Thus, to the extent any of the women alleging harassment were contractors and not employees, they would not have a claim under Title VII (although McMahon's actions might have otherwise been unlawful).

6. Sex Discrimination, Constitutional Law, and Lady Wrestlers   147

traveling circus it had once been. WWE had grown increasingly corporate over time, as evidenced by the fact that it now actually had a board of directors that could exert control over company policies and procedures. In theory, there should have been less toleration for sexual harassment in the wrestling business than there had been in the past.

New laws also emerged around this time that provided victims of sexual harassment with legal avenues that had previously been blocked. In November 2022, Congress passed the Speak Out Act, which prohibits the enforcement of non-disclosure agreements involving conduct that allegedly violates state or federal law.* Importantly, the Act also retroactively applies to NDAs involving alleged sexual harassment or sexual assault, thus permitting victims to speak out despite having previously signed an NDA. Also in November of 2022, New York passed the Adult Survivors Act, which gave victims of past sexual assault one year in which to bring lawsuits against the perpetrators despite the fact that such suits would ordinarily be barred by the state's statute of limitation. As a result, over 2,500 lawsuits alleging sexual abuse were filed in New York in the ensuing year.[115]

All of these forces conspired to produce even more problems for McMahon and WWE. In late 2022, former WWF referee Rita Chatterton sent a demand letter to McMahon, requesting $11.75 million for allegedly raping Chatterton in 1986. Chatterton had gone public with these allegations back in 1992 when the first wave of negative publicity hit the WWF, but McMahon filed (and later withdrew) a defamation action against Chatterton and Chatterton let the matter drop. But New York's Adult Survivors Act provided Chatterton with a new opportunity to pursue her claims. McMahon quickly settled with Chatterton.[116]

But in January 2024, McMahon and WWE were hit with a new bombshell. Janel Grant, one of the women with whom McMahon had entered into an NDA, filed a lawsuit in a New York federal court accusing McMahon and John Laurinaitis of a host of forms of sexual misconduct, including sex trafficking. Grant alleged that the NDA she had previously entered into was unenforceable due to the newly-enacted Speak Out Act as well as McMahon's alleged failure to make the payments agreed upon as part of Grant's settlement. Notably, Grant alleged in her complaint that "the WWE, and its most senior officials, knew about and fostered a culture where the venture of harassment and sexual exploitation of women was tolerated to further the business and financial interests of WWE."[117]

Grant's accusations were salacious and generated widespread media

---

* Notably, the preamble to the Act provides that it applies to independent contractors as well as employees.

coverage. They also prompted others to come forward and say, "me too." In February 2024, former WWF wrestler Nick Kiniski came forward to say that he had been repeatedly propositioned in the 1980s by former WWF official Terry Garvin, one of the individuals accused back in 1992 of having engaged in similar conduct. Kiniski claims to have complained to Vince McMahon about Garvin's behavior to no avail. Indeed, Kiniski claims, he suffered tangible harm for his refusals by being dropped from a live event to his financial detriment and was also made to start losing matches.[118] This, of course, contradicts McMahon's statements back in 1992 that he had never heard any complaints of sexual harassment involving Garvin at the time. Around this time, another story emerged involving former WWE performer Ashley Massaro.* As part of a separate lawsuit, Massaro provided a statement (that was not included in the lawsuit) in which she said McMahon punished her for not giving into his sexual advances by writing bad on-air material for Massaro that she says was written for the purpose of ruining her career. Massaro also claimed to have been raped by a doctor affiliated with WWE but was told by McMahon to keep quiet about the incident.[119]

McMahon had been engaged in an ongoing power struggle within WWE for some time when these events transpired. The 2024 scandal forced McMahon to resign, presumably for good. As this book prepared to go to press, Grant's legal case against WWE, McMahon, and Laurinaitis was still pending.

* * *

The law regarding sexual harassment evolved between 1992 and 2024, as did public perception of harassment. Nearly all employers adapted to these changes. For example, as early as 1997, 75% of U.S. companies had developed mandatory training programs for all employees on the subject of sexual harassment, and 95% had instituted internal procedures for dealing with complaints of sexual harassment.[120] Today, those numbers are almost certainly higher. Several states (including Connecticut where the WWE is headquartered) now *require* employers to provide training to employees regarding sexual harassment.[121] In the aftermath of the *#MeToo* movement, more workers believe that accusers are more likely to be taken seriously and that harassers are likely to be held accountable.[122]

If the allegations of those formerly associated with WWE are to be believed, one organization that did little to evolve on the issue of sexual harassment was WWE. Sexual harassment was tolerated and participated in at the highest levels of the company. Despite changes in the American

---

* Massaro died in 2019.

6. Sex Discrimination, Constitutional Law, and Lady Wrestlers 149

workplace, increased focus on the law regarding sexual harassment, and its status as a publicly-traded corporate entity, WWE allegedly continued to operate in a manner more in keeping with the olden days of the workplace in which employees had to endure sexual misconduct or risk losing their jobs. The law and public attitudes changed over time; World Wrestling Entertainment allegedly did not.

Chapter 7

Defamation

*Bollea v. World Championship Wrestling, Inc. (2005)**

> *Every fiction writer knows that his creation is in some sense false.*
> —*Guglielmi v. Spelling-Goldberg Productions,*
> 603 P.2d 454, 461 (Cal. 1979)

* * *

Turn on a television set today and you will find more reality TV shows than traditional fictional sitcoms and dramas. While the reality TV format first rose to prominence in the 1990s and exploded in the early 2000s, the roots of the genre extend further back. It's widely recognized that the first true reality TV show to air was *An American Family*, which aired in 1973 on PBS. *An American Family* focused on real-life, upper middle-class couple Bill and Pat Loud and their five children. Camera crews embedded themselves within the Loud household for seven months and filmed the daily life of an American family. But the show produced more than just a document of routine family fun and squabbles. The show captured the breakup of Bill and Pat's marriage as well as the coming out of son Lance as a homosexual.

The creator of the show insisted that "[e]verything happened as it happened.... No tricks. No retakes. There's more manipulation and staging in one segment of *60 Minutes* than there is in 12 hours of 'An American Family.'"[1] But as the reality TV genre evolved in the 1990s, the line between reality and fiction became increasingly blurred. Producers contrived situations in order to increase drama and conflict among participants. Reality

---

* An earlier version of this chapter appeared in the *Wake Forest Law Review*. See Alex B. Long, "All I Really Need to Know About Defamation Law in the 21st Century I Learned from Watching Hulk Hogan," 57 *Wake Forest Law Review* 413 (2022).

TV archetypes (the Innocent, the Manipulator, the Spoiled Brat, etc.) quickly developed and populated shows. Producers also became adept at creative editing (sometimes known as "frankenbiting") to re-sequence or combine different real-life events in order to tell a better story.

One result of consciously incorporating elements of fiction into reality TV has been the filing of defamation lawsuits by participants who have been presented in a negative light by the creative efforts of producers. Over the years, the producers of numerous reality TV shows have faced potential legal liability on a variety of legal theories, including defamation.[2] To cite but one example, Ellen Pearson Kardashian, widow of famed lawyer Robert Kardashian, sued producers and stars of the show *Keeping Up with the Kardashians* for statements made on the show. Kim, Kourtney, and Khloé Kardashian filed a lawsuit against Ellen for licensing Robert's diary entries without their permission. Ellen responded by suing the sisters and the show's production company for defamation. According to her lawsuit, "the Kardashians worked with the Production Company to craft and fully script the filing of the lawsuit and service of the summons as a sensational and dramatic scene for Season 8, Episode 2 of *Keeping Up with the Kardashians*."[3] Moreover, Ellen alleged that the show engaged in deceptive editing to create a false portrayal of Ellen's actions and that the Kardashians falsely attributed statements to Ellen that she had not made.[4]

Movies also sometimes blur the line. The award-winning movie *Fargo* begins with the following text on the screen: "This is a true story." It turns out that this famous introductory text is not substantially true. According to writer/producer Joel Coen, there were two real-life events that were used in the film (one involved a woodchipper, the other vehicle identification number fraud broadly defined), "[b]ut beyond that, the story is made up."[5] According to his brother Ethan, the film's director, "We wanted to make a movie just in the genre of a true story movie. You don't have to have a true story to make a true story movie."[6] Other filmmakers have similarly led audiences to believe that what they were witnessing onscreen was based on real events when, in reality, the films were entirely or almost entirely fictional. Horror movies, in particular, often use this convention, presumably because the more "real" events seem, the more viewers can empathize with the characters and be frightened by what they experience. Obvious examples include *The Blair Witch Project*, *The Amityville Horror*, and *The Strangers*.

For fans of professional wrestling, the notion of blending elements of reality and fiction in order to create compelling characters, generate emotion on the part of viewers, and advance interesting storylines undoubtedly sounds familiar. Indeed, this has been the wrestling business' stock and trade for decades. In this respect, professional wrestling was producing reality TV long before that term entered society's collective consciousness. But the blurring of fiction and reality in professional wrestling reached new heights in the mid–1990s, just prior to the reality TV boom. It culminated in a bizarre event at a pay-per-view event in 2000 that led to one of the more potentially interesting libel* lawsuits ever.

* * *

Part 1: Hulk Hogan and the Rise of the Worked Shoot

Hulk Hogan was born Terry Bollea, the chubby son of a construction worker father and stay-at-home mother. Raised in Tampa, Bollea was bullied as a child. When he got older, he tried to make a go of it as a professional musician but eventually decided to pursue a career as a professional wrestler. After wrestling under the names Terry Boulder and Sterling Golden, Bollea eventually settled on the name "Hulk Hogan" after going to work for promoter Vince McMahon, Sr., in 1979. By the mid–1980s, Hogan was not only the most famous professional wrestler in the world, he was one of the most famous people in the world. He appeared in movies, television shows, and on magazine covers. In 1987, Hogan, along with André the Giant, headlined the legendary Wrestlemania III pay-per-view event, which set a then-record for indoor attendance (over 93,000) and shattered previous pay-per-view buy-rates. In part by leveraging Hogan's celebrity, World Wrestling Entertainment (WWE)† was able to drive several of its competitors out of business. "Hulkamania" ran wild during the 1980s and into the early 1990s.

But by the early 90s, Hogan's routine was starting to grow stale. WWE fans had heard Hogan's catchphrases ("Whatchya gonna do when Hulkamania runs wild on you?") for years, and they had watched Hogan dispatch a host of heels in matches to the point that there few surprises left, either in the ring or on the microphone. Hogan eventually left the WWE in 1994 to join the organization's chief rival, World Championship Wrestling (WCW), owned by Ted Turner.

To say that the WCW was a legitimate rival to the WWE at the time would be generous. WCW was part of Ted Turner's media empire. But the "wrasslin'" company was viewed as something of an embarrassment by

---

* Slander is the spoken form of defamation. Libel is the written or more permanent form.

† The company was known at the time as the World Wrestling Federation (WWF).

Turner executives, who had long sought to kill off the company. A perpetual money-loser for Turner's company, WCW survived as an entity in large part because of Turner's fondness for professional wrestling.* The hope was that the signing of Hulk Hogan would breathe new life into the company.[7]

But by mid–1995, it was clear that Hogan's act had once again grown tired, despite the new stage WCW had provided. Tired of being bested by rival Vince McMahon, Turner gave the greenlight to WCW executives to develop a new program to air on Monday nights starting in September that would compete directly with McMahon's *Monday Night Raw* on the USA Network. The idea was to create "event programming" along the lines of *Monday Night Football* that fans would just *have to* tune in to watch.[8] The new show would be called *WCW Monday Nitro* and would broadcast live each week, with the goal of luring viewers by adding a strong dose of unpredictability to the broadcast.[9]

Hulk Hogan's role in this new undertaking would be crucial. In an effort to add to the unpredictability of *Nitro* and to revitalize Hogan's career, the WCW brain trust (led by Senior Vice President and on-air personality Eric Bischoff) devised perhaps the greatest "heel turn" in the history of professional wrestling. Hogan/Bollea had perfected his babyface routine over the years—famously urging kids to "say your prayers and eat your vitamins"—and was reluctant to give up his character. But Bischoff convinced Hogan that the time was now or never for him to turn "heel." And so, as part of the Bash at the Beach pay-per-view in 1996, it was revealed as part of the storyline that the character of Hulk Hogan had secretly been working with a group of former WWE wrestlers who were "invading" WCW. As trash hurled by fans rained down inside the ring, Hogan verbally spat on his former Hulkamaniacs and announced the formation of "the New World Order," a faction that planned to take over WCW.†

The heel turn worked. Over the next several years, the NWO (the New World Order) storyline would help propel *Nitro* and WCW past *Raw* and the WWE in the ratings and usher in the wrestling boom of the late 1990s. The competition prompted the WWE to reformulate its own approach, triggering huge ratings for both organizations. Perhaps not coincidentally, as the TV ratings for professional wrestling on Monday nights soared, the ratings for ABC's long-time juggernaut *Monday Night Football* declined precipitously.[10] Live wrestling broadcasts on Monday nights and

---

* Turner had built his original cable channel, TBS, on Atlanta Braves baseball, reruns of the *Andy Griffith Show*, and professional wrestling, and retained a soft spot for wrestling.

† Hogan actually botched the announcement of the organization's name at the time, referring to the group as "the New World Organization."

pay-per-view broadcasts became "must-see" events, sometimes featuring in-ring appearances from celebrities like Jay Leno and athletes like Mike Tyson, Karl Malone, and Dennis Rodman. And at the center of it all for WCW was Hulk Hogan.

* * *

> **Work (noun)**: *an event booked to happen, from the carnival tradition of "working the crowd." A work can also refer to the match itself. The opposite of a work is a shoot.*
> **Shoot (noun)**: *any "real" event in the world of wrestling....*
> —Pro Wrestling Fandom.com,
> Glossary of Professional Wrestling Terms

Unpredictability was a huge part of the success of the wrestling wars of the 1990s. Part of that unpredictability involved the incorporation of more elements of reality into the programming. Professional wrestling has always had a complicated relationship with reality. Back in the kayfabe days, the wrestling business went to great lengths to preserve the illusion of reality. For example, Florida promoter Eddie Graham supposedly told his wrestlers that if they got into a bar fight and lost, they would be fired; Graham's business thrived on the perception that his wrestlers were legitimate tough guys and he couldn't afford for his performers to be viewed as anything less.[11] This devotion to maintaining the perception of reality changed during the wrestling boom of the 1980s. Promoter Vince McMahon, Jr., taking over the WWE from his father, decided to forego any pretense that wrestling was on the level and started developing a more cartoonish and family-friendly form of wrestling that he pointedly referred to as "sports entertainment" instead of "wrestling."

But during the boom of the 1990s, both WCW and WWE started to incorporate more reality-based elements into their performances. Part of this trend had to do with the fact that the cartoon-based version of the product that had worked before was now no longer working as well. The pendulum naturally needed to swing back in the other direction a little bit. But the decision to weave elements of real-life into the simulated reality of professional wrestling also coincided with the rise of the Internet. Prior to the Internet, only a limited number of fans knew what was taking place behind the scenes in the world of professional wrestling. But the growth of the Internet enabled "smart" fans to become even smarter about what was happening behind the curtain. Wrestling websites soon sprang up, increasingly reporting behind-the-scenes rumors and leaked storylines and endings to matches.

WCW's product reflected this new reality. In the world of professional wrestling, that which is real is "a shoot." That which is part of the act is "a work." "Shoots" occasionally happened when, for example, one wrestler took offense to what his opponent had done in the ring and responded with something approximating a real punch. But otherwise, nearly everything that occurred at a wrestling event at the time was a work. During the boom of the 1990s, the wrestling business began to experiment with the so-called "worked shoot." As described by one source, a worked shoot is "a scripted segment that takes place in a show with elements of reality being exposed, such as an off-screen incident between wrestlers being used as fuel for an on-screen rivalry between them. It can also be a segment that fans are meant to believe is a shoot, but is not."[12] In other words, the worked shoot blurred the line between fiction and reality by bringing some measure of reality into the fantasy world of professional wrestling. It was a creative device that WCW would increasingly employ.*

One early example of a worked shoot from this era involved a match between Brian Pillman and Kevin Sullivan at a WCW pay-per-view event in February 1996. Pillman and Sullivan had been involved a long feud, which was to culminate in an "I Respect You" match. The idea was that the winner could only prevail by making his opponent say the words "I respect you" into the microphone, thereby acknowledging defeat. At the time, Sullivan was not only an in-ring performer but also the booker for WCW, meaning he was the person who set up matches and storylines. As part of an attempt to develop a new persona for Pillman—that of the "loose cannon"—Bischoff, Sullivan, and Pillman agreed to an unusual ending for the match. After about a minute of fighting in the ring, Pillman simply grabbed the microphone and announced, "I respect you, Bookerman" before leaving the ring.[13] By publicly referring to Sullivan as "Bookerman," Pillman was "exposing" the fact—already known to some fans who had been smartened by the Internet—that Sullivan was actually the booker for the promotion. The bizarreness of the incident had the desired effect, leaving some "smart" fans to wonder if what they had just witnessed was a genuine "shoot" by a possibly mentally unstable Brian Pillman.[14]

WCW increasingly blurred the line between shoot and work (or reality and fiction) over the years with varying degrees of effectiveness. For example, Bischoff and WCW stalwart Ric Flair were involved in a very real contract dispute in 1998. WCW had filed a breach of contract lawsuit against Flair for having failed to make a televised appearance. Bischoff ended up trashing ("shooting" on) Flair to other performers backstage

---

* WCW was hardly the first to incorporate "real life" into the world of professional wrestling. As an example, famed promoter Jerry Jarrett famously had a sign in his office in the 1970s reading "Personal issues draw money."

about the incident. As a result, Flair was off television for an extended period of time. Given Flair's absence from TV and the glut of Internet wrestling sites, these real events became public knowledge. When Flair eventually returned to TV, he delivered one of the all-time great worked-shoot promos. After fighting back what appeared to be very real tears after fans in Greenville, South Carolina, showed their genuine affection for the returning champion, Flair then channeled what looked for all the world like genuine hatred for Bischoff and delivered a scathing promo in which he told the crowd that "this is real! This is not bought and paid for!"[15] Even the smartest of smart fans had to wonder where reality ended and the storyline began as Flair called Bischoff—a man with something of a reputation for being obnoxious in real life—"an overbearing asshole" who had abused his power. Was this the real Ric Flair really shooting on the real Eric Bischoff? Or was this the character of "Ric Flair" performing a worked shoot on the character of "Eric Bischoff"?*

The blurring of reality only increased when Bischoff left the company for a period and creative duties were turned over to Vince Russo, a former writer for rival WWE. Russo increasingly looked to Internet wrestling sites for feedback on the product and geared more of the programming to the "smart marks" who populated such sites.[16] Russo increasingly injected real-life backstage politics into the "fictional" storylines of professional wrestling. One problem with this approach, however, was that these Internet-savvy smart marks did not make up anything close to the majority of WCW viewers. The vast majority of viewers did not understand many of the references that Russo included in the scripts, leaving many viewers confused as to what they were watching. Perhaps not coincidentally, by 2000, WCW's ratings had fallen precipitously from the peak of the early NWO invasion.

As the company continued to take on water, WCW eventually brought Bischoff back to work with Russo in an attempt to right the ship. The pair came up with a storyline that once again drew upon backstage politics. The idea was that there was a civil war within WCW, with the younger wrestlers (the New Blood) tired of being kept down by the older wrestlers (the Millionaire's Club), who refused to pass the torch.[17] The onscreen leader of the New Blood would be Vince Russo, playing an authority figure. And drawing upon real-life rumors that Hogan refused to make room for new talent, the onscreen leader of the Millionaire's Club would, of course, be Hulk Hogan. Complaining that the members of the New Blood "couldn't sell out a flea market," Hogan made it plain as part of the storyline that he was "not moving aside for anybody."[18]

---

  * A far less successful example of a worked shoot involving Flair occurred when Flair was told to fake a heart attack in the ring as a nod to Flair's advancing age.

* * *

Part of the intrigue of the New Blood/Millionaire's Club angle was that the real Hulk Hogan (Terry Bollea) was, in fact, widely believed to be unwilling to move aside for anybody in real life. In fact, his employment contract gave him that right. Bollea/Hogan's contract contained a "creative control" clause, which provided that "Bollea shall have approval over the outcome of all wrestling matches in which he appears, wrestles and performs, such approval not to be unreasonably withheld."[19] Therefore, if the real Hogan/Bollea did not want the Hulk Hogan character to lose a match, he could exercise his creative control and veto the plan proposed by the booker.

The real Hogan had a reputation as the consummate backstage politician. By this point, the reputation was known both within the locker room and among Internet smart marks. Other wrestlers involved in the creative process complained in real life about how difficult it was to advance new ideas due to Bollea/Hogan's creative control clause.[20] In one example, wrestling legend Bret Hart proposed an idea for an angle but was supposedly told that he would have "to convince Terry [Bollea]" first.[21] Once again, it was difficult to determine where the line between fiction and reality was when it came to Hogan and the Millionaire's Club.

* * *

Part 2: Defamation at the Beach

Fittingly enough, the real Hulk Hogan's legal troubles with WCW began at the same pay-per-view event where the character of Hulk Hogan had first turned heel four years earlier: Bash at the Beach. The plan was for Hogan to wrestle Jeff Jarrett, the world heavyweight champion. The problem was that no one could agree to a finish to the match. Bischoff, who was still closely aligned with Hogan in real life, planned to talk to Hogan the night before the event, but Bischoff's father died in the interim. Russo suggested several possible finishes to Hogan, all of which allowed Jarrett to retain the championship while still allowing Hogan to maintain the appearance of strength. Eventually, Hogan agreed to such a finish.[22] But Hogan subsequently changed his mind and, invoking his creative control clause, announced that he did not agree to Russo's planned finish.[23]

This is where memories start to differ and things become complicated. In retrospect, it is difficult to understand how the average wrestling fan was even supposed to make sense of what Russo supposedly had planned. But the short version is that Hogan agreed to a finish in which

Jarrett would literally lie down in the ring and allow Hogan to pin him, thus allowing Hogan to leave with the championship belt and setting up a future match with another wrestler, Booker T. Hogan would then deliver a promo accusing Russo of instructing Jarrett to lie down and ruining the company. According to the plan, Hogan would leave the arena in a huff, along with Bischoff, in an attempt to lead everyone to believe that Jarrett's act of lying down was a shoot and not part of the script. Russo would then later appear on the show and, in keeping with the New Blood/Millionaire's Club storyline, deliver a promo excoriating Hogan for being part of the old guard that refused to pass the torch.*

All of this went according to plan until, Hogan alleges, Russo went off script during his promo. Here is where reality and fiction once again became blurred. When Russo entered the ring, one of the announcers observed, "that's not Vince Russo, the character. That's Vince Russo, the boss!"[24] Another announcer informed viewers that "this is real-life here, fans."[25] Russo then delivered a promo in which he complained about the "bullshit of the politics behind that curtain" and advanced the storyline about the members of the New Blood, who actually "give a shit about this company," being held back by the veterans. And as an example of the veterans who didn't "give a shit about the company," Russo singled out "that goddamn politician Hulk Hogan." Russo then referenced the actual, real-life negotiations he had been having with Hogan over the planned match with Jarrett and complained about the real-life fact that "Hulk Hogan want[ed] to play his creative control card." Russo then promised the audience that they "would never see that piece of shit again." He explained to the crowd that the championship belt that Hogan left with was meaningless and that Jeff Jarrett would wrestle Booker T that night for the real championship. Russo ended his promo by addressing Hogan, saying "you big bald son of a bitch, kiss my ass!"[26]

The real Hulk Hogan was not amused. While he may have agreed to the bizarre finish to the match with Jarrett, he had not agreed to the substance of Russo's promo. So, Hogan filed a defamation suit in a Georgia state court against World Championship Wrestling and Russo styled *Bollea v. World Championship Wrestling, Inc. et al.*

* * *

The essence of a defamation claim is that the defendant published a false and defamatory statement about the plaintiff. Under Georgia law, a statement is "defamatory" where it would tend to injure the person's reputation and expose the person to contempt, hatred, or ridicule.[27] As the

---

* If all of that sounds incredibly convoluted, that's because it was.

7. Defamation

court filings suggest, the gist of Bollea's claim was that all of Russo's statements about Hulk Hogan playing "the creative control card" in order to keep down other wrestlers were false and "were designed to make Hogan less popular with wrestling fans and less employable by wrestling organizations in the future."[28] Bollea faced at least three interrelated challenges to success.

* * *

(1) Were Russo's Statements About Terry Bollea (and not "Hulk Hogan")?

One of the requirements of a defamation claim is that the defamatory statements must be "of and concerning the plaintiff."[29] Stated more simply, can the statements reasonably be interpreted as being about the plaintiff?[30] The fact that the defendant never mentioned the plaintiff by name or perhaps even used an incorrect name doesn't necessarily mean that the statement was not "of and concerning the plaintiff." Instead, it's enough that the "public acquainted with the parties and the subject would recognize the plaintiff as a person to whom the statement refers."[31] So, if people familiar with the plaintiff would recognize that the statement was referring to the plaintiff—even if the statement never specifically referenced the plaintiff—that would be good enough to satisfy the requirement.

The problem that Bollea faced was that Russo had never accused Terry Bollea of keeping other wrestlers down. Instead, Russo had accused "Hulk Hogan" of such conduct. So, were Russo's statements about Hulk Hogan (a.k.a. Terry Bollea), the real person, or "Hulk Hogan," the fictional character? Part of the difficulty in the case was that it wasn't always clear where Terry Bollea ended and Hulk Hogan began. For example, those who knew him at the time report that Bollea usually went by the name "Hulk Hogan" outside of the ring. Bollea also exhibited some of the same traits as the character of Hulk Hogan, for example, frequently referring to others as "brother."*

According to the law, the important question was whom members of the wrestling audience reasonably believed the statements to be about, not whom Russo actually intended to reference. If reasonable wrestling fans would believe that Russo was really referencing the actions of the real person portraying the character of Hulk Hogan, that should have been

---

* Adding to the complexity of the case was the fact that, according to his lawyers, Vince Russo "also portrayed the character of 'Vince Russo.'" Brief of Appellees, No. A04A1743, 2004 WL 5536503, *6 (Ga. Ct. App. June 21, 2004). So, was it the "character of Vince Russo" or the "real" Vince Russo who was talking about the "character of Hulk Hogan" or the "real" Hulk Hogan?

enough for Bollea/Hogan to satisfy this requirement. There are numerous examples of real-life individuals suing authors of works of fiction for basing their characters on the real-life individuals based on the fact that people in the community recognized the characters as being based on the real-life individuals.[32] For example, in one case from Georgia, the defendant wrote a book with a character who was presented as ""an unrehabilitated alcoholic ... foul-mouthed, insensitive and ill-mannered, a 'right-wing reactionary' and atheist, and a 'loose cannon' with a bad temper."[33] The plaintiff sued, claiming that the author stated facts about her when she referenced the character. In support of her claim, the plaintiff pointed out that the character bore so many similarities to the plaintiff, whom the author had known for 50 years, that the plaintiff's friends did not discuss the book around her because they did not want to embarrass her.[34] The Georgia Supreme Court held that if members of that community could reasonably believe that the book was stating actual facts about the real-life person—even though the facts were supposedly in reference to the fictional character—the plaintiff could proceed on her defamation action.

Applying that law to the facts of the case, a reasonable wrestling fan could pretty clearly believe that Russo was referring to the "real" Hulk Hogan (a.k.a. Terry Bollea) during his promo. For one thing, the announcers insisted to the viewers that Russo was not playing a character but was really being himself. ("That's not Vince Russo, the character. That's Vince Russo, the boss!") If that was true, then of course the "real" Vince Russo would logically address his comments to the "real" Terry Bollea/Hulk Hogan. Beyond that, WCW broadcasts leading up to Bash at the Beach had actually introduced to viewers the idea that there was Hulk Hogan, the real person (who also went by the name Terry Bollea), and "Hulk Hogan," the character. For example, one broadcast featured an interview with Hogan, in which both the interviewer and Hogan addressed real-life happenings in WCW.[35] The interview clearly meant to convey the impression that the interview was taking place with the "real" Hulk Hogan, not the character. At one point, the interviewer actually asked Hogan about the *character* of Hulk Hogan and whether that character was still viable. At another point, the interviewer asked Hogan a "personal" question: "Does Terry Bollea think that he needs to reinvent the persona of Hulk Hogan for the new millennium and, if so, how do *you* go about accomplishing that?"[36] Hogan (or Bollea) then proceeded to discuss the character of Hulk Hogan. Thus, viewers had been primed to recognize that there were two Hulk Hogans: the real-life person (who also went by the name Terry Bollea) and the character. Certainly then, a reasonable viewer might believe that when Russo talked about the Hulk Hogan who had creative control and tried to hold down younger wrestlers, he was talking about the "real" Hulk Hogan and not the character.

7. Defamation

But, most tellingly, a reasonable viewer could believe Russo was speaking about the "real" Hogan because Russo has since admitted that this is exactly what he wanted people to believe. Amazingly, Russo viewed Hogan's match against Jarrett and Hogan's subsequent promo on Russo as a worked shoot meant to confuse the other wrestlers—including Jeff Jarrett—as to what was really going on.[37] According to Russo, he actually wanted Jarrett and the other wrestlers to believe that Bollea/Hogan had, in real life, refused to let Jarrett win and that Jarrett's act of lying down was the only solution Russo could come up with.[38] And according to Russo, this is exactly what Jarrett believed in real life.[39] So, if one of the participants in the incident believed that Russo was actually "shooting" on the real Hulk Hogan/Terry Bollea, certainly a fan who tuned in that night and watched Russo deliver his promo could reasonably believe the same thing. So, logically, there was plenty of evidence that Russo's statement was "of and concerning" Terry Bollea as defamation law requires.

Somehow, all of this was lost on the courts in the matter. After Bollea filed his lawsuit, WCW moved for summary judgment on the defamation claim. The trial court granted this motion, thereby effectively ending Bollea's defamation suit pending an appeal. Bollea appealed this decision to the Georgia Court of Appeals. In affirming the lower court's decision, the Georgia Court of Appeals emphasized the fictional nature of professional wrestling and observed that "Russo never mentioned Bollea, only the fictional character Hogan."[40] In addition, the court pointed to Vince Russo's sworn affidavit, in which he said that he delivered his promo "solely as his on-air character" and not as the real-life Vince Russo.[41]* Remarkably, the court never considered how the average viewer might have perceived Russo's promo. Instead, in the court's view, there was a clear distinction between the real-life Hulk Hogan and the fictional Hulk Hogan and the real-life Vince Russo and the fictional Vince Russo. Despite all evidence to the contrary, the court seemed to believe that no one could reasonably be confused between the two. Therefore, the Georgia Court of Appeals, concluded that Russo's promo "could not be understood as stating actual facts about Bollea."[42]

* * *

(2) Were Russo's Statements Capable of Being Proved False?

The Georgia Court of Appeals' conclusion that Russo's statements could not be interpreted as being about Terry Bollea effectively ended the

---

 * Careful readers may note that what was said in the affidavit conflicts with what announcers told viewers at the time and also what Russo has since publicly said.

case. But there was always the possibility that Bollea might appeal to the Georgia Supreme Court, so the court went on to consider the other legal issues Bollea's attorneys had raised. In order to prevail on his defamation claim, Bollea would ultimately need to prove that Russo's statements were false. Therefore, one issue on appeal was whether Russo's scathing statements were actually capable of being proved false.

Not every nasty thing that one person says about another can form the basis of a defamation claim. To be actionable, a defamatory statement must be capable of being proven true or false.[43] Thus, as the Supreme Court has explained, mere insults, name-calling, "imaginative expression," "rhetorical hyperbole," and other forms of "loose" language are not actionable.[44] Likewise, courts have explained that a statement that cannot reasonably be interpreted as stating actual facts about a person cannot form the basis of a defamation claim.[45] So, for example, the statement "Vince Russo is the worst human being in the world" is not actionable because no one could reasonably interpret the statement as stating actual facts about Vince Russo. In addition, whatever one's thoughts are on Vince Russo, it is not possible to prove that he is literally the worst person in the world.

Based on prior court decisions, some of Russo's statements about Hogan could not be actionable as defamation. Russo's references to Hogan as "a goddamn politician" and a "big bald son of a bitch" were not actionable. It might be possible to prove, as an objective matter of fact, that Hogan was "big" and "bald." But the phrases "goddamn politician" and "son of a bitch" are the types of "rhetorical hyperbole," "imaginative expression," or "loose" language[46] that cannot form the basis of a defamation claim.

But Bollea's lawyers argued that there was at least one statement in Russo's promo that was provably false: Russo's statements to the effect that Hogan had used the creative-control clause in his contract to thwart the careers of other wrestlers.[47] Hogan's lawyers were absolutely correct. This is the sort of assertion that could theoretically be proven to be true or false based on the testimony of other witnesses. The interesting question was whether the assertion was actually false.

According to Bollea's lawyers, "Hogan had in fact never used his creative control rights for any purpose, much less to hold back other wrestlers"[48] In support of this argument, the lawyers produced an affidavit from Bollea in which "Hogan detailed eleven specific instances in which WCW/Russo caused Hogan to be beaten in confrontations with wrestlers of lesser stature than Hogan. In none of these matches did Hogan exercise creative control. He did not change the outcome of any match."[49] Hogan's assertion that he "never used his creative control rights for any purpose" flies in the face of the statements of his colleagues at the time and what is widely accepted as gospel among wrestling fans. Therefore, it would have been fascinating to watch this particular issue be litigated at trial.

Unfortunately, the Georgia Court of Appeals never allowed this to happen. The court committed what was almost certainly clear legal error in agreeing with the trial court's conclusion "that Russo's speech was made in a fictional context and asserted opinions amounting to hyperbole, which could not be proved false."[50] This, then, was strike two for Bollea on his appeal.

* * *

(3) Did Russo Make His Statements with Actual Malice?

The final legal issue in Bollea's lawsuit also exposed a shortcoming in modern defamation law. *New York Times Co. v. Sullivan* is perhaps the most important United States Supreme Court decision on the subject of defamation. Decided by the Court in 1964, *Sullivan* involved a claim brought by a public official—a police commissioner—against the *New York Times* for false statements appearing in an advertisement that ran in the Times that was critical of the official's performance of his duties.

The police commissioner in question was Lester Bruce ("L.B.") Sullivan, who was in the words of his critics, "a famous racist and hater of [B]lack people and anything they stood for."[51] As a staunch segregationist, Sullivan successfully ran for police commissioner in 1959 in Montgomery, Alabama, by attacking the incumbent for supposedly being too soft on Martin Luther King, Jr., and civil rights demonstrators in Montgomery.[52] When Freedom Riders arrived in Montgomery, Sullivan reportedly allowed a white mob to attack them with chains and clubs.[53]

When Sullivan sued the *New York Times* for printing what turned out to be false statements about Montgomery law enforcement's actions toward civil rights, the Court was concerned about the potential for other public officials to use the threat of defamation claims to stifle legitimate criticism of the official in the performance of his or her official duties. This was no imaginary threat. Sullivan's suit was actually part of a larger effort by segregationists to combat positive media coverage of the civil rights movement. By suing news outlets for libel over inaccuracies in reporting, segregationists hoped to chill media coverage of the movement.[54]

In order to prevent the threat of a defamation claim from having such a chilling effect on free speech, the Supreme Court held that when a public official, like Sullivan, seeks to bring a defamation action based on criticism of the official's actions in office, the public official must satisfy a demanding standard of proof. It's not enough that the critic *should have known* what he was saying about the public official wasn't true. Instead, the public official must prove that the critic acted with what the Court called "actual malice," meaning that the speaker either *knew* what he was saying was untrue or at least entertained serious doubts about the truth of what he was saying.[55] In practice, this "actual malice" standard has proven extremely difficult for public officials to satisfy.

Eventually, the Court expanded its "actual malice" standard to public *figures* as well as public officials. Thus, the spokesperson for a private interest group who thrusts herself into the midst of a public controversy in order to sway public opinion on the matter has to establish that a defendant who says something false about the spokesperson was either knowingly lying or at least entertained serious doubts about the truth of the statement.[56] Likewise, the super famous—those with "pervasive fame or notoriety"—have assumed some risk of public comment and criticism and must therefore also prove "actual malice" on the part of the speaker if they hope to prevail on a defamation claim.[57]

Hogan's lawyers conceded that Hogan was a public figure and was, therefore, required to prove that Russo made his statements with actual malice.[58] But according to the lawyers, this was a relatively easy burden to satisfy in this case. They argued that not only was it false for Russo to assert that Hogan had used his creative control power to keep down other wrestlers, Russo knew this assertion to be false. Hogan pointed to the fact that he had agreed to lose several matches to wrestlers of lesser stature heading in to Bash at the Beach, a fact that Russo was well aware by virtue of the fact that he, as part of the booking committee, helped set up those matches.[59]

But once again, the fictional nature of professional wrestling worked to Hogan's disadvantage. It was well-established by the time of Hogan's lawsuit that where a speaker intends a statement as a parody or caricature, the actual malice standard isn't satisfied; it doesn't make much sense to ask whether a speaker doubted that a statement was true when the speaker never intended the statement to be taken as stating actual facts to begin with.[60] So, for example, years earlier when *Hustler* magazine was sued for running an obvious parody of feminist author Andrea Dworkin, a federal court explained that Dworkin had not proved that *Hustler* acted with actual malice: "if a speaker knowingly publishes a literally untrue statement without holding the statement out as true, he may still lack subjective knowledge or recklessness as to the falsification of a statement of fact required by *New York Times* [*v. Sullivan*]."[61] This makes sense. When a speaker never intends for the recipient to believe a statement as stating actual facts, it makes little sense to inquire into what the speaker believed about the truth of the statement.

The Georgia Court of Appeals took this notion one step further. According to the court, statements *"made in a fictional setting* [] do not contain the necessary consciousness of falsity because the speaker does not think he is publishing a statement of fact."[62] This statement of law is fine insofar as it applies to more traditional forms of fictional works. In the case of a fictional book or play where both the producer and the audience know that what they are reading or watching is fictional, it makes little sense to ask whether the producer knew or entertained serious doubts about the falsity of the production. Of course he did. The producer never held out that the production to be true in the first place.

The problem with the Georgia Court of Appeals' statement of law as it applies to non-traditional fictional works—like professional wrestling—is that it ignores the intent of the speaker and the potential effect of the statement on the audience. And it certainly ignores the nature of WCW's product at the time. Not only did Russo know his statements were false, he intended to make the audience believe they were true. Professional wrestling may be fictional in the general sense, but for much of its existence, its goal has been to make viewers believe that what they were seeing was real. While the wrestling business largely discarded this goal for a period, Russo and company quite deliberately introduced a new form of wrestling that blurred the lines between fiction and reality in an attempt to confuse the viewer. Russo wasn't putting on a play in which the performers and the audience were both in on the fact that what was taking place was not real. Instead, Russo was putting on a performance in which only a few of the participants knew for sure what was real and what was not. If, as was the case, Russo intended to trick at least a portion of the audience into believing that what was going on in his promo was real and if, in fact, what he was saying was false, there is a good argument that he acted with actual malice.

Where a supposed work of fiction blurs the line between fiction and reality, some courts apply a different standard altogether. Where a defamatory statement is made in the context of what is supposedly a fictional work, some courts say that the supposedly fictional statement is actionable where the author intended that viewers would construe the statement as actually stating defamatory facts.[63] Thus, if the author intended to make viewers believe that what they are seeing was "the truth," the statement is actionable. Even where that was not the author's intent, if the author knew there was a high likelihood that the viewers would believe that what they were witnessing was "the truth," the false statements are actionable unless the author puts the audience on notice that the publication is really satire or fiction.[64] Given the fact that, by Russo's own admission, he intended to trick the audience into believing that what they were viewing was real, Russo's statements were unquestionably actionable.

Unfortunately, these sorts of subtleties were lost on the Georgia Court of Appeals, which viewed professional wrestling simply as another form of fiction. As a result, the court affirmed the trial court's decision to grant summary judgment to WCW. In the process, the court failed to add some important clarification the law of defamation.

* * *

Part 3: Conclusion

While Hogan's defamation claim failed, as the next chapter discusses, there was still more excitement remaining in the *Bollea v. World Championship Wrestling* saga. Unfortunately for defamation lawyers and scholars, the numerous interesting legal issues raised by Hogan's defamation case against WCW were never fully addressed. Sadly, fans of professional wrestling were also denied the chance to see the realities of the inner workings of one of more bizarre periods in professional wrestling played out in a courtroom.

As its declining rates at the time proved, WCW's efforts to attract viewers by blurring the lines between reality and fiction in a medium—professional wrestling—that had long blurred those lines ceased to work after a period of time. But it's worth noting that just as the "worked shoot" approach stopped yielding rates for WCW, the format of reality TV exploded. Just a little over a month before the Bash at the Beach fiasco involving Hogan and Russo, a little reality show on CBS called *Survivor* aired. The show soon became a cultural phenomenon and paved the way for the creation of countless reality TV shows. As these shows sought to carve out their own niches and lure viewers, they increasingly sought to develop more compelling storylines by blurring the line between reality and fiction. Producers took reality and through creative editing and sometimes outright creative fiction writing, developed reality TV heels, babyfaces, and babyfaces who completed heel turns in order to win love, money, or fame. While professional wrestling may not have always done these things better, it certainly did them first. And in doing so, the producers of reality TV exposed themselves to potential liability in the form of defamation claims in much the same way WCW did at Bash at the Beach.

* * *

This was not the last time the question of whether someone was referring to Terry Bollea or Hulk Hogan would pop in a legal proceeding. In October 2012, Gawker.com published a short excerpt from a video of Hogan having sex with his best friend's wife under the headline "Even for a Minute, Watching Hulk Hogan Have Sex in a Canopy Bed is Not Safe for Work but Watch it Anyway." Hogan eventually sued Gawker for having invaded his privacy. Gawker's defense? Hulk Hogan's sex life was not a matter of private concern because Hulk Hogan himself had made the details of his sex life public. From publicly bragging about the number of women he had slept with to the size of his penis, Hogan, a public figure, had voluntarily made his sex life a matter of public concern. So, a video that depicted him doing the things that he had bragged about was fair game for Gawker to publish.

Hogan's response? Yes, Hulk Hogan may have talked about his sex life on Howard Stern's show. And, yes, Hulk Hogan may have bragged about having a ten-inch penis. But Hulk Hogan is a character. He isn't a real person. And as a character, Hulk Hogan says things that aren't true. But "Terry Bollea is a normal person. Wrestling is his job. It's what Terry Bollea does for a living," testified Bollea/Hogan at trial.[65] And Terry Bollea tells the truth under oath.[66] Hulk Hogan may claim to have a ten-inch penis, but Terry Bollea, the real person, admits under oath that he does not.[67] Ultimately, Terry Bollea was having sex with Heather Clem on the video, not Hulk Hogan. And it was Terry Bollea's privacy that was invaded.

A Florida jury accepted this logic and awarded Bollea/Hogan a total of $140 million in damages. $115 million was allotted to compensate him for the harm he suffered. An additional $25 million covered punitive damages designed to punish Gawker for what the jury determined to be its egregious conduct.[68] Less than three months later, Gawker—with assets estimated at between $50 million and $100 million—was forced into bankruptcy as a result.[69]

Chapter 8

Breach of Contract

Bollea v. World Championship Wrestling, Inc. (2005)

Defamation was not the only weapon against WCW that Hulk Hogan had in his legal arsenal following the bizarre events at the Bash at the Beach. Hogan's creative control clause in his contract with WCW gave him the "approval over the outcome of all wrestling matches in which he appears, wrestles and performs."[1] According to Hogan, he had not approved what went on at Bash at the Beach. Therefore, WCW was in breach of contract.

* * *

Part 1: Read That Contract Before You Sign it!

Contracts have long played an important role in adding a measure of legitimacy to professional wrestling storylines. One longstanding trope involves a formal contract signing in the ring between two feuding wrestlers who sign a contract agreeing to a match to supposedly end the feud once and for all.* The signing of the contract marks the solemnity of the occasion. When a new character appeared in a wrestling show, it used to be fairly common for the promotion to generate fan interest in the character by holding some sort of contract signing ceremony in which a manager agreed to manage a wrestler's professional character. When Randy "Macho Man" Savage first appeared in the WWF, all of the established managers of the time (Bobby "the Brain" Heenan, "Classy" Fred Blassie, Mr. Fuji, etc.) spent time "scouting" Savage before holding a signing ceremony in

---

* There is also at least a 50/50 chance that the signing will end in one of the wrestlers attacking the other.

8. Breach of Contract

which Savage would announce his new manager and sign a personal services contract. But the "swerve" was that Savage chose not to be managed by any of the WWE's established managers but instead by "the lovely Miss Elizabeth," Savage's real-life wife. Savage quickly became one of the most popular stars in the promotion.

Another common wrestling trope involving a contract was the bounty storyline. Here, a wrestler or manager would place a "bounty" on the head of another wrestler after brandishing an open contract for anyone who could take out said wrestler. Similarly, sometimes a manager or wrestler would hire a fearsome outsider with a reputation for violence—say, Abdullah the Butcher—to take care of another wrestler.

But the contract-based wrestling storyline that relied most heavily on actual contract law was the fraud-in-the-execution storyline. Fraud in the execution (sometimes called "fraud in the factum") is a legal theory that alleges that one party to a contract tricked the other party into signing the contract by misrepresenting the substance of the contract. So, fraud in the execution of the contract would occur where Party A tells Party B that the contract contains a clause providing for an interest rate of 5 percent when, in reality, the contract provides that the interest rate is 20 percent. In such cases, the party who has been duped can void the contract and not perform her obligations. This situation needs to be contrasted with the situation in which one party simply fails to read the language of the contract and the other party did nothing to mislead the party as to its terms. Generally, the failure to read a contract is not a defense to one's obligations under the contract.[2]

Some version of this latter scenario played out dozens of times over the years in professional wrestling. For example, manager Jim Cornette somehow managed to repeatedly sign contracts without reading them, only to find out later that he had agreed to some type of stipulation that worked to the detriment of the wrestlers he managed or placed him in physical peril.[3] Cornette, who never seemed to learn the simple lesson that he should read a contract before signing it, would then rant about how he had been "tricked" into signing the contract and that his lawyers were looking to find a loophole to void the contract. In the most famous example, Cornette was "tricked" into signing a contract for a match between his team, the Midnight Express, and the Road Warriors that contained a clause providing that the match would take place on a scaffold above the ring and the only way one team could win was by throwing an opponent off the scaffold.*

---

* Cornette ended up being legitimately injured in the match when he dropped from the scaffold and landed wrong, none of which would have happened if he had just read the contract first.

* * *

So, when (as discussed in the previous chapter) writer/performer Vince Russo brought up the creative control clause in Hulk Hogan's contract during his promo at Bash at the Beach, he was carrying on a time-honored tradition in professional wrestling of using legal contracts to lend an air of legitimacy to the proceedings in the ring. But in Hogan's case, the contract that Russo referred to was quite real. Back in the day, contracts between wrestlers and promoters were fairly informal. In his trial against Ronnie Garvin in 1980 (discussed in Chapter 2), promoter Ron Fuller explained that in his entire time in wrestling, he had never seen a wrestler sign a contract and that the business was conducted entirely by handshakes.[4] But times had changed since 1980 and the economics of professional wrestling had grown more complicated. So, by the 1990s, contracts in the WWE and WCW were more detailed in nature.

For example, a WCW contract from around this time was eleven pages long. In addition to describing a wrestler's obligations under the contract (to appear at all events, to provide the wrestler's own wardrobe, props, and make-up, etc.) and WCW's obligations (to book the wrestler's performances, to sell tickets to those events, etc.), the contract covered a host of other terms:

- *Independent contractor status*: the contract provided that the wrestler was an independent contractor (not an employee) and was responsible for payment and withholding of any taxes;
- *Compensation*: the contract provided for a yearly salary;
- *Ownership of work product*: the contract provided that all themes, characters, routines, etc., developed by the wrestler during the term of the contract were the property of WCW;
- *Compliance with laws, rules, and regulations*: the wrestler agreed to comply with all WCW policies (including its substance abuse policy) and all relevant local, state, and federal law.
- *Indemnification*: the wrestler agreed that if WCW were to be sued as a result of the wrestler's actions, the wrestler would compensate WCW for any of its losses; and
- *Term and termination*: among other things, the contract (1) gave WCW the right to terminate the contract for any reason by giving the wrestler one month's notice, (2) limited the wrestler's right to terminate the contract to where WCW had materially breached the contract, (3) prohibited the wrestler from working for any other business (including non-wrestling businesses), and (4) prohibited the wrestler from working for another competitor for a period of 120 days following termination of the contract.[5]

* * *

Part 2: Hulk Hogan's Contract

Hulk Hogan's contract with WCW was no ordinary wrestler contract. Most relevant was his creative control clause, which, as mentioned, gave him the "approval over the outcome of all wrestling matches in which he appears, wrestles and performs." While at least a couple of other WCW performers (Kevin Nash and Scott Hall) may have had a contractual right to be *consulted* about creative matters involving them, only Hogan had creative control over the outcome of his matches.[6] In contrast, the typical WCW contract provided that a wrestler would "use his best efforts to perform the Services in a manner consistent with the customs of the professional wrestling industry [which involved a wrestler doing what the wrestler was told to do by the booker] and consistent with the *direction and advice of WCW*."[7]

Putting aside the creative control clause, the four-year contract extension Hogan signed with WCW in 1998 was remarkable in other ways.* For starters, Hogan received a $2 million signing bonus. Under the contract, Hogan would also be the "featured wrestler" at several pay-per-view events, including Bash at the Beach.[8] In addition, the contract provided that Hogan would receive the following:

- 15% of cable revenue from pay-per-view events or $675,000 per event, whichever was greater;
- 25% of ticket sales from televised appearances or $25,000 per event, whichever was greater;
- 50% of net revenue from the sale of Hulk Hogan-related merchandise;
- $20,000 a month for promoting the New World Order, the faction Hogan was a member of at the time; and (of course)
- First-class air travel, hotel accommodations, limousine service, and a $175 per diem while traveling for WCW.[9]

* * *

Part 3: Breach of Contract at the Beach?

One of the enduring popular misconceptions of the Bash at the Beach incident is that Hogan was unaware of Vince Russo's plan to have Jeff Jarrett to lie down and be pinned by Hogan. Hogan's on-camera reaction to

---

*According to one of Hogan's lawyers at the time, Hogan was not only business-savvy but also a "highly educated consumer of legal services" who took an active role in all matters.

Jarrett lying down certainly helped further the narrative that Russo had double-crossed Hogan. After pinning Jarrett, Hogan lashed out at Russo, telling Russo that "the company is in the goddamn shape it's in because of bullshit like this."[10] Indeed, as discussed in the previous chapter, Russo hoped that this is what fans and wrestlers alike would believe: Russo had double-crossed Hogan in real life.

In reality, Hogan admitted in his breach of contract lawsuit that he had agreed to this finish in the match with Jarrett.[11] According to the Georgia Court of Appeals, "In discussing the script for the Hogan–Jarrett match, it was decided that instead of Hogan and Jarrett actually wrestling, Jarrett would lie down in the ring so that Hogan would win by default. According to Bollea, this was to set up a tournament which would lead to the return of Hogan as the WCW champion."[12]

So, Hogan was not complaining about the fact that Jarrett had allowed himself to be pinned. Instead, Hogan alleged that WCW prevented Hogan from exercising his right of creative control and thereby breached its contract when Russo delivered his promo and declared the championship belt that Hogan held to be worthless. In other words, it was not the technical finish to the match that violated Hogan's creative control clause; it was what happened after the finish.

Hogan's claim raised an interesting factual issue as well as an interesting issue regarding interpretation of the contract. Hogan's contract gave him "approval over the outcome of all wrestling matches in which he appears, wrestles and performs."[13] WCW argued that wrestling promos are "used to develop the story lines and there is nothing in the Agreement that gives Bollea the right to approve the story lines which relate to his fictional character."[14] Hogan may have granted him approval over the outcome of his matches, WCW argued, but it did not give him approval over WCW's story lines and the content of the promos that furthered those story lines.

Hogan advanced two arguments in response. First, Hogan argued that by declaring the championship belt that Hogan held to be worthless, WCW had effectively changed the outcome of Hogan's match with Jarrett. As the trial court explained, "control over the outcome of the wrestling match is worthless if half an hour later the outcome is totally changed."[15] If Hogan and Russo had not agreed in advance that Russo would declare Hogan's belt to be worthless, Hogan was on pretty solid legal ground in arguing that WCW had prevented him from exercising his contractual right of creative control. The question is what Russo and Hogan agreed to. According to Russo, he and Hogan actually agreed that Hogan would leave with his championship belt and then as part of his promo, Russo would schedule a world championship match that night between Jeff Jarrett and Booker T. The agreed-upon idea was that there would be a match

8. Breach of Contract

at a future pay-per-view featuring Hogan versus the winner.[16] If that is true, this aspect of Hogan's breach of contract claim was frivolous.

Hogan's other argument was that his right to approve the outcome of all of his matches necessarily meant that he had the right to also control story lines. As WCW's lawyer pointed out, the literal language of the contract only gave Hogan the right to approve the outcome of his matches, not the story lines furthered by those matches. But Hogan testified in his deposition that he understood that his right to control "the outcome" of his matches included the right to approve how the overall story line would end, not just the match.[17]

* * *

Under what is known as "the objective theory of contract interpretation," unless the language of the contract is ambiguous, a court will interpret the language "based on what a reasonable person in the position of the parties would have understood the language to mean and not 'the subjective intent of the parties at the time of formation.'"[18] In other words, where the language of the contract has a clear and natural meaning, a party cannot argue that this was not the meaning they intended. Where, however, the language in question is ambiguous—where a reasonable person could ascribe more than one meaning to the language at issue—courts may look beyond the four corners of the contract itself and to outside evidence that might shed light on what the parties intended the language to mean.[19] This sort of outside evidence might include the circumstances surrounding the making of the contract and what is customary within the relevant industry.[20]

As a matter of contractual interpretation, there was a decent argument that the clause in Hogan's contract giving him "approval over the outcome of all wrestling matches in which he appears, wrestles and performs" was ambiguous. On the one hand, the word "outcome" typically means the end result of some process. Thus, the "outcome" of any athletic contest would be that one individual or team won and the other lost. Applied to Hogan's situation, the word "outcome" might imply that all Hogan could approve under this creative control clause was whether he won or lost a match. But not all outcomes or end results are the same. One football team may beat another team 7–6. That would be a very different outcome or end result than if the final score was 56–0. Professional wrestlers are often concerned about losing in a way that makes them appear weak. This is why a wrestler might have no objections to losing as a result of cheating on the part of an opponent but have strong objections if the same wrestler gets beaten cleanly and decisively by an opponent (let alone loses in a "squash match," a match in which one wrestler dominates the other). Thus, the word "outcome" in Hogan's creative control was arguably ambiguous.

The potential ambiguity of the term becomes even more apparent when one considers Hogan's specific case. Professional wrestling matches are simply a means of advancing or concluding story lines. The outcome of a particular match—including not only who wins or loses a match but how they win or lose—is analogous to a scene in a movie or novel. The hero may die, but the death may have greater meaning.* In Hogan's case, Hogan may have agreed to win the match. But the ultimate "outcome" of the match was that he was no longer champion and was denigrated in front of paying customers. If the ending of a match could be used to advance a story line that was diametrically opposed to what Hogan believed the ending was to be used for, Hogan's right to approve the outcome of a match was of considerably less value than he bargained for. So, Hogan had a good argument that the court should not find against him simply because the ending of his match against Jarrett transpired as he had agreed.

If Hogan's right of creative control really did include a right to approve story lines rather than simply whether he won or lost, the follow-up question was whether he had approved the story line advanced by Russo's promo. According to Russo, he and Hogan had actually agreed that Russo would cut a "scathing promo" on Hogan following Hogan's "match" with Jarrett. But Russo had apparently not explained to Hogan exactly what he planned to say. So, Hogan had not approved the gist of the story Russo was telling. From the perspective of Hogan and his ally Eric Bischoff, Russo's promo did not advance any story line and was instead "personal" and was meant to promote Russo "at the expense of the character, the story line, and the plan."[21] In other words, even if Hogan did agree to be the subject of a scathing promo, he didn't agree to the kind of promo Russo ultimately gave.

* * *

WCW moved for summary judgment on Hogan's breach of contract claim. The trial court denied the motion, and on appeal, the Georgia Supreme Court affirmed. According to the court, there were issues of fact for a jury to determine "as to whether WCW breached its agreement with Bollea by denying him approval of the outcome of the matches in which he participated."[22]

Hogan also alleged that WCW breached its contract with Hogan in another way. Hogan's contract also provided that he would be "the featured wrestler" at six pay-per-events.[23] According to Hogan, being the "featured wrestler" meant appearing in the final match of an event. Since

---

* Think Obi-Wan Kenobi in *Star Wars* or the death of Tom Hanks' character in *Saving Private Ryan*.

Hogan did not appear in the final match of the evening, Hogan alleged WCW breached the contract. The Georgia Court of Appeals denied WCW summary judgment on this issue and held that Hogan's claim should proceed to trial.

* * *

There also remained the question of what damages Hogan was entitled to if, in fact, WCW had breached the contract. In order to recover money in a breach of contract suit, a plaintiff must ultimately establish that the defendant's breach caused some kind of economic loss. Apparently, WCW had continued to pay Hogan for subsequent pay-per-view events in keeping with the contract despite the fact that it did not ask him to appear at any of those events. Thus, WCW argued, even if it had breached its contract, Hogan had suffered no damage as a result.

But the argument overlooked several other clauses in Hogan's contract that might have provided Hogan with additional revenue. For example, while Hogan was entitled to a minimum of $675,000 for each pay-per-view event, he was entitled to more if the event was successful and the buy rate exceeded a specified number. In addition, Hogan was entitled to merchandising revenue under the contract, which effectively dried up once Hogan no longer appeared on television or pay-per-view.[24]

WCW argued that these damages were speculative.[25] Perhaps the pay-per-view buy rates would have been substantial enough for Hogan to have earned more than his base pay of $675,000, but perhaps they would not. According to WCW, Hogan could not establish with any measure of reasonable certainty how much money, if any, he lost. And in any event, Hogan had sat around his Tampa, Florida, home collecting paychecks from WCW for nine months for pay-per-view events he did not appear on without ever complaining about WCW's supposed breach. Therefore, WCW argued, he had waived his claim for breach of contract.[26]

The universal contract law rule is that a party seeking to recover for lost profits in a breach of contract action must prove lost profits with "reasonable certainty."[27] The majority of courts have adopted a rule that basically says that where a plaintiff can prove that a defendant's breach of contract definitely caused at least some lost profits, the fact that the plaintiff cannot prove the precise amount of lost profits does not necessarily bar recovery. The plaintiff doesn't necessarily have to prove lost profits with mathematical certainty.[28] Instead, it's enough that the plaintiff provides enough evidence to permit the jury to have a "reasonable basis" for computing an award or to permit the jury to make "a fair estimate of the amount of damage."[29]

At the same time, this "reasonable certainty" rule may have some teeth in practice, particularly when it comes to sports and entertainment. For example, back in 1926, Jack Dempsey was the Hulk Hogan of boxing. His only rival in terms of fame in the sports world more generally at the time was Babe Ruth.* His first match against Gene Tunney that year brought out 120,000 paying customers who watched the fight outdoors in the rain.[30] Dempsey entered into a contract for a boxing match with contender Harry Wills to take place in Chicago. Dempsey refused to perform, so the promoter of the match sued for breach of contract. The problem the promoter faced was in proving lost profits from the event. The promoter estimated lost profits of $1.6 million. But according to the court, the promoter lacked the evidence to prove that this estimate was anything more than just guesswork:

> The profits from a boxing contest of this character, open to the public, is dependent upon so many different circumstances that they are not susceptible of definite legal determination. The success or failure of such an undertaking depends largely upon the ability of the promoters, the reputation of the contestants and the conditions of the weather at and prior to the holding of the contest, the accessibility of the place, the extent of the publicity, the possibility of other and counter attractions and many other questions which would enter into consideration. Such an entertainment lacks utterly the element of stability which exists in regular organized business.[31]

As a result, the promoter's claim for lost profits failed.

Hogan faced similar problems. While it was possible that Russo's supposed master plan pitting the New Blood against the Millionaire's Club would have generated huge buy rates for future events featuring Hogan, there were too many variables involved to predict with any degree of certainty that this would be the case. Indeed, common sense suggests that it was unlikely that the show would have generated substantial profits. WCW was effectively a dumpster fire around the time of Bash at the Beach. Pay-per-view buy rates had been steadily declining to pre–*Nitro* numbers in the preceding year.[32] However, the Georgia Supreme Court of Appeals did not seem particularly troubled by the speculative nature of Hogan's claims. According to the court, "Bollea was an established wrestler with a long history of past earnings. He can therefore submit evidence of an amount of lost profits sufficient to enable a jury to calculate the amount of damages with reasonable certainty."[33] In addition, there were some claimed damages that were definitely capable of being proven with reasonable certainty. For example, Hogan was supposed to appear on episodes of *Nitro* and be paid $25,000 per appearance. Since he was no longer booked on these shows, these damages were easily provable.

---

* Interestingly, Dempsey was something of a heel for much of his career for having supposedly dodged the draft in World War I, a fact that promoters played up early in his career in order to generate interest in his matches.

8. Breach of Contract

The court was equally dismissive of WCW's argument that Hogan had waived any breach of contract claim against WCW by failing to complain after not being featured in events while still collecting money for those events. According to the court, given all of the conflicting testimony as to what Hogan agreed to at Bash at the Beach, the question of waiver was for the jury to decide.[34]

* * *

So, while Hogan's defamation claim was dead, Hogan lived to fight another day on his breach of contract claim. Ultimately, it would be up to a Georgia jury to decide whether WCW had breached its contract through Russo's promo and, if so, what damages that breach caused Hogan. The fact that the case was headed for trial where juries sometimes did unpredictable things gave both sides an incentive to settle.* Not surprisingly, the two sides reached a settlement.

* * *

Part 4: Conclusion

Hulk Hogan never worked for WCW again following Bash at the Beach. Eric Bischoff also quit the company. A few months after Bash at the Beach, Russo was gone, too. By the time the case of *Bollea v. World Championship Wrestling* finally settled in 2005 World Championship Wrestling had ceased to exist. The organization limped along for the rest of 2000 and into 2001 before finally being bought out by long-time rival Vince McMahon of the WWE.

Less than two years after Bash at the Beach, Hogan returned to the WWE, where he tried to catch lightning in a bottle a second time by reforming the New World Order. Hogan was featured prominently in WWE events. But a little over a year later, Hogan was gone once again, due to creative differences with those who controlled the story lines.[35]

Postscript: Breach of Contract, Unjust Enrichment, and Fraud

Ventura v. Titan Sports, Inc. (1995)

Hulk Hogan and WCW were arguing over whether WCW had breached enforceable provisions in Hogan's contract. But sometimes a party

---

* According to one of the attorneys involved, the litigation was highly contentious.

may not be able to point to a provision in a contract that the party has a right to enforce against another party. Maybe that's because the two sides never entered into an enforceable contract to begin with. Or maybe there was a contract, but it didn't address some key point. Or maybe there was a contract, but it was not legally enforceable for some reason. But despite the absence of some enforceable contractual provision that the other party violated, the law sometimes proceeds from the assumption that a party deserves some form of compensation. And then there is the relatively straightforward case where one party just deceives another party when the two sides enter into a contract. In such cases, the law proceeds from the assumption that the party that was defrauded deserves some form of compensation.

Back in the early 1990s, a Minnesota jury awarded wrestler-turned-commentator-turned-governor Jesse "the Body" Ventura close to a million dollars on both of those legal theories in his lawsuit against the WWF.

* * *

In 1984, Ventura entered into an oral contract with Vince McMahon to wrestle for the WWF. Shortly afterward, the WWF entered into a number of licensing agreements with companies to produce WWF action figures, video games, etc. One of these agreements was with a company to produce videotapes of WWF matches, some of which featured Ventura. Such deals were not industry custom at the time, and Ventura had no knowledge that McMahon and the WWF had entered into such arrangements with other companies. Ventura's deal with McMahon hadn't mentioned these videos or any other licensing agreement. After getting injured, Ventura became a heel commentator for the WWF under an oral contract that paid him $1,000 a week. In 1985, he signed a booking agreement as a wrestler. Ventura took some time off from the ring to make movies with Arnold Schwarzenegger before coming back to the WWF once again in late 1986 as a heel commentator under a new oral contract. None of these agreements mentioned anything about royalties from licensing agreements.[36]

Ventura eventually learned about the WWF's videotape deal. When Ventura split from the WWF in August 1990, he decided that he wanted a cut of the money McMahon and the WWF had made from the videotapes and other products featuring Ventura. So, in 1991, he sued the WWF for royalties in state court in Minnesota. The case was eventually removed to federal court and tried in front of a jury. Among the legal theories Ventura asserted was the theory of unjust enrichment (also sometimes referred to as quantum meruit).*

---

* *Quantum meruit* is a Latin phrase meaning "as much as one has earned" or "as much as one deserved."

8. Breach of Contract 179

This unjust enrichment theory is all about fairness. Essentially, the theory allows a party to recover in certain situations where it would be unfair to deny the party compensation. In order for the theory to apply, there must be no existing, enforceable contract between the parties concerning the subject in question.[37] In other words, the party alleging unjust enrichment can't be asserting a breach of contract. In addition, the party alleging unjust enrichment must have provided the other party with some sort of valuable benefit in the form of goods or services rendered. But it's not enough just that the party provided a benefit to the other party. The party receiving the benefit must have been "unjustly enriched." As the Minnesota courts have explained, this could be the case where it would be "morally wrong" to permit "one party to enrich himself at the expense of another."[38] This could be the case where the party's conduct was similar to fraud in nature or was in bad faith, or, in some cases, where it would simply be unjust to permit the party to retain the benefit without having to pay.[39] The remedy in such cases is the reasonable value of the benefit or services received by the defendant.[40]

In Ventura's case, there were a number of contracts between Ventura and the WWF that did address compensation for the services—wrestling and commentating—that Ventura provided. Therefore, the WWE argued that the unjust enrichment theory did not apply because there were express contracts covering the subject matter in question. In other words, the unjust enrichment theory does not protect one party from the consequences of having entered into a bad bargain.

But here, the United States Court of Appeals for the Eighth Circuit concluded, the contracts were silent on the issue of the benefits that Ventura provided to the WWF. Ventura had not just provided the WWF with the benefits of his commentary. He had provided the company with the benefits of his right of publicity.[41] As discussed in the Postscript to Chapter 4, the law recognizes a right to control one's own name and likeness and to prevent others from using those qualities for their own commercial gain. While the contracts may have addressed the labor that Ventura was to provide, they said nothing about the issue of who got to control Ventura's right of publicity. So, there was no existing, enforceable contract between the parties concerning the subject of Ventura' right of publicity.

Ventura had provided the WWF with the benefit of his name and likeness, so the next question was whether the WWF was unjustly enriched through the receipt of this benefit. In the court's view, the fact that Ventura had a right of publicity and the WWE violated that right made the WWF's enrichment from the videotapes "unjust."[42]

* * *

Ventura also alleged that WWE had engaged in another form of misconduct with respect to its videos. In 1987, Ventura hired an agent to represent him in contract negotiations with the WWF. The agent inquired about the possibility of Ventura receiving royalties from the videos but was told that the only performers who received such royalties were those who were the featured performers of a video.[43] So, for example, Hulk Hogan might receive royalties from sale of the "Best of Hulk Hogan" video, but his opponents in the matches in the video would not. Not wanting these royalties to be a dealbreaker, Ventura's agent did not push the point. When the agent negotiated other contracts over the next few years, he asked again about the royalties and was again told that only featured performers received such royalties. This turned out not to be true. The WWF did, in fact, pay non-featured performers royalties.*

As discussed in Chapter 8, a fraud-in-the-execution theory exists where one party lies to the other party about what is actually contained in the contract. In contrast, a fraudulent *inducement* theory applies where one party lies to the other party about other facts in an effort to induce the party to enter into a contract. That was the kind of fraud that Ventura alleged the WWF had engaged in. The WWF may not have lied about what was actually in the contract, but, according to Ventura, it had lied about who received compensation from the videos that were the subject of the contract. The trial court agreed with Ventura. The court found that had Ventura known about the WWE's actual practices, he would not have entered into the deals and that his reliance on the WWF's representations to his agent was justified.[44]

At the end of the day, Ventura's expert witness estimated that the royalty rates Ventura was owed ranged from over $800,000 up to over $1.8 million. As in the Hogan breach of contract case, the WWF argued that these damages were too speculative in nature. But, as in the Hogan case, the court rejected this argument.[45] Ultimately, the jury awarded Ventura over $809,000.

* * *

The WWF tried to appeal the decision to the United States Supreme Court, but the Court declined to hear the case. Ventura's lawsuit undoubtedly helped influence modern WWE contracts. Today, WWE contracts go into great detail concerning the various ways the WWE may use a performer's name, image, and likeness (videos, photos, books, movies, etc.) and the royalties the performer receives.[46]

---

* According to the court, the company "paid videotape royalties to all 54 wrestlers appearing in the 'Survivor Series,' to all 57 wrestlers appearing in 'Wrestlemania IV,' and to all 38 wrestlers appearing in 'Summer Slam '88'" despite the fact that none of these videotapes had featured performers. *Ventura v. Titan Sports, Inc.*, 65 F.3d 725, 733 n.10 (8th Cir 1995).

CHAPTER 9

Concussions, Fraud, and Statutes of Repose

McCullough v. World Wrestling Entertainment, Inc. (2006)

* * *

On the weekend of June 22, 2007, professional wrestler Chris Benoit murdered his wife, Nancy, in the couple's Georgia home. He then killed his seven-year-old son, Daniel. Benoit placed a Bible alongside both bodies and then took his own life.

The list of professional wrestlers who died an early death is long. There have been numerous suicides and even a few murders in the wrestling world. But the Chris Benoit murder/suicide is probably the most tragic incident in the history of professional wrestling. At the time, Benoit was one of the most respected and popular wrestlers in the business. Therefore, the murders and suicide attracted international attention.

One common theme in the stories that followed was the "why." Why had Benoit done it? What caused his seemingly inexplicable behavior? Some stories focused on the possible connection between the murders and Benoit's abuse of anabolic steroids, questioning whether the murders were the results of "roid rage." But eventually, the focus shifted to another possible cause: the neurological disorder chronic traumatic encephalopathy (CTE). The Sports Legacy Institute, an organization that researches the long-term effects of concussions, conducted testing on Benoit's brain tissue and found evidence of extensive brain damage consistent with repeated blows to the head. "These extreme changes throughout Chris Benoit's brain are enough to explain aberrant behavior, including suicide and even homicide," said the chairman of neurosurgery at West Virginia University and a member of the Institute. Another neurosurgeon, Dr. Bennet Omalu, reported that at the time of his death, Benoit had the brain of a man aged 80 or older with "very severe" Alzheimer's disease. "His was the most extensively damaged of the brains we have examined so far."[1]

Benoit was not the first professional athlete to be diagnosed with CTE upon death. But his case was the most shocking to that point. The Benoit incident and the attention it brought to the long-term impact of concussions on professional athletes eventually helped lead to a massive lawsuit against World Wrestling Entertainment (WWE).

* * *

Part 1: CTE

The first time many people heard the initials CTE was following the death of NFL Hall of Famer Mike Webster in 2002. Webster exhibited strange behavior prior to his death. He would forget to eat; wander off for days or weeks at a time, living under bridges; and shock himself with a Taser in order to fall asleep.[2] Following his death at age 50, an examination of his brain yielded an unusual finding. As far back as 1928, medical science had noted the tendency of some boxers to become "punch drunk" later in their careers and upon retirement. In 1973, a neuropathologist observed damage to the brain tissue of dead fighters and gave the condition an official name: *dementia pugilistica*.[3] Following Webster's death, Dr. Bennet Omalu examined Webster's brain. What Omalu observed in Webster's brain was similar to *dementia pugilistica* but different. At first glance, the boxers' brains were clearly bruised and damaged, whereas Webster's was not. But upon inspection under a microscope, the brain tissue of the two groups looked the same.[4] The condition soon became known as CTE.

CTE involves a buildup of tau protein. These clumps of tau protein, as described by one author, act "kind of like sludge, clogging up the brain and killing healthy cells," including "cells in regions responsible for mood, emotions, and executive functioning."[5] Symptoms include "memory loss, confusion, personality changes (including depression and suicidal thoughts), erratic behavior (including aggression), problems paying attention and organizing thoughts, and difficulty with balance and motor skill."[6] Today, the National Institutes of Health and the Center for Disease Control and Prevention recognize that there is a causal connection between CTE and repeated traumatic brain injuries.[7]

But it is not necessarily the severity of the impacts that puts one at the greatest risk of developing CTE; it is also the number of head injuries one sustains.[8] While concussions may lead to CTE, head impacts that do not result in a concussion (known as sub-concussive head impacts) also

9. Concussions, Fraud, and Statutes of Repose 183

increase the risk of CTE. For example, linebackers in the NFL experience more concussions but are hit in the head less frequently than defensive and offensive linemen, like Mike Webster.* Yet, linemen have higher rates of CTE. Thus, it is the number of blows one sustains to the head that is the better predictor of whether one will develop CTE.

CTE symptoms may not develop until years after one suffers the injuries to the brain.[9] Importantly, the disease is currently impossible to definitively diagnose until the brain can be analyzed after death. Thus, one may have the condition for years before experiencing symptoms and die before there can be a conclusive diagnosis.

* * *

The death of Mike Webster was followed by the suicides of former NFL players Andre Waters in 2005 and Terry Long in 2006, both of whom were later determined to have been suffering from symptoms related to CTE. But Chris Benoit's case in 2007 was perhaps the most high-profile CTE-related event up to that point. More studies emerged during this time linking football to brain injuries and long-term consequences, such as depression.[10]

As more scientific and anecdotal evidence of a connection between repeated head trauma and CTE began to accumulate, the NFL responded by calling into question the connection. In 1994, the NFL formed the Mild Traumatic Brain Injury (MTBI) Committee to study the effect of brain injury upon players. The NFL's commitment to this mission has been called into question. The chair of the MTBI Committee, Dr. Elliot Pellman, was a rheumatologist with no experience with brain science and who was also the team doctor for the New York Jets.[11] Pellman downplayed the seriousness of concussions at the time, stating that drinking (among other things) was a bigger issue than brain injuries for NFL players and that concussions were an occupational risk of the profession.[12] Commissioner Paul Tagliabue similarly downplayed the issue, describing concussions in the NFL as a "pack journalism issue" and describing the number of concussions among players as "relatively small."[13]

As incidences of CTE caught the public's attention following the deaths of Webster, Benoit, and others, the MTBI published a string of articles downplaying the issue. Between 2003 and 2009, the MTBI published 16 articles in a medical journal that concluded, among other findings, that there was no connection between football and brain damage.[14]

---

* It is estimated that linemen are hit 1,000 times a year over the course of their football careers at a force equal to driving a car into a brick wall at 35 m.p.h. Mikayla Paolini, "NFL Takes a Page from the Big Tobacco Playbook: Assumption of Risk in the CTE Crisis," 68 *Emory L.J.* 607, 612–13 (2019).

A 2004 article actually claimed that NFL players were less susceptible to brain injuries than members of the general population.[15] In 2009, a study of former players funded by the NFL found that players were 19 times more likely than the general population to have dementia. Shortly afterward, the NFL disavowed its own report as being flawed.[16] Later that year, Tagliabue's replacement as commissioner, Roger Goodell, testified before Congress concerning the issue. Goodell refused to acknowledge a link between football and subsequent brain problems.[17]

Facing congressional and public blowback following Goodell's testimony, the NFL took a new approach. The league appointed new chairs to the MTBI Committee (which it renamed the Head, Neck and Spine Committee) and appointed the author of a paper that had earlier found football players to be at a significantly higher risk of depression.[18] And in December 2009—just two months after Goodell refused to acknowledge a link between brain injuries and long-term consequences—the NFL did just that in a public statement. Despite repeated past denials, an NFL spokesperson told the *New York Times* that "[i]t's quite obvious from the medical research that's been done that concussions can lead to long-term problems."[19] The league stopped short of acknowledging a connection between football and CTE. But for the first time ever, it did acknowledge that concussions may have long-term effects.

* * *

The NFL attracted most of the CTE-related public attention during this period. But professional wrestling drew its fair share. Chris Nowinski performed in WWE from 2002 until his retirement in 2004. Prior to that, he had been a football player in high school and college. Nowinski suffered several concussions while in WWE, but it was after a match in June 2003 that he began experiencing serious problems. After taking a few weeks off, he lied about the post-concussion effects he was feeling in order to get back into the ring. This naturally meant that he took more blows to the head and, according to Nowinski, his condition grew worse. He stopped wrestling, but his condition did not improve over the next 12 months. So, Nowinski retired. He continued to experience headaches for the next five years and even ten years later would wake up in the middle of the night fearing that he was choking to death.[20]

After his wrestling career ended, Nowinski became an outspoken advocate for research into the field. He went on to get his Ph.D. in Neuroscience and became a co-founder of the Concussion Legacy Foundation, a non-profit organization established to support all those "affected by concussions and CTE, to promote smarter sports and safer athletes through education and innovation, and end CTE through prevention and research."

9. Concussions, Fraud, and Statutes of Repose 185

In 2006, Nowinski would also publish the book *Head Games: Football's Concussion Crisis from the NFL to the Youth Leagues*. While focused primarily on the connection between football (at all different levels) and long-term neurological damage, the book also details Nowinski's experiences in the wrestling world and the head injuries he suffered. Nowinski began experiencing serious problems after being accidentally kicked in the head during a match. But there are dozens of ways wrestlers can experience concussive and sub-concussive head trauma. The most obvious is the "chair shot," in which one performer hits another over the head with (what is usually) a folding chair. There is the "protected" chair shot, in which the wrestler on the receiving end is able to raise his arms and absorb most of the blow that way. But with an "unprotected" chair shot, the wrestler simply gets hit on the head. Until fairly recently, chair shots—protected and unprotected—were simply a part of the business, despite the obvious potential for head injuries.

* * *

It was Chris Nowinski who reportedly suggested to authorities that they examine Chris Benoit's brain to see if damage to the brain had played a role in Benoit's murder of his family and subsequent suicide in 2007. Benoit definitely took his fair share of chair shots over the course of his career. But Benoit was also closely associated with another move that almost certainly resulted in at least sub-concussive injuries: the diving head butt. While his opponent was lying flat on his back in the middle of the ring, Benoit would climb to the top rope and dive headfirst, hitting his opponent somewhere in the vicinity of the head with his own head. Regardless of where Benoit's head actually landed, his neck would invariably snap back upon impact. Benoit may not have performed his diving head butt in every match of his 22-year career. But, like an NFL linemen, his head and neck were thrust back in a violent collisions hundreds of times when performing the diving head butt. With what we know about CTE today, it's hard to believe that these collisions did not produce some type of lasting damage to his brain, exclusive of the potential damage caused by a career's worth of chair shots and other impacts.

* * *

In March of 2009, while Nowinski was working to bring attention to the problem of brain injuries in professional wrestling and the NFL was still trying to downplay the link between football and brain injuries, former professional wrestler Andrew "Test" Martin died of a drug overdose. Tests following his death revealed that Martin's brain showed signs of CTE, thus making Martin the second WWE superstar linked to the condition.[21]

Martin's death brought further attention to the link between CTE and professional wrestling. In response to this media coverage, WWE followed the NFL's playbook at the time and responded by questioning the diagnosis:

> While this is a new emerging science, the WWE is unaware of the veracity of any of these tests, be it for Chris Benoit or Andrew Martin. Dr. Omalu claims that Mr. Benoit had a brain that resembled an 85-year-old with Alzheimer's, which would lead one to ponder how Mr. Benoit would have found his way to an airport, let alone been able to remember all the moves and information that is required to perform in the ring.[22]

* * *

Part 2: The NFL Concussion Lawsuit

The first concussion-related lawsuit against the NFL was filed in 2011. After that, hundreds of former players and family members began suing the NFL. Eventually, all of the cases were consolidated into one action in a Pennsylvania federal court, titled *In re National Football League Players' Concussion Injury Litigation*. The gist of the suits was that "despite the NFL's awareness of the risks of repetitive head trauma, the League ignored, minimized, or outright suppressed information concerning the link between that trauma and cognitive damage."[23] As an example, the players cited the work of the Mild Traumatic Brain Injury Committee in 1994, which players characterized as being "at the forefront of a disinformation campaign that disseminated 'junk science' denying the link between head injuries and cognitive disorders."[24]

The players' lawsuit advanced several legal theories, but at the heart of the lawsuit was the allegation of fraudulent concealment: the NFL knew about the special long-term dangers posed by concussive and sub-concussive injuries but actively concealed these risks from players. Among the damages the players sought to recover were medial monitoring costs: the costs of future medical check-ups the players would need to undergo to monitor for CTE and related conditions. For its part, the league denied that it knew of the link between head injuries and CTE. But in late 2012, something very much like a smoking gun emerged that undercut the NFL's position. Working together, ESPN's *Outside the Lines* and PBS's *Frontline* uncovered the fact that the league's Retirement Board had awarded disability benefits in the late 1990s and 2000s totaling around $2 million to former players after concluding that their brain injuries were caused by football.[25]* In other words, at the same time the NFL was denying any link

9. Concussions, Fraud, and Statutes of Repose   187

between football and permanent and disabling brain damage, the league itself had actually found just such a connection and awarded disability benefits to the three players.

Faced with this new evidence, the league reached a settlement with the players in 2013.[26] After extensive legal wrangling, the parties agreed on a settlement of over $1 billion. In 2016, the NFL acknowledged for the first time that there is a link between football and CTE. A 2017 study of brains donated by family members of former NFL players found evidence of CTE in 110 out of 111 brains.[27]

* * *

Part 3: The WWE Lawsuit

In 2014, former wrestler Billy Jack Haynes brought a lawsuit against WWE in federal court in Oregon. Soon thereafter, a number of other former WWE performers filed a number of other complaints in different courts that largely tracked the allegations in Haynes' complaint.[28] The complaints borrowed heavily from the complaint filed in the NFL litigation.* Specifically, among other claims, the wrestlers alleged that WWE officials knew about the link between wrestling and CTE but actively concealed this information from performers.[29] And like the NFL players, the former WWE wrestlers were not seeking compensation for the discrete head injuries they suffered while wrestling but the increased risk of developing CTE and related permanent neurological conditions.

The procedural history of the case is incredibly complicated. And Konstantine Kyros, the lead attorney for the wrestlers, would anger Judge Vanessa L. Bryant at multiple points throughout the process. But eventually, the separate complaints would be consolidated and end up in federal court in Connecticut with over 60 former wrestlers—including Road Warrior Animal (Joseph Laurinaitis), Jimmy "Super Fly" Snuka, "Mr. Wonderful" Paul Orndorff, and King Kong Bundy (Christopher Pallies)—and family members of former wrestlers joining the class action against WWE.

* * *

---

* Actually, some of the allegations were literally copied and pasted from the NFL case, with the result being that the complaint sometimes accidentally referred to the NFL instead of the WWE. In another instance, the complaint referred to former Pittsburgh Steeler Mike Webster as a wrestler. *McCullough v. World Wrestling Entertainment, Inc.*, CIVIL ACTION NO. 3:15-CV-1074 (VLB), CIVIL ACTION NO. 3:15-CV-994 (VLB), CIVIL ACTION NO. 3:16-CV-1209 (VLB), 2018 WL 4425977, *5 (D. Conn. Sept. 17, 2018).

In 2015, WWE filed a motion to dismiss the complaint on the grounds (among others) that the complaint was barred by the statute of limitations. A statute of limitations is like a stopwatch. It is a law passed by a legislature that sets the time a plaintiff has to file a lawsuit. The stopwatch starts running upon the happening of a designated event, and the plaintiff has until a designated moment in time to file a claim. The Connecticut statute of limitations relevant to the concussion litigation provided that "[n]o action to recover damages for injury to the person ... shall be brought but within two years from the date when the injury is first sustained or discovered or in the exercise of reasonable care should have been discovered...."[30]

Statutes of limitations encourage injured parties not to "sit on their rights" and instead to bring their claims for compensation in a timely manner. That way, it's less likely that memories concerning the events will fade or that evidence will be lost over time. Importantly, Connecticut's statute of limitations (like many other states) only starts to run when a party is injured or *should have* discovered the injury through the exercise of reasonable care. This provision limits the unfairness that would result if a party could have suffered an injury that did not materialize until years later, like in the case of exposure to harmful chemicals that only results in cancer years later. So, as explained by one court, "the statute of limitations begins to run when the claimant has knowledge of facts which would put a reasonable person on notice of the nature and extent of an injury and that the injury was caused by the wrongful conduct of another."[31]

In 2016, the trial court in the case denied WWE's motion to dismiss the plaintiffs' claims on the basis of the statute of limitations. The court acknowledged that the former wrestlers may have been aware of the fact that they had suffered concussions more than two years before suit was filed. But knowledge of a concussion is not the same thing as knowledge that one has CTE or is at an increased risk of developing CTE. The court concluded that it was plausible that the plaintiffs had no reason to know of these facts more than two years prior to filing suit.[32] So, the plaintiffs had managed to clear the first hurdle WWE placed before them.

* * *

But the former wrestlers faced at least three other significant obstacles. One of these was Connecticut's statute of repose. A statute of repose is similar to, but different from, a statute of limitation. A statute of repose sets a time at which a plaintiff a plaintiff loses the right to bring a claim *even if* the plaintiff has not discovered the injury or could not reasonably have discovered it. In other words, a statute of repose sets an almost absolute limit on the time a party has to bring suit. Even more dramatically, a statute of repose bars a claim even if the plaintiff hasn't yet suffered any

9. Concussions, Fraud, and Statutes of Repose 189

injury resulting from the defendant's conduct. So, for example, a company might negligently expose an individual to a chemical that may increase the risk of cancer in the future. The statue of repose in the jurisdiction is three years. Even if the individual had no reason to know they had been exposed to the chemical until more than three years later and had not developed cancer within those three years, the statute of repose would bar any claim against the defendant.

State legislatures began enacting statutes of repose in the late 20th century as part of the tort reform movement.[33] Tort reform is concerned with the perceived unfairness of the civil litigation system toward defendants. Certain kinds of civil cases in particular, most notably lawsuits based on dangerous products (products liability) and medical malpractice, drew much of the attention of tort reformers. The purpose of these statutes is to provide some measure of *repose* (or peace of mind) for defendants. A business can rest more easily knowing that it won't be subject to liability some 20 years down the road for an act of negligence. State legislatures listed a host of other supposed "social and economic evils" resulting from businesses being forced to defend against lawsuits brought years later. These included the cost of maintaining liability insurance far into the future, the cost of storing documents for years on end in case litigation eventually results, and the adverse impact that such suits have on the willingness of business to innovate and develop new products.[34]

The downside for the injured party, however, is that such statutes limit their right to recover, including in situations in which an injury did not actually materialize until years later. For example, in a case from Tennessee, the plaintiff used the defendant's diet drug for 90 days between 1996 and 1997. In 2005, she was diagnosed with Primary Pulmonary Hypertension (PPH), a fatal disease. The plaintiff alleged that the pharmaceutical company knew of the risks of PPH associated with its product before it marketed it but concealed and downplayed those risks. The plaintiff filed her lawsuit shortly after being diagnosed with PPH. Tennessee's statute of repose provided that a lawsuit "must be brought within ten (10) years from the date on which the product was first purchased for use or consumption, *or within one (1) year after the expiration of the anticipated life of the product*, whichever is the shorter."[35] The "anticipated life of the product" is the "expiration date placed on the product by the manufacturer."[36] The expiration date for the defendant's drug was three years from the date of the manufacturer. The last date of manufacture of the drug was September 1997. So, "one (1) year after the expiration of the anticipated life of the product" would have been September 2001 at the absolute latest. Because the plaintiff did not file her lawsuit until 2005, Tennessee's statute of repose barred her claim, even though she did not discover the fact that she had PPH (or have any reason to know she had the disease) until nearly eight years after consuming the product.[37]

Given these kinds of harsh effects of statutes of repose, some state courts have declared them to be unconstitutional.[38] Other states have chosen not to enact such statutes or have carved out exceptions to them.[39] The statutes that do exist are typically limited to certain kinds of lawsuits (such as construction, medical malpractice, or products liability cases). In states that have them, the statutes typically tend to run for fairly long periods of time. Ten years is common.

In Connecticut, where the WWE concussion litigation took place, the applicable statute of repose runs for *three years*, one of the shortest timeframes in the country.[40] Unlike most states, Connecticut's statute is not limited to product liability claims or medical malpractice claims or claims based on faulty construction. Instead, the statute applies to *any* claim stemming from a defendant's negligence or reckless or wanton misconduct.[41] This makes Connecticut's statute of repose one of (if not the) strictest in the country.

Since the plaintiffs all claimed to have suffered head injuries more than three years before filing suit, the fact that they had no way of knowing that their concussion put them at a heightened risk of CTE was irrelevant.

* * *

The second obstacle the performers faced was also related to the statute of repose. Connecticut courts had previously held that the statute of repose was tolled (or paused) where the defendant fraudulently concealed the existence of the plaintiffs' right to sue. So, in order to escape the limitations imposed by the statute of repose, the WWE performers needed to show that WWE (1) had actual awareness of the facts that established the basis of the plaintiffs' claim against WWE, (2) intentionally concealed those facts from the plaintiff, and (3) concealed those facts for the purpose of delaying the filing of an action against WWE.[42] This exception to the statute of repose obviously tied back to the gist of the plaintiffs' claims against WWE: did WWE officials actually know about the connection between head injuries and CTE and, despite this knowledge, did it conceal this information from the performers?

The plaintiffs' complaint cited several examples of statements and actions from WWE officials that the plaintiff claimed demonstrated knowledge of the link between CTE and efforts to conceal this link. These included:

- the fact that between 2003 and 2006, Chris Nowinski worked for the WWE after retiring as an in-ring performer and, during this

time, Nowinski researched the connection between concussions and permanent degenerative neurological conditions[43];
- 2007 testimony by WWE Executive Stephanie McMahon Levesque* before the Committee on Oversight and Government Reform of the U.S. House of Representatives that there were "no documented concussions in WWE's history."[44]
- WWE's 2009 statement questioning how Chris Benoit "would have found his way to an airport, let alone been able to remember all the moves and information that is required to perform in the ring" had he been suffering from CTE;
- statements made by Vince and Linda McMahon on CNN further questioning the finding that Benoit had CTE[45];
- 2015 public statements made by Dr. Joseph Maroon, a neuroscientist and head injury specialist for the NFL who was hired to head the WWE's Wellness Program, to the effect that while the problem of CTE was real, "it is being overexaggerated."[46]

* * *

The third obstacle the plaintiffs faced was that by the time the WWE filed a motion to dismiss the plaintiff's complaint in 2016, the plaintiffs' lawyer, Konstantine Kyros, had thoroughly annoyed the presiding judge. The litigation had been contentious from the start. WWE attorney Jerry McDevitt had gone on the attack in 2015, accusing Kyros of "trolling around looking for people to sue." According to McDevitt, until Kyros began reaching out to former wrestlers encouraging them to join the suit, WWE "didn't have one person, none, claiming they had any kind of traumatic brain injuries, or dementia or ALS or any of the kind of stuff you see associated with the NFL." For its part, the WWE released a statement accusing Kyros of misleading and exploiting the wrestlers in question.[47]

But Kyros had also gotten off on the wrong foot with Judge Bryant early in the litigation through what Bryant described as a "vexatious and transparent attempt" on Kyros' part to avoid having the case end up in front of Bryant in federal court in Connecticut in the first place. "Forum shopping" is a term lawyers use to describe the practice of filing a case in a court that the lawyer believes will be most sympathetic to the plaintiff's claims. Sometimes, there might be multiple courts that conceivably have jurisdiction (or authority) to hear a case. So, some lawyers tend to look around (or shop) for the court (or forum) that is most likely to be friendly toward the plaintiff's claim. In the case of the WWE CTE litigation,

---

* McMahon Levesque is the daughter of Vince McMahon.

Kyros filed complaints in multiple federal courts in different states in what Judge Bryant referred to as an attempt to evade the jurisdiction of her court. When the case eventually landed in federal court in Connecticut, Kyros attempted to prevent the case from being assigned to Judge Bryant.[48]*

While forum shopping has a bad name, the reality is that lawyers on both sides routinely try to make sure that a case ends up in the forum they believe will be most likely to lead to the best outcome for their clients. While plaintiffs' lawyers usually bear the brunt of the criticism when it comes to forum shopping since they are the ones who decide in which court to file the initial complaint, defense lawyers will routinely try to get a case that was filed in state court transferred (or "removed") to federal court when they believe it will be advantageous to do so. For his part, Kyros could hardly be blamed for wanting to stay as far away from Connecticut's ultra-short statute of repose as possible. But what makes Kyros' actions so unusual are (1) the lengths to which he went in trying to avoid ending up in federal court in Connecticut and (2) his decision, once he wound up there, to try to keep the case away from Judge Bryant. Judges are, of course, supposed to be impartial and not permit their personal feelings toward the lawyers or the parties influence their decisions. But any lawyer will tell you that, as a matter of common sense, it's best to avoid getting on the wrong side of the judge who is hearing your case.

As the litigation progressed, Bryant grew increasingly frustrated with Kyros for reasons having little to do with his forum-shopping. At one point, she chided Kyros for including "superfluous, hyperbolic, inflammatory opinions and references to things that don't have any relevance" in his complaints. According to Bryant, the complaints contained "numerous allegations that a reasonable attorney would know are inaccurate, irrelevant, or frivolous."[49] At one point, she even suggested to Kyros on the record that he reacquaint himself with the rules of procedure governing the filing of complaints and read some decisions concerning those rules.[50] Kyros had definitely gotten on the wrong side of Judge Bryant.

* * *

Whatever Judge Bryant's personal opinions regarding Kyros, her initial rulings at least give the appearance that she was bending over

---

* Judge Bryant was appointed to the federal bench by President George W. Bush, making Bryant the first Black federal judge in New England. Prior to the WWE litigation, Bryant was most known for having ruled that the federal government's Defense of Marriage Act, which defined marriage exclusively in terms of union between a man and woman, violated the Equal Protection Clause of the Constitution. *Pedersen v. Office of Personnel Management*, 881 F.Supp.2d 294 (July 31, 2012).

9. Concussions, Fraud, and Statutes of Repose 193

backward to be unbiased. She allowed Kyros to go back and amend his initial complaint. She also denied WWE's initial motion to dismiss the plaintiffs' claims. When WWE filed a new motion to some of the claims on the grounds that the complaint was frivolous, Judge Bryant again gave Kyros and his clients another chance to amend the complaint before ruling on WWE's motion.[51] But roughly three years after the litigation in Connecticut commenced, Judge Bryant dropped the hammer.

By this point, the plaintiffs' case was starting to unravel. In order to toll the statute of repose and prevail on their lawsuit, the plaintiffs needed to establish that WWE knew of the connection between concussions and CTE and concealed that connection from its performers. The plaintiffs alleged that the WWE learned about the link between concussions and CTE sometime between 2003 and 2006 while Chris Nowinski was writing his book *Head Games* while also working for the WWE. However, according to Nowinski, his involvement with the WWE during this time was limited, and there was no evidence establishing that anyone at the WWE knew about Nowinski's research.* As the facts developed, Judge Bryant concluded that there was no evidence "to support a finding that WWE knew of a risk that repeated head injuries incurred while performing as a professional wrestler could cause permanent degenerative neurological conditions prior to September 5, 2007"—the date it was revealed that Chris Benoit had been diagnosed with CTE.[52]

What's more, the supposed facts that helped establish that WWE officials had attempted to conceal the connection between wrestling and CTE turned out not to carry as much weight as the plaintiffs suggested. For example, one of the facts the plaintiffs had relied on to establish that WWE officials had known of the connection between head injuries and CTE for years and were trying to conceal it was the 2007 congressional testimony by Stephanie McMahon Levesque to the effect "that there were no documented concussions in WWE's history," a statement that was obviously untrue. However, it turned out that McMahon Levesque's statement had been in response to a question asking about the number of concussions documented *after* the WWE's adoption of its wellness policy in 2006. Judge Bryant referred to the plaintiffs' characterization of McMahon Levesque's testimony as "deliberately misleading."[53]

Other facts emerged that tended to undermine the plaintiffs'

---

* Judge Bryant suggested that there was no evidence to suggest that the WWE was aware of Nowinski's research until September 2010. In fairness to Kyros and the plaintiffs, it seems hard to believe that the WWE was not aware of Nowinski's research until 2010 in light of the fact that Nowinski's book had come out four years earlier and at least touched on his own experiences with concussions while still a wrestler. In 2013, the WWE donated over $1 million to the Sports Legacy Institute, a research program at Boston University's Center for the Study of Traumatic Encephalopathy co-founded by Nowinski.

argument that WWE officials were concealing the truth about the connection between wresting and CTE. In 2009, Vince McMahon and Stephanie McMahon Levesque both publicly questioned the validity of Chris Benoit's CTE diagnosis. But a year earlier, the WWE had hired Dr. Joseph Maroon, a neurosurgeon with an extensive background in concussion assessment, and was conducting regular neurological testing of its workers.[54] Between 2010 and 2015, Nowinski and Maroon gave several presentations to WWE performers regarding traumatic brain injuries.[55] Whatever WWE officials may have said publicly about CTE, in the locker room, they were providing at least some testing and training on the risks of permanent neurological damage. What's more, while all of this was taking place, the NFL concussion litigation had generated widespread attention to the issue, including the revelation in 2012 that the NFL had previously awarded disability benefits to former players suffering from neurological damage.

In short, absent clear evidence that WWE was denying any link between wrestling and CTE while talking to performers in the locker room, at some point it is difficult to believe that the WWE could have concealed the long-term risks of concussions even if it wanted to. Unfortunately for the plaintiffs, they had no such evidence. Over the course of several decisions, Judge Bryant dismissed each of the plaintiffs' claims.

* * *

Part 4: Conclusion

Kyros would file numerous appeals in the ensuing years, none of which were successful. In April 2021, the United States Supreme Court declined to hear the case, thus putting an end to the plaintiffs' claims.

WWE lawyers had filed a motion for sanctions against Kyros earlier in the litigation based on the filing of allegedly frivolous complaints and the failure to adequately respond to discovery requests. Judge Bryant initially denied the motion but indicated that she was open to reconsidering her decision if Kyros continued with his "bad habits." Eventually, Judge Bryant referred the question of sanctions to a different judge, who found that Kyros had engaged in various forms of misconduct. For example, during the pre-trial discovery phase, a party can file an "interrogatory" that asks the other side a specific question, to which the other side must respond. WWE lawyers filed an interrogatory asking Kyros to identify each public statement or article in which WWE downplayed the long-term health risks associated with concussions. According to the judge, Kyros instead "steer[ed] WWE to random publications and documents

9. Concussions, Fraud, and Statutes of Repose   195

with little specificity or guidance," including a reference to the entire book *Head Games*.

The reviewing judge concluded that sanctions were warranted, a conclusion with which Judge Bryant agreed.[56] Eventually, another judge imposed sanctions in the amount of $312,143.55 (which was less than the over $500,000 WWE was seeking).[57]

CHAPTER 10

Race Discrimination

Sporty Harvey, Joe Dorsey, Bobo Brazil, and Sputnik Monroe v. Jim Crow

> "I figured there would be kids coming along who didn't have the problems that I had. And there have been.... I did something to make me feel good. I did something."
> —I.H. "Sporty" Harvey, 1997[1]

Professional wrestling and race discrimination go way back. The sport has a long history of trafficking in racist tropes, like the recurring gimmick of the Black wrestler being able to withstand or deliver a particularly vicious headbutt because, you know, Black people have really hard heads. Promoters frequently offered fans crudely stereotypical characters, such as Black wrestlers who supposedly hailed from the jungles of Africa (see Kamala the Ugandan Giant), were headhunters (see Saba Simba), or were witch doctors (see Papa Shango).[2] Mexican wrestlers wore sombreros and had finishing moves like the Flying Burrito; wrestlers who were supposedly German had Nazi overtones; announcers would complain about a Japanese wrestler's "sneak attack" or "Pearl Harbor job" on another wrestler; and if a promoter put an Italian wrestler in a headdress, the wrestler suddenly became an American Indian. Heels were not above employing blatantly racist language and taunts in an effort to get heat (see Roddy Piper pretending to feed bananas to a poster of Mr. T and telling Mr. T that he was going to "whip him like a slave").[3] It wasn't until 1992 when Ron Simmons became World Champion in World Championship Wrestling that a Black wrestler was recognized as a world champion.[4]

Professional wrestling and boxing also go way back. Throughout most of the 20th century, state athletic commissions regulated both businesses, and boxers would sometimes work part-time in the wrestling game. Sometimes the two fields would overlap more formally, such as when Muhammad Ali took on Antonio Inoki in a bizarre boxer-meets-wrestler match in 1976. Both sports also had unsavory reputations. But, at least behind closed doors, wrestling was honest about its crookedness. Boxing, while nominally a legitimate sport, had a long history of corruption. Indeed, this corruption is partly why state legislatures felt it necessary to give state athletic commissions the authority to regulate the two businesses. And like wrestling, boxing had its own history of using racism to promote the business.

Despite these unsavory traits, the two businesses played a role in breaking down institutionalized segregation in the South during the civil rights era. The story of the civil rights struggle in the U.S. involves a combination of individual bravery and legal action. The same is true of the process of breaking down racial barriers in the wrestling and boxing worlds. In some instances, performers were able to break down racial barriers through sheer talent and bravery. In other instances, they used the legal system.

Part 1: Sports and Jim Crow

Plessy v. Ferguson[5] is on virtually every legal scholar's short list for the worst Supreme Court decision of all time. The 1896 decision involved the constitutionality of Louisiana's Separate Car Act, which required that railroad companies provide "equal but separate" railway cars for black and white passengers. Only 30 years earlier, Congress had approved the Fourteenth Amendment to the federal Constitution. The Fourteenth Amendment was one of three post–Civil War amendments designed to address the effects of slavery. Importantly, the first section of the amendment prohibits a state from denying "to any person within its jurisdiction the equal protection of the laws." In a 7–1 decision, the Supreme Court held in *Plessy* that Louisiana's Separate Car Act did not violate the Equal Protection Clause, despite the fact that the Act, on its face, required differing treatment of black and white passengers.[6] According to the Court, the differential treatment required by the Act did not imply the inferiority of black passengers.

In reaching the decision, the Court dismissed the idea that legislation prohibiting segregation was an effective means of addressing discrimination. The majority opinion rejected the idea that "social prejudices may be overcome by legislation, and that equal rights cannot be secured to the negro except by an enforced commingling of the two races."[7] This was an idea that would be put to the test in the ensuing decades.

The Court's conclusion that state-mandated "separate but equal" treatment of the races did not violate the Constitution helped institutionalize the practice of segregation. In particular, the *Plessy* decision sanctioned Jim Crow laws throughout the South.* For example, a 1908 Louisiana statute prohibited the sale of intoxicants to "white and colored men on the same premises."[8] These were laws that barred black citizens from visiting public parks, forced them to use separate hotels, and established "colored only" sections within places of public accommodation. Of course, it was obvious to anyone paying attention that the separate opportunities and accommodations provided to African American citizens were often not equal to those afforded white citizens and that the denial of hotel rooms and meals to African American customers most definitely did, in fact, imply inferiority.

* * *

Plessy v. Ferguson involved a segregation law impacting public transportation. There were also Jim Crow laws that applied specifically to recreational and athletic activities. For example, an Atlanta ordinance made it unlawful "for any amateur white baseball team to play baseball in any vacant lot or baseball diamond within two blocks of a playground devoted to the negro race, and it shall be unlawful for any amateur colored baseball team to play ... within two blocks of a playground devoted to the white race."[9] An Oklahoma statute gave a state commission "the right to make segregation of the white and colored races as to the exercise of rights of fishing [and] boating."[10] An Alabama statute prohibited white and black citizens from something as trivial as engaging in "any game of cards, dice, dominoes or checkers."[11] Louisiana had a sweeping law on the books that prohibited any individual from putting on "athletic training, games, sports or contests and other such activities involving personal and social contacts, in which the participants or contestants are members of the white and negro races."[12] This law would impact Louisiana sports in significant ways, including causing the University of Wisconsin's football team to cancel a 1956 game against Louisiana State University in Baton Rouge because Wisconsin's quarterback and star wide receiver were both black.[13]

One scholar has noted that "prohibitions against blacks attending white colleges and universities effectively excluded the black athlete from playing for predominantly white southern institutions."[14] But the reach of Jim Crow also extended beyond the South. Some athletic conferences had gentlemen's agreements that excluded black athletes from participation,

---

* The term "Jim Crow" was derived from a minstrel show character. Michelle Alexander, *The New Jim Crow* 44 (The New Press 2020).

while some northern schools imposed quotas on the number of black student-athletes on a team.[15]

Jim Crow also impacted professional sports. As sociologist Harry Edwards has noted, "there were never any formal rules or regulations barring Blacks from mainstream professional baseball, basketball, or football."[16] But informal agreements and customs worked to prevent Black professional athletes from competing with and against their white counterparts. For example, in 1887, a group of minor league baseball owners voted to exclude Black players from participating in their league.[17] Other organizations followed to the point that "by the early to mid–1890s, African Americans were prohibited from playing organized professional baseball in the United States."[18] As Professor Edwards put it, "[l]argely as a result of 'separate but equal' legal rulings and the power of custom, convention, and connivance ... there developed a national Black sports institution paralleling that of mainstream White society" that emerged following the Civil War.[19]

The most obvious example of this sort of paralleling was the Negro Leagues of professional baseball. In 1885, the Cuban Giants became the first black professional baseball team. The Negro National League started in 1920 and various Negro Leagues existed over the course of the next three decades. Lesser known were the Black Fives, the black professional basketball teams that competed shortly after the beginning of the 20th century until 1950.

Importantly, Jim Crow not only prevented white and Black athletes from taking the field of competition against each other, it also sometimes prohibited white and Black attendees from interacting with each other at sporting events. For example, an Alabama statute prohibited the owner, operator, or person in charge of a "yard, court, ball park or other indoor or outdoor place" to permit "any ... athletic contest of any kind whatsoever, unless such place has entrances, exits and seating or standing sections set aside for and assigned to the use of negroes, by well defined physical barriers, and unless the members of each race are effectively restricted and confined to the sections set aside for and assigned to the use of such race."[20] Griffith Stadium in Washington, D.C., was home to both the Washington Senators and the Homestead Grays of the Negro National League. But when the Senators played at home, Black fans were restricted to the right field pavilion or the left field bleachers.[21]

* * *

Professional wrestling was also segregated during this time. Following the Civil War and early into the 20th century, professional wrestling matches were largely legitimate athletic competitions. But there were few Black performers.[22] Viro Small is generally regarded as the first Black professional wrestler in the United States. Born into slavery in South Carolina, Small eventually made his way North following the Civil War to St. Albans, Vermont, and New York City where he earned a living wrestling and boxing between 1870 and 1885.* Wrestling as "Black Sam, the Colored Champion of the World," Small won the Vermont Collar and Elbow Championship and wrestled in county fairs in New England, dingy Bowery bars, and the first incarnations of Madison Square Garden.[23] According to one account, Small was as adept in dealing with rowdy Northeastern customers as he was professional opponents. Small had "almost uncanny talents for removing pistols or knives and replacing drawn weapons with fractured arms or wrists or tranquilizing uppercuts, but always, of course, in a courteous manner."[24]

By the 1920s, professional wrestling events had evolved from true athletic competitions to matches involving pre-determined outcomes.[25] Professional boxing saw an increase in Black fighters following the success of Jack Johnson, who became the world champion in 1908. But the wrestling business remained comprised mostly of white wrestlers competing against each other for the next few decades.[26]

Interestingly, boxing and wrestling attracted special attention from segregationists. A 1933 Texas criminal statute prohibited anyone from "knowingly permit[ing] any fistic combat match boxing, sparring or wrestling contest or exhibition between any person of the Caucasian or 'White' race and one of the African or 'Negro' race."[27] The Louisiana State Athletic Commission had a virtually identical rule.[28] The stated justification for these rules was the desire to prevent racial violence among fans.[29] The concern was not entirely farfetched. Back in 1910, Jack Johnson faced off against white Jim Jeffries in the first "Fight of the Century." The fact that this was a contest between Black and white participants took center stage. Johnson had appeared unstoppable in his previous fights against white opponents, and Jeffries was dubbed the first "Great White Hope." Racial pride was very much on the line, with white media outlets consistently playing up racist stereotypes concerning Johnson.[30] The result was that when Johnson battered Jeffries to win the title, white fans around the country responded with riots that resulted in the deaths of several individuals and many more injured.[31]

* * *

---

* Legend has it that one of Small's opponents in New York was so outraged after a match that he shot Small while Small was sleeping. Small survived.

Part 2: Post–World War II Attitudes, *Brown v. Board of Education*, and Other Legal Attacks on Jim Crow

Jim Crow laws would remain deeply rooted in the South until the 1960s. But America's involvement in World War II two decades earlier helped lay the groundwork for societal and legal change. The most dramatic example of that legal change would be the Supreme Court's 1954 decision in *Brown v. Board of Education,* a decision that would help pave the way for other legal challenges to segregationist laws, including those impacting boxing and professional wrestling.

* * *

World War II and Post-War Segregation

The desegregation movement had some of its origins in World War II. As the U.S. supplied Great Britain's war effort and began preparing for its own eventual entry into the war in 1941, the nation's defense industry kicked into high gear. This growth created a need for new employees. But Black applicants for these new positions in the defense industry faced widespread discrimination. Facing pressure from civil rights leaders, President Franklin D. Roosevelt issued Executive Order 8802, which prohibited discrimination in the defense industry on the basis of race.

From the time the U.S. entered the war in December 1941 until the end of the war in 1945, over 1 million Black Americans served in the U.S. military. But like American society more generally, the U.S. military also engaged in Jim Crow discrimination. Black soldiers were assigned separate barracks and relegated to non-combat support positions during the first years of the war. But as casualties mounted and more soldiers were needed on the front lines, more Black units served in combat roles. Some African American units were kept separate from white soldiers, but other units were integrated with white troops.[32] This service helped shape attitudes among fellow white soldiers as well as white officers. A U.S. Army survey near the end of the war revealed that the overwhelming majority of white officers and non-commissioned officers believed that Black soldiers had fought well and could perform as well as white soldiers given equal training and equipment.[33]

When Black soldiers returned home after risking their lives overseas, they returned to a country where institutionalized racism was still present. As Professor Edwards put it, "the stark contradiction of the United

States fighting for democracy and against racist tyranny abroad, while maintaining a race-based oppressive caste at home, became ever more politically untenable."[34] While it would take years to end formal segregation throughout the country, World War II provided some of the impetus for desegregation efforts.

* * *

Segregation slowly began to give way in professional sports in the years following the war. When the Cleveland Rams of the National Football League (NFL) were preparing to move to Los Angeles in 1946, the NFL remained segregated. Black journalists complained about the fact that the taxpayer-funded Los Angeles Coliseum, where the Rams would play, would be used to further racial segregation. In an effort to placate the public, secure a lease, and increase ticket sales among Black fans, the Rams agreed to sign black players. They fulfilled this promise by signing Kenny Washington that year, thus making the NFL the first major professional sports league to break the color barrier.[35]

Similarly, Brooklyn Dodgers' president and general manager Branch Rickey's belief that desegregation was immoral fit nicely with his desire to increase ticket sales. These forces led to the signing of Jackie Robinson and the desegregation of professional baseball in 1947.[36] Finally, Chuck Cooper became the first Black player drafted by a National Basketball Association (NBA) team in 1950. Nat "Sweetwater" Clifton became the first Black player to sign an NBA contract and Early Lloyd became the first Black player to actually play in an NBA game later that year.[37]* Once again, economics played a big role in the decision of NBA owners to desegregate. By 1950, the NBA attracted fewer fans than college basketball, and all-Black teams like the Harlem Globetrotters were earning big money. Thus, desegregating professional basketball made good business sense.[38]

* * *

While the most popular sports in the country were making strides during this era in terms of desegregation, professional wrestling lagged behind. Boxing—professional wrestling's more socially acceptable cousin—had already seen several Black world champions by the end of World War II, Joe Louis being the most obvious example. But Black professional wrestlers had far more limited opportunities.

It's worth noting that while the major professional sports leagues had all been desegregated by 1950, the number of Black players in the leagues

---

* The first non-white player in the NBA was Wat Misaka, an Asian-American point guard who played briefly for the New York Knicks in 1947.

was still fairly small. There were only around a dozen African American ballplayers playing in Major League Baseball in 1950. The Los Angeles Rams added a second Black player to the team in 1946 but it wasn't until 1949 that another NFL team (the Detroit Lions) drafted a Black player.[39] But at least these players were fully integrated within their respective leagues, playing on the same fields and courts against white players.

Professional wrestling was different. The number of Black professional wrestlers during this era was similarly limited, but the business was also more segregated than other sports. The wrestling business by this time was largely made up of different geographic territories. The level of segregation that existed within the business depended upon the territory in question. Black performers were often relegated to lower slots on the card. A black performer might become the "U.S. Colored Champion" or the "World Negro Heavyweight Champion" but could not compete to be the "U.S. Champion" or "World Champion."[40] In some instances, promoters ran all-Black shows for all-Black audiences. In others, Black wrestlers performed on the same card as white wrestlers but were restricted to wrestling each other.[41] For example, Black wrestlers Luther Lindsey and Shag Thomas were in the same promotion during this period. Lindsey described his schedule (presumably only partly in jest): "Monday I wrestle Shag Thomas in Portland, Tuesday I wrestle Shag Thomas in San Francisco, Wednesday I wrestle Shag Thomas in Dallas, Thursday I wrestle Shag Thomas in Houston, Saturday I wrestle Shag Thomas in Memphis."[42]

There were exceptions. Probably the first Black wrestler to break the color barrier after wrestling switched from sport to entertainment was "the Black Panther" Jim Mitchell. A newspaper story reveals that Mitchell wrestled and defeated a white performer named Speedy O'Neal back in 1932 in Kokomo, Indiana.[43] According to Mitchell's biographer, "there simply weren't enough black wrestlers working in the 1930s for a color barrier to exist."[44] Mitchell would perform with white wrestlers throughout the decade in Ohio and Michigan before eventually moving out west. Over time, more Black performers entered the sport. But professional wrestling remained segregated in the South immediately after World War II. So, while Mitchell might have been able to face white opponents while wrestling in California, when he performed in his hometown of Louisville and other more southern locations, he faced only other Black performers.[45]

Brown v. Board of Education and Desegregation

The NAACP Legal Defense Fund began its efforts to overturn *Plessy v. Ferguson*'s "separate but equal" standard in the 1930s.[46] Lawyers for the

NAACP, including future Supreme Court Justice Thurgood Marshall, devised a strategy that initially focused on segregation in public education. They would whittle away at *Plessy v. Ferguson*'s "separate but equal" standard by first challenging segregation laws and policies at the graduate and professional school level by showing that the few separate programs offered to Black students were not, in fact, equal. Eventually, they would argue that segregation in public education and elsewhere was inherently unequal.[47]

Plessy v. Ferguson's "separate but equal" notion took a hit 1950 with two Supreme Court decisions decided on the same day. In the first, *Sweatt v. Painter*,[48] Herman Sweatt was denied admission to the University of Texas Law School on the grounds that the school only admitted white students. Sweatt sued to be admitted, claiming that the law school's segregation policy violated the Fourteenth Amendment's Equal Protection Clause. Instead, the Texas trial court gave the State of Texas six months to establish a Black-only law school.[49] But the interim law school paled in comparison to the University of Texas Law School in terms of resources and reputation. Therefore, even under *Plessy*'s "separate but equal standard," Texas' relegation of Black applicants to its Black-only law school violated the Equal Protection Clause.[50]

That same day, the Court decided *McLaurin v. Oklahoma State Regents*.[51] There, a Black doctoral student, George McLaurin, was originally denied admission to the University of Oklahoma on the basis of a state statute that made it a crime to operate a racially mixed school. After McLaurin successfully challenged the constitutionality of the statute, the Oklahoma legislature amended the statute to permit Black students to attend the same university as white students but on a segregated basis.[52] McLaurin was admitted to the university but was forced to attend class separately.[53] McLaurin was required to sit apart from his classmates in class; to sit at a designated desk in the library, but not to use the desks in the regular reading room; and to sit at a designated table and to eat at a different time from the other students in the school cafeteria.[54] McLaurin challenged the constitutionality of this arrangement. The Supreme Court concluded that the restrictions faced by McLaurin "impair and inhibit his ability to study, to engage in discussions and exchange views with other students, and, in general, to learn his profession."[55] In other words, his learning environment was separate and not equal. Thus, the Court concluded that the university's treatment of McLaurin denied McLaurin equal protection of the law.[56]

Importantly, in neither case did the Court reject *Plessy v. Ferguson*'s "separate but equal standard." Indeed, in *Sweatt*, the Court specifically declined to reconsider this standard.[57] But this was about to change.

The single most important Supreme Court decision regarding desegregation—and indeed one of the most important judicial decisions of the 20th century—was the Court's 1954 decision in *Brown v. Board of Education of Topeka*.[58] A group of Black students in four states sought admission to the public schools in their communities on a nonsegregated basis after having been denied admission to schools attended by white children.[59] The students alleged that state laws that required or permitted segregation of public school students according to race violated the Equal Protection Clause of the Fourteenth Amendment.

By 1954, Black public schools were at least in the process of being equalized in terms of buildings, the qualifications of teachers, and all of the others things that make up a public school. But there remained the concern "the effect of segregation itself on public education" might deny Black students equal opportunities.[60] So, the Court considered several studies on the impact of segregation upon public education. These studies revealed that segregated schools were "inherently unequal" because of the adverse psychological impact they had upon African-American children.[61] Segregated schools, by their nature, suggested the inferiority of Black children and generated "a feeling of inferiority as to their status in the community that may affect their hearts and minds in a way unlikely ever to be undone."[62] Therefore, the Court concluded that state laws requiring or permitting the segregation of public schools deprived students "of the equal protection of the laws guaranteed by the Fourteenth Amendment."[63] In short, *Plessy v. Ferguson*'s "separate but equal" idea no longer had any force in the public education setting.

Part 3: Sporty Harvey v. Jim Crow

> *When he fights, he fights for groceries and that is what this case is about—groceries and liberty.*
> —Plaintiff's court filing, *Harvey v. Morgan*

On its face, *Brown v. Board of Education* only addressed segregation in public schools. But the Supreme Court's decision impacted Jim Crow laws as they applied in other settings. This included boxing and professional wrestling. On August 13, 1953—nine months before the Supreme Court announced its decision in *Brown*—boxer I.H. "Sporty" Harvey filed suit seeking to compel the Texas Commissioner of Labor Statistics to grant Harvey a boxing license. A month earlier, Harvey, a Black heavyweight, had been denied a license to fight against a white opponent on the grounds that Texas law prohibited "any fistic combat match boxing, sparring or wrestling contest or exhibition between any person of the Caucasian or 'White' race and one of the African or 'Negro' race."[64] Like the plaintiffs in *Brown*, Harvey argued that the Texas law deprived him of equal protection under the law in violation of the Constitution.

The Texas legal system had a rather ugly history when it came to race discrimination. For example, a local ordinance in Fort Worth made it unlawful "for any white person and any Negro to have sexual intercourse with each other" within city limits.[65] In 1941, a Texas appellate court ruled that a white woman who had been wrongfully excluded from an elevator reserved for white people and "forced" to ride in an elevator with Black visitors could bring a lawsuit against the owners of the building.[66] And, of course, there was also the blanket exclusion of Black applicants to institutes of higher learning at issue in *Sweatt v. Painter*. It was against this backdrop that Speedy Harvey sought help from the Texas court system.

* * *

Harvey was represented by Maury Maverick, Jr., a liberal white Texas lawyer who practiced law at a time when liberal white Texas lawyers were a rarity.[67] Maverick served in the Texas Legislature from 1951 to 1955. When the body passed a resolution inviting red-baiting Senator Joe McCarthy to visit, Maverick introduced his own resolution inviting Mickey Mouse to visit. "If we're going to invite a rat," Maverick said, "why not invite a good rat?"[68]

There were few white lawyers in the South who both believed in desegregation *and* were willing to run the professional and personal risks associated with representing Black clients seeking to assert their civil rights.[69] Maverick was one of those lawyers. Earlier that year, Maverick had introduced a bill that would have repealed the Texas statute prohibiting interracial boxing and wrestling matches. The bill died a quick death in committee.[70] Sporty Harvey sought out Maverick after hearing of Maverick's efforts in the Texas legislature. Still bitter over failure to repeal the ban, Maverick was more than willing to represent Harvey.

Maverick reached out to the NAACP, which agreed to help pay for some of Harvey's court costs. But Maverick would anger NAACP lawyers by rejecting their strong advice to file Harvey's suit in federal court where all of the NAACP's previous successful actions had been filed.[71] Instead, Maverick filed in state court. According to a friend, Maverick chose state court because he "wanted to win civil-liberties cases in state court because he wanted to change the mind-set of Texas juries and jurists." Or maybe it was simpler than that. "I wanted to whip 'em in a Texas court," said Maverick.[72]*

* * *

When Harvey first sought legal representation, he informed Maverick that he wanted to talk to him about filing a lawsuit and about "dignity for [his] people."[73] Harvey's wife would later say that she feared for her husband's safety after he filed suit but that he was doing what he thought was right.[74] While Harvey seems to have been motivated by a sense of justice, he also had a practical reason for filing suit: he wanted to make more money.[75] Since he could not fight white opponents, Harvey was sometimes forced to drive to Mexico to fight.[76] Harvey was no great prospect. He got knocked out in his first four professional fights and lost his first eight.[77] At a hearing, Maverick, his own lawyer, referred to him as a "mediocre fighter." But according to witness testimony, there were more mediocre white fighters in Texas than there were mediocre Black fighters. Therefore, a mediocre Black fighter like Sporty Harvey couldn't get as many fights and earn as much money as mediocre white fighters under Texas law.[78] Harvey wanted dignity for his people, but he also wanted to be able to buy enough groceries to feed his family.

M.B. Morgan, the Texas Commissioner of Labor Statistics who had denied Harvey's application to fight a white boxer, cited the Texas statute prohibiting "mixed race" boxing and wrestling matches. Morgan took the position that the purpose of the statute preventing white and Black boxers and wrestlers from competing against each other "was to prevent situations which engendered racial feelings and tended toward racial riots."[79] There was conflicting evidence presented at trial on the question of just how likely there was to be resulting racial violence. There had been amateur events during this time featuring contests between fighters of different races without any resulting racial violence.[80] The Supervisor for the State Boxing and Wrestling Commission, Austin, testified that permitting white and Black pugilists and wrestlers to compete against each other would increase racial tension and cited as an example an incident in which

> there was a white boy got a decision over a Latin American, and there was a near riot, and, in my opinion, if a colored boxer was boxing a white fighter,

---

* Maverick's father was a former New Deal Democrat who represented South Texas in the U.S. House of Representatives and went on to become mayor of San Antonio. The elder Maverick is widely credited with coining the term "gobbledygook" back in 1944 to describe vague and self-important language. The Maverick family can also lay claim to being the inspiration for the word "maverick," meaning an independent-minded person or one who does not follow the herd. Maury Maverick, Jr.'s great-grandfather, Samuel, was a cattle rancher who did not brand his cows, thus leading his cattle being called "mavericks" when they wandered off.

there would even be—or even a Latin American, there would be a greater tension. That is strictly my opinion.[81]

However, a Deputy Boxing Commissioner testified that the "high feeling at a boxing match" had little to do with the races of the combatants and was instead simply a function of the nature of the event itself.[82]

* * *

The question of whether the fear of race riots was what was really driving the concerns in Texas over racially mixed boxing and wrestling events is an interesting one. On the one hand, there was most definitely a longstanding fear that race-based violence might erupt at professional wrestling matches. Fan violence at professional wrestling matches during this time was not an entirely rare occurrence. It was around this time, for example, that wrestling fans in Virginia, angered by the tactics of the heel that night, turned violent, resulting in a woman being hit in the head by a flying whiskey bottle.[83]

As mentioned, professional wrestling events were segregated in many territories. But even in territories where a white wrestler might take on a Black wrestler, the Black performer during this era almost always played the role of the fan favorite and the white performer the role of the dastardly heel. The most obvious reason was that, in light of wrestling fans' tendency to resort to violence when outraged, promoters feared that white fans would react violently to a Black wrestler cheating in order to defeat a white wrestler.[84] For example, when white wrestler Penny Banner first started wrestling Black wrestler Babs Wingo, she was told by the promoter that Banner would need to assume the role of heel and Wingo the role of babyface "because the fans would riot if a black rulebreaker beat a pretty blonde 'good girl.'"[85]

Another possible explanation involved money. Promoters may have been less worried about white fans rioting than they were about white fans not showing up at events where Black performers were cheating to win against white performers. The job of a heel is to get heat—or a negative reaction—from the crowd. But there is the kind of heat that makes fans spend money to show up to an event in the hopes that the heel will lose and the kind of heat—known as "go-away heat" or "go-home heat"—that causes fans to not want to come to the match at all. Promoters of the era may have been worried that Black heels facing white babyfaces would generate go-away heat.

There was at least one instance of fan violence at a professional wrestling event around this time that broke down along racial lines. In August 1949—just a few years before Harvey brought his claim in the Texas courts—the Black Panther, Jim Mitchell, squared off against Gorgeous

George, the most famous heel wrestler of the era, in Los Angeles. As was common, Mitchell played the role of rule-abiding babyface.* As was his wont, "the Gorgeous One" employed some despicable tactics against Mitchell, which ultimately resulted in the referee stopping the match after Mitchell was tossed out of the ring. George apparently did his job as a heel a little too well, because a fan charged the ring, looking to get at him. Thus, the initial cause of fan violence seems to have had little to do with race. But eventually, the scene degenerated into what one news story described as a "full-scale riot,"[86] with the arena splitting along racial lines.[87] At least one person was stabbed.[88] Apparently, casting the Black performer as the good guy was no guarantee that race-based violence would not erupt.

The history of interracial boxing matches also presents something of a mixed picture in terms of the potential for such matches to trigger racial violence. There was, of course, the race-based violence that erupted following the Jack Johnson–James Jeffries fight in 1910. But nearly two decades earlier, another widely hyped interracial match that attracted national attention produced little in the way of race-based violence. Back in 1892, Black boxer George "Little Chocolate" Dixon fought white boxer Jack Skelly in New Orleans for the World Featherweight Championship before a segregated crowd. The interracial nature of the match took center stage in media accounts, with the *Boston Globe* observing that the fight would "test the color line at New Orleans."[89] A Dixon victory, the *Globe* reported, "would make the negro simply unbearable. It would be a local calamity."[90] The club where the fight was held had never previously allowed black spectators but was doing so on this occasion based upon Dixon's insistence.[91] (Black spectators were relegated to general admission seats in the upper deck.[92]) The fight ended up being a one-sided affair, with the *Chicago Daily Tribune* reporting that "the little darky" Dixon pummeled Skelly, prompting, in the words of the *Boston Globe*, "thousands of long faces among the whites."[93]

Some predicted that angry white fans would exact retribution against Black Dixon supporters, many of whom celebrated in the streets.[94] But no serious violence erupted. A Black Dixon fan was knocked down by "an indignant white man" after "imprudently talking too loud of Dixon's victory."[95] But there were no widespread clashes in the streets of New Orleans following the match.

However, the pride of some white southerners had been damaged. The president of the club where the Dixon–Skelly fight had taken place told reporters that the event had prompted members of the club to conclude

---

* For a brief period of time, Mitchell performed elsewhere as heel, thus probably making him the first Black wrestler to play the role of a heel.

that "there will be no more colored men fighting before the club."⁹⁶ In the eyes of many in the white press, it had been a mistake to match the two contestants in the first place because the result was that "thousands of vicious and ignorant negroes regard the victory of Dixon over Skelly as ample proof that the negro is equal, and superior to the white man."⁹⁷

Only two months earlier, racial order in New Orleans had been maintained when Homer Plessy was pulled off a train bound for Covington, Louisiana, and arrested for violating Louisiana's Separate Act, thus ultimately leading to the Supreme Court's decision in *Plessy v. Ferguson*. George Dixon had upset that order.

* * *

M.B. Morgan's official position in Sporty Harvey's case was that Texas's prohibition on interracial boxing and wrestling represented a valid exercise of the state's police power and was designed to prevent interracial violence. But other parts of his testimony suggest that there may have been other factors at play. Morgan testified that he feared that "the pleasant [read 'white'] customer who is now paying an admittance to see these contests" would lose interest and stop attending if there were interracial matches. He also feared that "[t]he papers will become disinterested and withdraw their support."⁹⁸ In short, M.B. Morgan didn't "think the people of Texas [were] quite ready for us to abandon our present segregation and restriction on boxing and wrestling."⁹⁹

The State of Texas prevailed at trial, but Harvey appealed. By this point, the United States Supreme Court had decided *Brown v. Board of Education*, thus calling into question the entire premise on which the "separate but equal doctrine" was based. The decision would have ramifications for Speedy Harvey.

On appeal, the Texas Court of Civil Appeals in Austin concluded that whatever the Texas Legislature's fears may have been about permitting interracial boxing and wrestling, those fears had proven unfounded over the years.¹⁰⁰ But the court went on to hold that "*[e]ven if* riotous conditions did result from mixed boxing exhibitions," the Supreme Court's decision in *Brown v. Board of Education* just five months earlier established that the state's racial classification was unconstitutional. The Texas court drew upon the language from the Supreme Court's decision in *Brown* and prior cases to the effect that the Fourteenth Amendment gave Black citizens the right to be free from "unfriendly legislation against them" that implied their inferiority in civil society and lessened "their enjoyment of the rights which others enjoy."¹⁰¹ The court concluded that it had "no hesitancy in declaring [the statute] to be in violation of the Fourteenth Amendment to the Constitution of the United States and is null and void."¹⁰² Sporty Harvey had prevailed.

* * *

The court's decision in *Harvey v. Morgan* helped end *de jure* (by law) segregation in the State of Texas as applied to boxing, wrestling, and other sporting events. Only a few months later, Harvey fought Buddy Turman in Dallas, Texas, in the first sanctioned professional boxing match between an African American and white fighter. Harvey lost that fight as, apparently, he did the majority of his other later fights.[103]* Nonetheless, Sporty Harvey—at best a mediocre fighter with a sixth-grade education—had established important legal precedent and delivered an important blow to Jim Crow. Others would follow in his footsteps.

* * *

Part 4: Joe Dorsey v. Jim Crow

Joe Dorsey was a popular Black fighter based in New Orleans. At one point, he was the eighth-ranked light heavyweight in the country. But like Speedy Harvey, he couldn't get enough decent fights in his home state to put food on the table due to Louisiana State Athletic Commission Rule 26, a rule that prohibited boxing or wrestling matches "between any person of the Caucasian or 'white' race and one of the African or 'Negro' race." Rule 26 further prohibited Black and white contestants from appearing on the same card.[104] "There were times when I didn't have money to buy food for my family," Dorsey would later say.[105] As a result Dorsey, who like Harvey had only a sixth-grade education, would work as a janitor for $45 a week in order to make ends meet. At the time, Dorsey was earning only $600 a year as a fighter when similarly ranked white fighters were earning much more.[106] So, like Harvey before him, Dorsey decided to sue for the right to fight white opponents.†

Dorsey was represented by Israel Meyer Augustine, Jr., who would go on to become the first Black elected criminal district judge in Louisiana, and Louis Berry, a Black civil rights lawyer who would go on to serve as dean of Southern University Law Center.[107] Dorsey's legal team filed suit on July 28, 1955, in the United States District for the Eastern District of Louisiana, alleging that the Commission's rule violated the Equal Protection Clause of the Fourteenth Amendment. The following year, the Louisiana legislature passed a new, broader piece of legislation, known as Act

---

* According to one source, Harvey's career record was 10–23–2.

† Several local sportswriters helped raised the necessary $350 to cover the costs of filing the case in federal court by passing a cigar box around Dorsey's neighborhood, seeking donations. A local barber reportedly donated $300 himself.

579, that extended beyond boxing and wrestling and prohibited any individual from putting on "athletic training, games, sports or contests and other such activities involving personal and social contacts, in which the participants or contestants are members of the white and negro races."[108] In other words, the law required that all athletic events in Louisiana be segregated. So, Dorsey amended his complaint to also challenge the constitutionality of this new law.

By this point, Louisiana had to contend not only with the Supreme Court's decision in *Brown v. Board of Education* but all of the subsequent lower court decisions applying the Court's holding from the case. Lower courts held that the Court's decision in the public school setting applied with equal force to a host of other settings, including race-based classifications at public golf courses, parks, beaches, swimming pools, buses, streetcars, and, of course, boxing and wrestling matches as reflected in *Harvey v. Morgan*.[109] So, Louisiana, faced an uphill battle. Just as the State of Texas had argued a few years earlier, Louisiana argued that the rule and the statute "were adopted under the State's police power as a necessary measure to preserve peace and good order."[110] But, drawing upon an earlier decision from the U.S. Fifth Circuit Court of Appeals, a three-judge panel of the court responded that "use of the term police power works no magic in itself."[111]

In the court's view, this was an easy case:

> Act 579 does not raise difficult issues involving the meaning of a law or the unconstitutional application of a statute apparently constitutional. Act 579 is not intended to circumvent desegregation by clever verbiage or by adroit administrative techniques. Act 579 is in the teeth of the School Segregation Cases, *Brown v. Board of Education of Topeka*, and other cases stemming from that decision; a clear challenge to the validity of those cases when a state legislature invokes the police power. In these circumstances this Court must hold with the plaintiff that, as to athletic contests, Act 579 of 1956 is unconstitutional on its face in that separation of Negroes and whites based solely on their being Negroes and whites is a violation of the Equal Protection Clause of the Fourteenth Amendment of the Constitution of the United States. Rule 26 is of course no less unconstitutional.[112]

Undaunted, the defendants appealed to the United States Supreme Court.[113] They argued that the holding from *Brown v. Board* and subsequent lower court decisions should not be extended to professional boxing. The provision of public education and the operation of golf courses, public parks, and similar government services are "generally considered to be beneficial in the community." In contrast, boxing has a sordid past, having "again and again, in many states in these United States, been declared an unlawful act."[114] Likewise, the Georgia Supreme had observed in 1946 that

10. Race Discrimination

professional wrestling by its nature is "brutal in character and dangerous to human life, and to affect the public peace, order, and morality of the community."[115] As a result, state athletic commissions had wide latitude to regulate boxing and wrestling.

As an example, the defendants pointed out that only a few years earlier, the Supreme Court of Oregon had ruled in *State v. Hunter* that the decision to deny a professional wrestling license to a woman—specifically on the grounds that she was a woman—did not amount to a violation of the Equal Protection Clause.* There, the Oregon Supreme Court explained that

> [t]here is no inherent right to engage in public exhibitions of boxing and wrestling. Both sports have long been licensed and regulated by [criminal] statute, and in some cases, absolutely prohibited. It is axiomatic that the 14th Amendment to the U.S. Constitution does not protect gross liberties which civilized states regard as properly subject to regulation by [criminal] law.[116]

In short, the boxing and wrestling rings were a far cry from classrooms and public parks, according to Louisiana and Oregon.

On May 25, 1959, the United States Supreme Court, without a written opinion, affirmed the district court's decision that Louisiana's Act 579 and Rule 26 were unconstitutional.[117] Dorsey had won.† Louisiana could no longer lawfully prohibit Black and white athletes from competing against each other. Reflecting upon the case years later, one of Dorsey's lawyers, Louis Berry, would say that he "was so thrilled when he heard the news that he pulled his car over to the side of the road and found himself laughing and crying at the same time."[118]

Dorsey's victory had implications for future court decisions. Future litigants and courts would go on to cite *Dorsey v. State Athletic Commission* in a number of cases, including other segregation claims,[119] claims by college football players who were disciplined for wearing black armbands in protest of race discrimination,[120] and voting rights.[121]

Part 5: Professional Wrestling and the Fight Against Jim Crow Outside of the Courtroom

Of course, the fact that Sporty Harvey and Joe Dorsey won their court cases didn't automatically mean that segregation in sports ended. Segregation backed by the force of law may have been declared to be

---

* The case is discussed in more detail in Chapter 6.
† Despite his victory in court, Joe Dorsey did not fight for six years following the Supreme Court's decision. According to his family, promoters blackballed Dorsey and prevented him from fighting.

unconstitutional, but de *facto* discrimination—or discrimination that took place as a result of custom and culture—remained solidly in place throughout the South. While state governments could no longer lawfully engage in segregation, some nonetheless continued to do so in defiance of the law. And private entities—restaurants, hotels, and sports arenas—remained free to discriminate.

After the Supreme Court held that segregation in public schools violated the Constitution in *Brown v. Board of Education* in 1954, the Court issued a second opinion a year later to explain how its decision needed to be implemented. Recognizing that public education consisted of a patchwork of regional, state, and local approaches, the Court decided against imposing a deadline or a one-size-fits all standard and instead declared that individual states must desegregate schools "with all deliberate speed."[122]

Southern politicians responded with a call for "massive resistance" to desegregation efforts.[123] In 1956, over 100 members of Congress—all from states that formerly comprised the Confederacy—signed the so-called "Southern Manifesto," a document attacking the Court's decision in *Brown* and urging resistance to integration.[124] In an extreme example of the resistance to desegregation efforts, officials in Prince Edward County, Virginia, closed down its public school system rather than comply with *Brown*'s integration order.[125]

* * *

Ultimately, the civil rights movement was as much about non-lawyers being willing to run a gauntlet of jeering protesters on the way to class, sit at segregated restaurant counters, and risk imprisonment and police brutality as it was lawyers and elected officials changing the law. Sports also played a significant role in helping to bring about the end of desegregation.

Jackie Robinson famously broke the color line in Major League Baseball in 1947, and he just as famously had to endure a wide range of racist behavior targeting him in the process. Those who followed behind him may have had an easier time of things, but they still had to regularly confront segregationist practices as they traveled around the country. And while the color line in baseball may have been broken, Black players still faced some resistance. For example, it would take the Boston Red Sox twelve years from Jackie Robinson's signing and five years from the *Brown v. Board of Education* decision to put their first Black player, Pumpsie Green, into a game. Many minor league baseball stadiums still had segregated seating going into the 1960s.[126]

Full integration came slowly in other sports as well. The Washington

Redskins were the last NFL team to finally integrate—under direct pressure from the federal government—when they signed wide receiver Bobby Mitchell in 1962.* It was not until 1961 that Professional Golfers' Association (PGA) removed its "Caucasian-only" clause from its bylaws that prevented non-white golfers from competing on the PGA Tour. Charlie Sifford became the first Black member of the Tour three years later but still could not eat at some of the clubhouses at courses where he played.[127] It was not until 1975 that golfer Lee Elder broke the color barrier at Augusta National at the Masters golf tournament. He received death threats for doing so.[128] Again, it took a small number of brave individuals willing to endure the subtle and overt forms of discrimination to put a meaningful dent in segregated sports.

* * *

The wrestling world had its own set of trailblazers. There was "Sailor" Art Thomas, who was able to draw a huge crowd in Chicago in 1961 facing white wrestler "Nature Boy" Buddy Rogers.[129] There was Luther Lindsay, widely recognized as the first Black wrestler to wrestle white competitors south of Washington, D.C., in the 1950s. Lindsay was the first to wrestle an interracial match in Texas back in 1955 and the first Black wrestler to challenge for the National Wrestling Alliance World Heavyweight Championship.[130] When he came to Kingsport, Tennessee, in 1965 to wrestle white heel Ron Wright, the National Guard was brought in to ensure order. But as a testament to the talents of Lindsay and Wright, the white East Tennessee crowd rallied behind Lindsay.[131]

There was Bearcat Wright, a boxer turned wrestler who was suspended by the Indiana Athletic Commission after announcing during a show in Gary, Indiana, in 1960 that he would no longer participate in racially segregated matches.[132] The NAACP took up Wright's cause and, according to Wright at the time, "mixed wrestling" began "opening everywhere."[133] There was another Bearcat—Bearcat Brown—who played in important role in the desegregation of the business. In 1963, Birmingham, Alabama's Commissioner of Public Safety, Eugene "Bull" Connor, famously ordered police to release attack dogs to disperse civil rights protesters. It was around that same time Brown and his white tag-team partner, Len Rossi, integrated wrestling in Birmingham by teaming together, reportedly resulting in bomb threats at the venue.[134]

But the Black wrestler who perhaps did the most to integrate professional wrestling during this era was Bobo Brazil. Standing six feet six

---

* *Washington Post* sportswriter Shirley Povich once observed that the team's colors were "burgundy, gold, and Caucasian."

inches, Brazil was a big draw throughout the country during the 1950s and 1960s. Often referred to as the "Jackie Robinson of professional wrestling," Brazil attracted Black and white fans alike and frequently competed with and against white wrestlers during this era.[135] As author David Shoemaker put it, Brazil "became so popular wherever he went that race hardly seemed to matter in his feuds."[136]

While Brazil may have been accepted in the ring while competing against white wrestlers, he still had to endure the indignities of Jim Crow laws as he made his way around the country. Wrestler Killer Kowalski explained

> Some of these hotel managers had come to the arenas and paid to see him wrestle me and cheered Brazil, but then when he wanted to rent a room to sleep for the night, they apologized and refused him. I'd later quietly sneak him into my room to share it with me later on in the middle of the night, which I did many, many times. It was very ugly, an ugly time, and it happened in so many towns around the country.[137]

It wasn't until October 9, 1970, that the city of Atlanta saw a racially mixed wrestling match, which, naturally, featured Brazil.[138]

In short, it took the willingness of men like Brazil, Lindsay, Wright, Brown, and Thomas to endure the indignities of racial discrimination to truly break down the racial barriers in the wrestling business, particularly in the South. Said Kowalski, "Bobo or Bearcat Wright or 'Sailor' Art Thomas acted like it didn't bother them, but you always knew in your heart that it hurt them very deeply. I could feel their disappointment in their fellow man and the hurt."[139]

* * *

> "If he thought somebody was getting a raw deal, he'd jump in and try and help."
> —Jo Ann Brumbaugh, speaking about her husband, Sputnik Monroe.[140]

Memphis, Tennessee, was one of those cities that was still dragging its feet when it came to desegregation following *Brown v. Board of Education*. In 1960, a group of plaintiffs had sued in federal court to force Memphis to desegregate its municipal parks and other city-owned places of recreation. The City responded by saying it needed more time to do so and that it needed to proceed at slow and gradual pace. The trial court largely bought the City's argument and gave the City six months to develop a new plan for desegregating the facilities. Under the City's proposed plan, desegregation of city-owned facilities would not be complete until 1971.[141] The plaintiffs appealed, but the U.S. Court of Appeals for the Sixth Circuit sided with the City.¹⁴² Ultimately, it took a decision from the United States Supreme Court in 1963—some nine years after *Brown* was decided—to declare that the City had stalled long enough and that it was time to fully desegregate its parks and recreational facilities.¹⁴³

* * *

It was against this backdrop that wrestler Sputnik Monroe performed at the Ellis Auditorium in Memphis. Legend has it that in 1957, the white "Rock Monroe" picked up a Black hitchhiker on his way to a television taping in Mobile, Alabama. Once inside, Monroe would pull back the curtain and pretend to kiss the hitchhiker on the cheek in order to antagonize the crowd.¹⁴⁴ A white woman was so outraged that she responded with an unusual insult inspired by the Soviet Union's recent success in launching the first satellite: she called Monroe "a damn Sputnik."¹⁴⁵ Henceforth, "Rock" Monroe would go by the first name "Sputnik." When he arrived in Memphis, Monroe was a fully formed heel, boasting about being "235 pounds of twisted steel and sex appeal."¹⁴⁶

Monroe's act caught on and attendance at wrestling shows increased. News reports at the time described Monroe as "the most hated man in Memphis," which, of course, was good for business.¹⁴⁷ "When he came to Memphis, they were averaging 300 people a night (at wrestling shows). By the time he started wrestling, 7,000 people were coming out to see him," said one of Monroe's friends years later. "He could've run for mayor and could've been elected. That's how big he was in this town."¹⁴⁸ A 1959 match between Monroe and babyface Billy Wicks with boxing great Rocky Marciano as the guest referee drew a reported crowd of 13,749 fans, an indoor-arena attendance record in Memphis that reportedly stood for more than 30 years.¹⁴⁹*

When he wasn't wrestling, Monroe was hanging out in bars populated almost exclusively by Black patrons, where he would sometimes hand out tickets to his matches. According to a news report, Monroe was arrested in 1960 on a charge of disorderly conduct for the apparent crime of "drinking in a negro café with [Negroes]."¹⁵⁰ He hired Russell B. Sugramon, Jr., a Black lawyer who would go on to become a judge, as his attorney in what the trial judge said was "the first time he [could] recall that a white man was represented in City Court by a negro attorney." Monroe ended up being fined $26.¹⁵¹

* * *

---

* Monroe was something of a Memphis folk hero. One story has Monroe dyeing a goose pink, placing a rhinestone collar around its neck, and then walking the goose down Beale Street in Memphis on a leash.

Monroe owed much of his success to Black wrestling fans. Memphis' Ellis Auditorium ran regular wrestling events at the time. Seating was segregated. Black patrons would enter through a side entrance and watch from the balcony while white patrons sat below.[152] Ever the contrarian, Monroe would play to the balcony. Despite ostensibly being a heel, Monroe was a fan favorite among Black fans in Memphis. "Sputnik wouldn't even look at the white people who were booing him when he came into the ring," said one of his friends. "Then all of sudden out of nowhere he'd would look up and raise both arms in the air to the balcony. And every single black person in the balcony would stand up and raise their hands and cheer him."[153]

By this point, Monroe had some leverage due to his ability to draw fans, and he decided to use it. Seating in the balcony for black patrons was limited. "[T]hey had a guy counting the white door and a Black counting the black door," said music producer and Sputnik Monroe fan Jim Dickinson.[154] And there were more Black fans than there were seats in the balcony. Monroe first tried to appeal to the business sense of promoters, arguing that they could make more money if they let in more Black fans who could help fill the seats on the floor. When that apparently didn't work, Monroe bribed an employee to let more Black fans in the auditorium so that there was no room for them all in the balcony.[155] Eventually, Monroe threatened to quit unless promoters opened up the lower level. "I had the power because I'm selling out the place, the first guy that ever did, and they damn sure wanted the revenue," Monroe would say.[156] The promoters caved.[157]

* * *

Although Monroe's act of defiance didn't magically end segregation in Memphis, it was, in the words of his former lawyer, Russell Sugarmon, "the first domino to fall in integrating public entertainment in Memphis."[158] While the City of Memphis continued to stall the desegregation of its public parks, segregation in other settings slowly started to give way. Sugarmon recalled trying to purchase theater tickets around this time with his wife and being denied. According to Sugarmon, "The committees that were working on those things said 'Well, we have to integrate these things slowly; we don't want to upset the unwashed masses.' And we said, 'Well, the unwashed masses are getting along quite fine sitting alongside each other at the wrestling matches!'"[159]

A plaque at the Rock 'n' Soul Museum in Memphis, a music museum, celebrates the accomplishments of this bad-guy wrestler: "Sputnik Monroe played a major part in destroying the color lines in Memphis entertainment venues."[160]

* * *

Part 6: Conclusion

It took the efforts of individuals who were willing to fight for their rights in the courts, the lawyers who represented them, and individuals who were willing to risk their well-being and careers for the cause of civil rights to put the first significant dents in the Jim Crow South. Their efforts helped pave the way for the most important piece of civil rights legislation in U.S. history: the Civil Rights Act of 1964.

President Lyndon Johnson signed the Civil Rights Act of 1964 on July 2, 1964. Title II of the Act covers places of public accommodation—hotels, restaurants, and movie theaters as well as "sports arena[s], stadium[s] or other place[s] of exhibition or entertainment."[161] Congress may not have had professional wrestling and boxing specifically in mind when it considered Title II, but the new legislation prohibited segregated wrestling and boxing events as well as segregated lunch counters and hotels.

The twin punch of Title II and *Brown v. Board of Education* would help put an end to Jim Crow practices in the South, including in the athletic and entertainment fields. But it took time. For example, it wasn't until 1968 that a YMCA in Raleigh, North Carolina, was forced to desegregate when lawyers successfully relied upon Title II to put an end to the facility's discriminatory membership practices.[162] And it wasn't until 1969 that a parish in Louisiana was forced to construct decent athletic fields for predominately Black schools.[163]

It also took decades for the most blatant forms of racism in professional wrestling to subside. Racist stereotypes involving Black wrestlers would persist for years after *Brown v. Board of Education* and the passage of the Civil Rights Act of 1964. It wasn't until 1992 that professional wrestling recognized its first Black World Heavyweight Champion when Ron Simmons won the WCW crown. And it wasn't until years later that the presence of a Black World Heavyweight Champion ceased to be an unusual occurrence. But in order for that to happen, it took people like Viro Small, Jim Mitchell, Thurgood Marshall, Sporty Harvey, Maury Maverick, Jr., Joe Dorsey, Bobo Brazil, and Sputnik Monroe to pave the way.

Chapter Notes

Chapter 1

1. Peter W. Kaplan, "TV Notes: ABC Reporter May Sue Wrestler Who Sued Him," *N.Y. Times*, Feb. 23, 1985, https://www.nytimes.com/1985/02/23/arts/tv-notes-abc-reporter-may-sue-wrestler-who-hit-him.html.

2. David Margolick, "Lawyers Go to the Mat in the Battle Between Hulk Hogan and a 98-Pound Comedian," *N.Y. Times*, Jan. 5, 1990, https://www.nytimes.com/1990/01/05/us/law-bar-lawyers-go-mat-battle-between-hulk-hogan-98-pound-comedian.html; Lifetime Network, Hot Properties (first aired March 27, 1985), https://www.youtube.com/watch?v=i7n_SHrK408.

3. Vice TV, "David Schultz & the Slap Heard Round the World" (first aired April 28, 2020).

4. Margolick, *supra* note 2; Hulk Hogan, *Hollywood Hulk Hogan* 156 (2002), https://books.google.com/books?id=ctSR_k_960UC&pg=PA156&lpg=PA156&dq=RICHARD+BELZER+%22CHEZ+HOGAN%22&source=bl&ots=-FNC98Da9Q&sig=ACfU3U3wp0EC0tyrzH-C2sb7q3WzpO9m_w&hl=en&sa=X&ved=2ahUKEwjV5OGpz_btAhUHWq0KHfVyADc4ChDoATAMegQIARAC#v=onepage&q=RICHARD%20BELZER%20%22CHEZ%20HOGAN%22&f=false; ESPN, *Up Close with Roy Firestone* (first aired 1990), https://www.youtube.com/watch?v=7ICoZV4ZEjg; Jesse Ellison, "Richard Belzer on His Debut Novel, Hulk Hogan, and Not Being Related to the Fonz" (Oct. 4, 2008), *Vulture*, https://www.vulture.com/2008/10/richard_belzer_on_his_debut_no.html.

5. *Belzer v. Bollea*, 571 N.Y.S.2d 365 (N.Y. Sup. Ct. 1990).

6. Shaun Assael & Mike Mooneyham, *Sex, Lies, and Headlocks* 11 (2002).

7. Wrestling Perspective, http://wrestlingperspective.com/working/1898/brookeag1106.html.

8. Tim Hornbaker, *National Wrestling Alliance: The Untold Story of the Monopoly that Strangled Pro Wrestling* 6 (ECW Press 2007).

9. David Shoemaker, *The Squared Circle: Life, Death, and Professional Wrestling* 18–19 (2013).

10. *Id.* at 23 (quoting Joel Sayre, "The Pullman Theseus," *The New Yorker*, March 5, 1932, at 26).

11. Gerald F. Hess, "Heads and Hearts: The Teaching and Learning Environment in Law School," 52 *J. Legal Educ.* 75, 78–79 (2002).

12. Thomas C. Galligan, Jr., "The Tragedy in Torts," 5 *Cornell J.L. & Pub. Pol'y* 139, 148–49 (1996).

13. Iman Zekri, "Respectfully Dissenting: How Dissenting Opinions Shape the Law and Impact Collegiality Among Judges," 94 *Fla. B.J.* 6, 9 (Sep./Oct. 2020).

14. *White v. Frenkel*, 615 So. 2d 535, 539 (La. Ct. App. 1993); *Bergeron v. State Boxing and Wrestling Com'n*, 829 So.2d 620, 621 (La. Ct. App. 2002).

15. *Massey v. Jim Crockett Promotions, Inc.*, Plaintiffs' Petition for an Appeal from a Final Order of the Circuit Court of Raleigh County, West Virginia, Oct. 12, 1989; *Poffo v. Gulas et al.*, Civil Action No. 79-147, *Deposition of Jerry Jarrett*, at 24 (Dec. 16, 1981).

16. *Silvia v. Woodhouse*, 248 N.E.2d 260, 263 (Mass. 1969).

17. *Langness v. Ketonen*, 255 P.2d 551, 554 (Wash. 1953).
18. *Myers v. George*, 271 F.2d 168, 171 (8th Cir. 1959).
19. *Id.* at 174.
20. Peter Kerr, "Now it Can Be Told: Those Pro Wrestlers Are Just Having Fun," *N.Y. Times*, Feb. 19, 1989, at A1; Assael & Mooneyham, *supra* note 6, at 83.
21. Keenan Salla, *Shoot Interviews and the Emerging Oral History of American Professional Wrestling*, https://www.academia.edu/20146442/Shoot_Interviews_and_the_Emerging_Oral_History_of_American_Professional_Wrestling.
22. *Id.*
23. "Jarrett Suits Hit TAC, Gulas," *The Commercial Appeal*, Feb. 16, 1978, at 50.
24. Nancy J. Knauer, "Legal Fictions and Juristic Truth," 23 *St. Thomas L. Rev.* 70, 119 (2010).
25. Ryan Holiday, *Conspiracy* 225 (Portfolio/Penguin 2018).

Chapter 2

1. Model Rules of Pro. Conduct rs. 3.1, 3.3 (Am. Bar Ass'n 2020).
2. Bobby Matthews, "Ron Garvin and Bob Roop: How Stealing the Title Led to a Rebellion," *Pro Wrestling Stories* https://prowrestlingstories.com/pro-wrestling-stories/ron-garvin-boob-roop-rebellion/.
3. *NWA Southeastern Wrestling Inc. v. Garvin*, No. 66591, Trial Transcript at 8 (Knox County Chancery Court, Feb. 13, 1980).
4. *Id.* at 5–7.
5. *Id.* at 7.
6. *NWA Southeastern Wrestling Inc. v. Garvin*, No. 66591, Complaint ¶ 3, June 6, 1979.
7. "Write or Wrong," *The Knoxville News-Sentinel*, June 17, 1979, at 38 (Letters to the Editor).
8. *NWA Southeastern Wrestling Inc. v. Garvin*, No. 66591, Amendment to Complaint, June 18, 1979.
9. Matthews, *supra* note 2.
10. *NWA Southeastern Wrestling Inc. v. Garvin*, No. 66591, Trial Transcript at 6 (Knox County Chancery Court, Feb. 13, 1980).
11. *Id.* at 15–17.
12. *Id.* at 22–23.
13. *Aegis Investigative Grp. v. Metro. Gov't of Nashville & Davidson Cnty.*, 98 S.W.3d 159, 162–63 (Tenn. Ct. App. 2002).
14. *Burton v. City of Spokane*, 482 P.3d 968, 970 (Wash. Ct. App. 2021).
15. *NWA Southeastern Wrestling Inc. v. Garvin*, No. 66591, Trial Transcript at 9 (Knox County Chancery Court, Feb. 13, 1980).
16. Matthews, *supra* note 2.
17. *Mason v. Evans*, 1 N.J.L. 182, 186 (N.J. Sup. Ct. 1793).
18. *Keystone Driller Co. v. Gen. Excavator Co.*, 290 U.S. 240, 244–45 (1933).
19. *Kendall-Jackson Winery Ltd. v. Superior Court*, 90 Cal. Rptr. 2d 743, 749 (Cal. Ct. App. 1999).
20. *Blain v. Doctor's Co.*, 272 Cal. Rptr. 250, 256–57 (Cal. Ct. App. 1990).
21. *NWA Southeastern Wrestling Inc. v. Garvin*, No. 66591, Trial Transcript at 37–39 (Knox County Chancery Court, Feb. 13, 1980).
22. *Id.* at 39.
23. *Id.* at 41–42.
24. *Id.* at 42.
25. Matthews, *supra* note 2.
26. "Judge Pins Fake Wrestling Scheme," *Knoxville News-Sentinel*, Feb. 13, 1980, at 46.
27. *NWA Southeastern Wrestling Inc. v. Garvin*, No. 66591, Complaint ¶¶ 3–5, June 6, 1979.
28. *ABF Freight Sys., Inc. v. NLRB*, 510 U.S. 317, 323 (1994).
29. https://www.youtube.com/watch?v=s-I3ugh_KWE.
30. Peter Kerr, "Now it Can Be Told: Those Pro Wrestlers Are Just Having Fun," *N.Y. Times*, Feb. 19, 1989, at A1.
31. Jim Wilson, *Chokehold: Pro Wrestling's Real Mayhem Outside the Ring* 38–39 (2003).
32. *Kathleen Crass v. Ronald Welch a/k/a Ron Fuller & Southeastern Gulf Coast Wrestling, Inc.*, No. 1-141-87, Complaint at ¶ 7 (Knox County Circuit Court March 11, 1987).
33. *Id.* at ¶ 8.
34. *Kathleen Crass v. Ronald Welch a/k/a Ron Fuller & Southeastern Gulf Coast Wrestling, Inc.*, No. 1-141-87, Deposition of Ronald Edward Welch a/k/a Ron Fuller at 9, Nov. 21, 1988.
35. *Id.* at 15.
36. *Id.* at 20.

37. *Id.*
38. *Id.* at 13.
39. *Id.* at 21.
40. *Id.* at 30–31.
41. *Kathleen Crass v. Ronald Welch a/k/a Ron Fuller & Southeastern Gulf Coast Wrestling, Inc.*, No. 1-141-87, Motion in Limine, Jan. 12, 1989.

Chapter 3

1. For a story about the incident following the death of Ox Baker, see Doug Brown, "Wrestling Legend Ox Baker—Whose 1974 Match Caused a Riot in Cleveland—Dies at 80," *Cleveland Scene*, Oct. 20, 2014, https://www.clevescene.com/scene-and-heard/archives/2014/10/20/wrestling-legend-ox-baker-whose-1974-match-caused-a-riot-in-cleveland-dies-at-80.
2. *Massey v. Jim Crockett Promotions, Inc.*, 400 S.E.2d 876, 878 n.5 (W. Va. 1990) (per curiam).
3. *Id.* at 881 n.8.
4. *Id.* at 881 n.9.
5. *Id.* at 878 & n.6.
6. *Massey v. Jim Crockett Promotions, Inc.*, Plaintiffs' Petition for an Appeal from a Final Order of the Circuit Court of Raleigh County, West Virginia, *8, Oct. 12, 1989.
7. *Massey*, 400 S.E.2d at 881 n.10.
8. *Id.* at 878.
9. *Id.* at 880.
10. *Id.* at 880.
11. Mahala Strauss, "Trial Date Set for Raleigh Man's Suit Against Tag Team Wrestlers," *Beckley Register-Herald*, Apr. 7, 1989, at 9A.
12. *Id.*
13. *Massey*, 400 S.E.2d at 878.
14. *Camp v. Rex, Inc.*, 24 N.E.2d 4 (Mass. 1939); *Lawson v. Clawson*, 9 A.2d 755 (Md. 1939); *see also Begin v. Georgia Championship Wrestling*, 322 S.E.2d 737 (Ga. Ct. App. 1984) (involving spectator who was injured at a professional wrestling event when she tripped and fell on plastic sheets on the floor).
15. Restatement (Second) of Torts § 315(b) (1965); *Isaacs v. Huntington Memorial Hosp.*, 695 P.2d 653, 657 (Cal. 1985).
16. *Whitfield v. Cox*, 52 S.E.2d 72, 73 (Va. 1949).
17. *Reynolds v. Deep South Sports, Inc.*, 211 So. 2d 37, 39 (Fla. Ct. App. 1968) (quoting *Stevenson v. Kansas City*, 360 P.2d 1 (Kan. 1961).
18. *Whitfield v. Cox*, 52 S.E.2d 72, 73 (Va. 1949).
19. *Id.* at 74. *But see Sample v. Eaton*, 302 P.2d 431 (Cal. App. 2d. 1956) (denying summary judgment to promoter where customer was hit by a flying Coca Cola bottle after fans had been throwing items into the ring for several minutes and no one made any effort to stop the behavior).
20. *Whitfield*, 52 S.E.2d at 76.
21. *Id.* at 75.
22. *Murphy v. Steeplechase Amusement Co.*, 166 N.E. 173 (N.Y. 1929).
23. *Id.* at 174.
24. *Id.*
25. *Id.*
26. *Whitfield*, 52 S.E.2d at 75–76.
27. *Pierce v. Murnick*, 145 S.E.2d 11, 12 (N.C. 1965) (per curiam) (emphasis added).
28. *Id.* at 12.
29. *C. & M. Promotions v. Ryland*, 158 S.E.2d 132 (Va. 1967).
30. *Id.* at 135.
31. *Id.* at 134.
32. *See, e.g., The T.J. Hooper*, 60 F.3d 737 (2d Cir. 1932) (stating an industry "never may set its own tests. ... Courts must in the end say what is [reasonable]").
33. Mike Mooneyham, "Attempted WWE Fan Attack Evokes Memories of Bygone Era, "*The Post and Courier* (Charleston, SC), Aug. 20, 2016, https://www.postandcourier.com/staff/mike_mooneyham/attempted-wwe-fan-attack-evokes-memories-of-bygone-era/article_822fb223-fda0-57f6-b9dd-877ebc60b617.html; "Wrestler Ole Anderson Stabbed," *Greenville News*, May 25, 1976 (reproduced at https://www.midatlanticwrestling.net/resourcecenter/gateway_remembers/oleandersonstabbing/5-25_article.htm.
34. Mike Gibson, "Pro Wrestling Peaked in Knoxville Long Before the WWE," *Metro Pulse* (Knoxville, TN), March 4, 2004, https://monkeyfire.com/mpol/dir_zine/dir_2004/1410/t_cover.html.
35. Jack Encarnacao, "In City's Wrestling Prime, No Holds were Barred," *Boston Globe*, Sep. 26, 2004, http://archive.boston.com/news/local/massachusetts/articles/2004/09/26/in_citys_

wrestling_prime_no_holds_were_barred/?page=full.

36. *See Ramsey v. Kallio*, 62 So. 2d 146 (La. Ct. App. 1952) (involving alleged attack by wrestler upon fan); *Frick v. Ensor*, 557 So.2d 1022 (La. Ct. App. 1990) (involving alleged attack by professional wrestler Buddy Landell upon fan); *Johnson v. Mid-South Sports, Inc.*, 806 P.2d 1107 (Okla. 1991) (involving attack by one fan upon another); *Smith v. McDaniel*, 503 F. Supp. 13 (N.D. Ga. 1980) (involving lawsuit stemming from an alleged attack by wrestler Chief Wahoo McDaniel upon a fan); *Sills v. Mid-South Sports*, 550 So. 2d 909, 911 (La. Ct. App. 1989) (involving attack upon a fan by Hacksaw Jim Duggan after the fan had allegedly thrown a cup of ice at Duggan); "Wrestler Sued by Spectator," *Knoxville News-Sentinel*, Dec. 29, 1983, at 10 (detailing lawsuit by fan against wrestler Ronnie Garvin). *Frick v. Ensor*, 557 So. 2d 1022, 1024 (La. Ct. App. 1990).

37. *Massey v. Jim Crockett Promotions, Inc.*, Plaintiffs' Petition for an Appeal from a Final Order of the Circuit Court of Raleigh County, West Virginia, *13, Oct. 12, 1989.

38. A video of the interview Cornette gives in which he says this (and lots of other mean things about West Virginia) is available on YouTube. https://www.youtube.com/watch?v=glll1qH20SI.

39. *Massey v. Jim Crockett Promotions, Inc.*, 400 S.E.2d 876, 880 (W. Va. 1990) (per curiam).

40. *See Sills v. Mid-South Sports*, 550 So. 2d 909 (La. Ct. App. 1989). ("The Monroe Civic Center requires the promoters of wrestling matches to hire off-duty uniformed policemen to escort the wrestlers to and from the ring and provide them protection from the fans whom the bad guys have intentionally incited and made unruly.")

41. Podcast, *Jim Cornette Experience*, Episode 364, Jan. 15, 2021.

42. *Massey v. Jim Crockett Promotions, Inc.*, Plaintiffs' Petition for an Appeal from a Final Order of the Circuit Court of Raleigh County, West Virginia, *7, Oct. 12, 1989.

43. Restatement (Second) of Agency § 228 (1958).

44. *Massey*, 400 S.E.2d at 882.

45. *See, e.g., LeBrane v. Lewis*, 292 So. 2d 216 (La. 1974) (holding that supervisor who stabbed subordinate on company premises in the course of a work-related dispute acted within the scope of employment).

46. In one instance, a 77-year-old fan was injured by a referee after tapping the referee on the shoulder on his way back to the dressing room. *Ulrich v. Minneapolis Boxing & Wrestling Club*, 129 N.W.2d 288 (Minn. 1964).

47. *Langness v. Ketonen*, 255 P.2d 551, 553 (Wash. 1953).

48. *Id.*

49. *Id.* at 555.

50. *Wiersma v. City of Long Beach*, 106 P.2d 45 (Cal. Ct. App. 1940).

51. *Id.* at 46.

52. *Id.* at 48.

53. "Some Defendants Dismissed From Suit Against Wrestlers," *Beckley Register-Herald*, May 25, 1989, at 5A.

54. "Man Calls Wrestling Incident an Attack," *Beckley Evening Post*, Page 2 A, June 3, 1987.

55. "'Express' Suit Settled," *Times-Picayune*, Aug. 19, 1991, at C-7, https://infoweb-newsbank-com.proxy.lib.utk.edu/apps/readex/doc?p=EANX&sort=YMD_date%3AA&page=7&fld-base-0=alltext&val-base-0=%22stan%20lane%22&val-database-0=&fld-database-0=database&fld-nav-0=YMD_date&val-nav-0=&docref=image/v2%3A1223BCE-5B718A166%40EANX-16D4905FC-9C6E87C%402448484-16D37DA8C-3F41A08%4094-16D37DA8C-3F41A08%40&firsthit=yesm.

56. http://www.thesmokinggun.com/file/ackerman-lawsuit.

Chapter 4

1. Wayne D. Collins, "Trusts and the Origins of Antitrust Legislation," 81 *Fordham L. Rev.* 2279, 2280–81 (2013).

2. *Id.* at 2281.

3. *Id.* at 2293.

4. *Id.*

5. *Id.* at 2308–09.

6. 15 U.S.C. § 1 et seq.

7. 15 U.S.C. § 1; *Standard Oil Co. of N.J. v. United States*, 221 U.S. 1, 58 (1911).

8. Patrick Donathen, "Post-and-Hold Laws: Has the Second Circuit Authorized

Liquor Cartels in the Face of the Sherman Antitrust Act?," 83 *U. Pitt. L. Rev.* 167, 170 (2021).

9. 15 U.S.C. § 2.

10. 15 U.S.C. § 15(a) (b).

11. Tim Hornbaker, *National Wrestling Alliance: The Untold Story of the Monopoly that Strangled Pro Wrestling* 22–23 (ECW Press 2007).

12. *See Continental TV, Inc. v. GTE Sylvania, Inc.*, 433 U.S. 36 (1977).

13. Benjamin J. Larson, "Antitrust for All: A Primer for the Non-Antitrust Practitioner," *Colo. Law.*, October 2014, at 20.

14. Rochella T. Davis, "Talent Can't Be Allocated: A Labor Economics Justification for No-Poaching Agreement Criminality in Antitrust Regulation," 12 *Brook. J. Corp. Fin. & Com. L.* 279, 294 (2018).

15. *United States v. Topco Assoc., Inc.*, 405 U.S. 596, 607–608 (1972).

16. *Eastern States Retail Lumber Dealers' Ass'n v. U.S.*, 234 U.S. 600 (1914).

17. Hornbaker, *supra* note 11, at 25.

18. Hornbaker, *supra* note 11, at 15–16.

19. Jim Wilson, *Chokehold: Pro Wrestling's Real Mayhem Outside the Ring* 244 (2003).

20. Hornbaker, *supra* note 11, at 145–47.

21. *National Wrestling Alliance v. Myers*, 325 F.2d 768, 772 (8th Cir. 1963).

22. *Id.* at 772.

23. Hornbaker, *supra* note 11, at 147–48.

24. Hornbaker, *supra* note 11, at 159.

25. Wilson, *supra* note 19, at 239.

26. Wilson, *supra* note 19, at 245.

27. *United States v. National Wrestling Alliance*, Civil Action No. 3–729, 1956 Trade Case (CCH) P68,507 (S.D Iowa October 15, 1956).

28. *Contos v. Capitol Wrestling Corp.*, Civil Action No. 576–60, 1963 Trade Cas. (CCH) P70,737 (D.D.C. April 10, 1963).

29. Wilson, *supra* note 19, at 188–89.

30. Wilson, *supra* note 19, at 193–95.

31. Wilson, *supra* note 19, at 272–75.

32. Wilson, *supra* note 19, at 275.

33. *Von Poppenheim v. Portland Boxing and Wrestling Commission*, 442 F.2d 1047 (9th Cir. 1971); *Murdock v. City of Jacksonville, Fla.*, 361 F. Supp. 1083 (M.D. Fla. 1973); *International Wrestling Association & John Powers v. Jim Crockett Promotions, Inc.*, No. C-C76-32 (W.D.N.C. Jan. 26, 1976); *James M. Wilson v. National Wrestling Alliance*, no. C-76-1625A (N.D. Ga. Sep. 20, 1976); *James M. Wilson v. National Wrestling Alliance*, no. -79-1210A (N.D. Ga. July 17, 1979); *Gunkel Enterprises, Inc. v. National Wrestling Alliance, Inc.*, no. C-76-2059A (N.D. Ga. Dec. 17, 1976); *Angelo Poffo et al. v. Nick Gulas et al.*, no. 79-147 (E.D. Ky. August 22, 1979).

34. Wilson, *supra* note 19, at 274.

35. "Promoter Gulas Retires from Wrestling Work," *The Tennessean*, Aug. 30, 1980, at 16; Max York, "The King of Wrestling," *The Tennessean*, May 18, 1975, at 151.

36. Larry Woody, "Mat Men: Gulas Pioneered the Sport," *The Tennessean*, July 10, 1985, at 11; Max York, "The King of Wrestling," *The Tennessean*, May 18, 1975, at 151.

37. Wilson, *supra* note 19, at 280–81.

38. Wilson, *supra* note 19, at 275.

39. Wilson, *supra* note 19, at 281 (2003).

40. Joel Bierig, "Tug of War Is on for Memphis Wrestling Limelight," *The Commercial Appeal*, March 20, 1977, at 37.

41. Ron Russell, "The Grapple Capital," *The Commercial Appeal*, Nov. 26, 1978, at 307.

42. Jerry Jarrett, *The Best of Times* 32–33 (2011).

43. *Id.* at 54.

44. *Id.* at 60.

45. *Id.* at 103–07.

46. *Id.* at 116–19.

47. *Id.* at 124.

48. Joel Bierig, "Tug of War Is on for Memphis Wrestling Limelight," *The Commercial Appeal*, March 20, 1977, at 37.

49. Mark James, *Memphis Wrestling History Presents: 1977 The War for Memphis* 56–57 (2014). According to this account, WHBQ feared there would be a lawsuit as a result of the Gulas/Jarrett split and "didn't want to be associated publicly with a lawsuit over a lowbrow wrestling company." *Id.* at 56.

50. Ron Cobb, "Wrestling Camps Fight for Home," *Memphis Press-Scimitar*, April 28, 1977, at 23.

51. *Id.*

52. "Jarrett Suits Hit TAC, Gulas," *The Commercial Appeal*, Feb. 16, 1978, at 50.

53. *Id.*

54. "Promoter Charges Wrestling Balks," *The Tenneseean*, 16, May 27, 1978.

55. *Gulas Wrestling Enterprises, Inc. v. Louie Heinman a/k/a Las Vegas Louie, Ron Garfield a/k/a Earl White, Don Garfield a/k/a/ Don Garfield Kalt a/k/a Don Fargo, Jarrett Enterprises, Inc., Welch Enterprises, Inc., Jarrett Welch Wrestling Co. and their Agents*, No. 78-79-1, Complaint at 8-9 (Davidson County Chancery Court May 28, 1978).

56. *Trau-Med of Am., Inc. v. Allstate Ins. Co.*, 71 S.W.3d 691, 701 (Tenn. 2002).

57. *Gulas Wrestling Enterprises, Inc. v. Louie Heinman a/k/a Las Vegas Louie, Ron Garfield a/k/a Earl White, Don Garfield a/k/a/ Don Garfield Kalt a/k/a Don Fargo, Jarrett Enterprises, Inc., Welch Enterprises, Inc., Jarrett Welch Wrestling Co. and their Agents*, No. 78-79-1, Exhibit A (Davidson County Chancery Court May 28, 1978).

58. *Speakers of Sport, Inc. v. ProServ, Inc.*, 178 F.3d 862, 865 (7th Cir. 1999).

59. *Gulas Wrestling Enterprises, Inc. v. Louie Heinman a/k/a Las Vegas Louie, Ron Garfield a/k/a Earl White, Don Garfield a/k/a/ Don Garfield Kalt a/k/a Don Fargo, Jarrett Enterprises, Inc., Welch Enterprises, Inc., Jarrett Welch Wrestling Co. and their Agents*, No. 78-79-1, Complaint at 6 (Davidson County Chancery Court May 28, 1978).

60. *Gulas Wrestling Enterprises, Inc. v. Louie Heinman a/k/a Las Vegas Louie, Ron Garfield a/k/a Earl White, Don Garfield a/k/a/ Don Garfield Kalt a/k/a Don Fargo, Jarrett Enterprises, Inc., Welch Enterprises, Inc., Jarrett Welch Wrestling Co. and their Agents*, No. 78-79-1, Exhibit A (Davidson County Chancery Court May 28, 1978) (emphasis added).

61. *White v. Mederi Caretenders Visiting Servs. of Southeast. Fla., LLC*, 226 So. 3d 774, 785 (Fla. 2017).

62. *Gulas Wrestling Enterprises, Inc. v. Louie Heinman a/k/a Las Vegas Louie, Ron Garfield a/k/a Earl White, Don Garfield a/k/a/ Don Garfield Kalt a/k/a Don Fargo, Jarrett Enterprises, Inc., Welch Enterprises, Inc., Jarrett Welch Wrestling Co. and their Agents*, No. 78-79-1, Notice of Dismissal (Davidson County Chancery Court Oct. 31, 1979).

63. James, supra note 49, at 95.

64. "Fuller Challenges Lawler for Title," *The Commercial Appeal*, May 15, 1977, at 44.

65. Joel Bierig, "Jarrett's Wrestling Show Sets a Monday Night Date," *The Commercial Appeal*, June 1, 1977, at 47.

66. Ron Russell, "The Grapple Capital," *The Commercial Appeal*, Nov. 26, 1978, at 307.

67. Bobby Matthews, "Ron Garvin and Bob Roop: How Stealing the Title Led to a Rebellion," *Pro Wrestling Stories* https://prowrestlingstories.com/pro-wrestling-stories/ron-garvin-boob-roop-rebellion/.

68. Marvin West, "Wrestling Rift's A Rather Tricky Affair," *The Knoxville News-Sentinel*, July 6, 1979, at 20.

69. "Write or Wrong," *The Knoxville News-Sentinel*, June 23, 1979, at 11 (Letters to the Sports Editor).

70. *NWA Southeastern Wrestling, Inc. & Robert Welch a/k/a Robert Fuller v. All Star Championship Wrestling, Inc., Ronnie Garvin, Bob Orton, Jr., Bob Roop, and Ron Wright*, No. 67652, Complaint at 3 (Knox County Chancery Court Oct. 3, 1979).

71. *NWA Southeastern Wrestling, Inc. & Robert Welch a/k/a Robert Fuller v. All Star Championship Wrestling, Inc., Ronnie Garvin, Bob Orton, Jr., Bob Roop, and Ron Wright*, No. 67652, Complaint at 4-5 (Knox County Chancery Court Oct. 3, 1979).

72. *NWA Southeastern Wrestling, Inc. & Robert Welch a/k/a Robert Fuller v. All Star Championship Wrestling, Inc., Ronnie Garvin, Bob Orton, Jr., Bob Roop, and Ron Wright*, No. 67652, Complaint at 6-7 (Knox County Chancery Court Oct. 3, 1979); *see also* "Wrestler Sues Rivals; Restraining Order Issued," *Knoxville News-Sentinel*, Oct. 5, 1979, at 24.

73. *NWA Southeastern Wrestling, Inc. & Robert Welch a/k/a Robert Fuller v. All Star Championship Wrestling, Inc., Ronnie Garvin, Bob Orton, Jr., Bob Roop, and Ron Wright*, No. 67652, Complaint at 9-10 (Knox County Chancery Court Oct. 3, 1979).

74. *NWA Southeastern Wrestling, Inc. & Robert Welch a/k/a Robert Fuller v. All Star Championship Wrestling, Inc., Ronnie Garvin, Bob Orton, Jr., Bob Roop, and Ron Wright*, No. 67652, Amendment to Complaint at 1-2 (Knox County Chancery Court Oct. 10, 1979).

75. *NWA Southeastern Wrestling, Inc. & Robert Welch a/k/a Robert Fuller v. All Star Championship Wrestling, Inc., Ronnie*

Garvin, Bob Orton, Jr., Bob Roop, and Ron Wright, No. 67652, Complaint at 9–10 (Knox County Chancery Court Oct. 3, 1979); *NWA Southeastern Wrestling, Inc. & Robert Welch a/k/a Robert Fuller v. All Star Championship Wrestling, Inc., Ronnie Garvin, Bob Orton, Jr., Bob Roop, and Ron Wright*, No. 67652, Amendment to Complaint at 2–3 (Knox County Chancery Court Oct. 10, 1979).

76. *NWA Southeastern Wrestling, Inc. & Robert Welch a/k/a Robert Fuller v. All Star Championship Wrestling, Inc., Ronnie Garvin, Bob Orton, Jr., Bob Roop, and Ron Wright*, No. 67652, Agreed Opinion (Knox County Chancery Court Nov. 9, 1979).

77. *NWA Southeastern Wrestling, Inc. & Robert Welch a/k/a Robert Fuller v. All Star Championship Wrestling, Inc., Ronnie Garvin, Bob Orton, Jr., Bob Roop, and Ron Wright*, No. 67652, Memorandum Opinion (Knox County Chancery Court Dec. 21, 1979).

78. "Bob Polk Buys SE Wrestling," *Knoxville News-Sentinel*, Nov. 11, 1979, at 41.

79. See *Poffo v. Gulas et al.*, Civil Action NO. 79–147 (E.D. Ky [Lexington]), Deposition of Roger Barnes, Feb. 19, 1980, at 10.

80. *Poffo v. Gulas et al.*, Civil Action NO. 79–147 (E.D. Ky [Lexington]), Deposition of Robert Roop, Feb. 19, 1980, at 22–26; *id.*, Deposition of Roger Barnes, Feb. 19, 1980, at 9.

81. John Woestendiek, "Wrestling's 'Outcasts' Looking for Respect Riches," *Lexington Herald-Leader*, 30, March 3, 1981.

82. *Id.*

83. *Id.*

84. *Id.*

85. *Poffo v. Gulas et al.*, Civil Action No. 79–147, Complaint (E.D. Ky [Lexington], Aug. 22, 1979).

86. *Id.* ¶ 14.

87. *Id.* ¶ 15.

88. *Id.* at 12; *see also* "Poffos' Lawsuit Hits Promoters," *The Tennessean*, Aug. 25, 1979, at 18.

89. *Poffo v. Gulas et al.*, Civil Action No. 79–147, Complaint (E.D. Ky (Lexington) Aug. 22, 1979), *Motion of Defendants Gulas and Renestro, Affidavit of Nick Gulas* at 5.

90. *Id.* at 3–5.

91. *Id.* at 4–5.

92. *Id.*; *see also* "Wrestling Promoter Gets Order Temporarily Halting Interference," *The Courier-Journal* (Louisville, KY), Aug. 24, 1978, at 4.

93. *Poffo v. Gulas et al.*, Civil Action No. 79–147, Complaint (E.D. Ky (Lexington), Aug. 22, 1979), Motion of Defendants Gulas and Renestro, Affidavit of Nick Gulas at 5.

94. *Poffo v. Gulas et al.*, Civil Action No. 79–147, Deposition of Robert Roop, at 22–26 (Feb. 19, 1980).

95. *Poffo v. Gulas et al.*, Civil Action No. 79–147, Deposition of Roger Barnes, at 9 (Feb. 19, 1980).

96. *Id.* at 9.

97. *Id.* at 49.

98. *Id.* at 59–62.

99. *Poffo v. Gulas et al.*, Civil Action No. 79–147, Deposition of Deborah Szostecki, at 5 (Feb. 19, 1980).

100. *Poffo v. Gulas et al.*, Civil Action No. 79–147, Deposition of Mark Sciarra, at 13 (Feb. 19, 1980).

101. *Poffo v. Gulas et al.*, Civil Action No. 79–147, Deposition of Eddie Farhat, at 9–10 (Dec. 28, 1981).

102. *Id.*

103. *Id.* at 12.

104. *Poffo v. Gulas et al.*, Civil Action No. 79–147, Memorandum Opinion and Order (Oct. 15, 1982).

105. Justin Barrasso, "Jim Crockett Jr. Reminisces About His Battles with Vince McMahon," *SI*, Nov. 8, 2019, https://www.si.com/wrestling/2019/11/08/jim-crockett-promotions-starrcast-interview; David Bixenspan, "Starrcade vs. Survivor Series: The Fight for Thanksgiving that Changed Wrestling," *Bleacher Report*, Nov. 27, 2013, https://bleacherreport.com/articles/1868129-starrcade-vs-survivor-series-the-fight-for-thanksgiving-that-changed-wrestling.

106. *MLW Media LLC v. World Wrestling Entertainment, Inc.*, Case 3:22-cv-00179-KAW, Complaint (N.D. Cal. Jan. 11, 2022), https://www.courthousenews.com/wp-content/uploads/2022/01/mlw-wwe-complaint.pdf.

107. *MLW Media LLC v. World Wrestling Entertainment, Inc.*, Case 5:22-cv-00179-EJD, First Amended Complaint, ¶¶ 84–86 (N.D. Cal. March 6, 2023), https://storage.courtlistener.com/recap/gov.uscourts.cand.390399/gov.uscourts.cand.390399.64.1.pdf.

108. *Id.* ¶ 85.
109. *NWA Southeastern Wrestling, Inc. & Robert Welch a/k/a Robert Fuller v. All Star Championship Wrestling, Inc., Ronnie Garvin, Bob Orton, Jr., Bob Roop, and Ron Wright*, No. 67652, Complaint at Exhibit A (Knox County Chancery Court Dec. 21, 1979); *see also Knoxville News-Sentinel*, Sept. 21, 1979, at 29; *Knoxville News-Sentinel*, Oct. 5, 1979, at 22.
110. *NWA Southeastern Wrestling, Inc. & Robert Welch a/k/a Robert Fuller v. All Star Championship Wrestling, Inc., Ronnie Garvin, Bob Orton, Jr., Bob Roop, and Ron Wright*, No. 67652, Complaint at 8–10 (Knox County Chancery Court Dec. 21, 1979); *see also* "Wrestler Ron Fuller Loses Court Tussle," *Knoxville News-Sentinel*, Feb. 4, 1980, at 4.
111. *Roberson v. Rochester Folding Box Co.*, 64 N.E. 442, 442 (N.Y. 1902).
112. Samuel D. Warren & Louis D. Brandeis. "The Right to Privacy," 4 *Harv. L. Rev.* 193 (1890).
113. *Roberson*, 64 N.E. at 448.
114. N.Y. Civil Rights Law §§ 50, 51.
115. *Pavesich v. New England Life Ins. Co.*, 50 S.E. 68, 68 (Ga. 1905).
116. *Id.* at 69.
117. *Id.* Syl. Pt. 11.
118. *Martin Luther King, Jr. Ctr. for Soc. Change, Inc. v. Am. Heritage Prods., Inc.*, 296 S.E.2d 697, 703 (Ga. 1982).
119. *Cabaniss v. Hipsley*, 151 S.E.2d 496, 503–04 (Ga. Ct. App. 1966).
120. *Memphis Development Foundation v. Factors Etc., Inc.*, 616 F.2d 956, 957 (6th Cir. 1980).
121. *Id.*
122. *Memphis Development Foundation v. Factors, Etc., Inc.*, 441 F. Supp. 1323, 1330 (W.D. Tenn. 1977).
123. *NWA Southeastern Wrestling, Inc. & Robert Welch a/k/a Robert Fuller v. All Star Championship Wrestling, Inc., Ronnie Garvin, Bob Orton, Jr., Bob Roop, and Ron Wright*, No. 67652, Memorandum Opinion (Knox County Chancery Court Dec. 21, 1979).
124. 418 S.W.2d 660 (Tenn. 1967).
125. *Id.* at 664.
126. *NWA Southeastern Wrestling, Inc. & Robert Welch a/k/a Robert Fuller v. All Star Championship Wrestling, Inc., Ronnie Garvin, Bob Orton, Jr., Bob Roop, and Ron Wright*, No. 67652, Order (Knox County Chancery Court March 4, 1980).

Chapter 5

1. *See, e.g., Frick v. Ensor*, 557 So. 2d 1022, 1023 (La. Ct. App. 1990) (noting, in 1984, that contract between promoter and wrestler referred to wrestler as an independent contractor).
2. *Fuller v. U.S. Aircraft Ins. Group*, 530 So.2d 1282, 1293 (La. Ct. App. 1989).
3. *Koch Ref. Co. v. Chapa*, 11 S.W.3d 153, 155 (Tex. 1999).
4. *Dusckiewicz v. Carter*, 52 A.2d 788, 790 (Vt. 1947).
5. 29 U.S.C. § 151.
6. 29 U.S.C. § 157.
7. 29 U.S.C. § 158.
8. 29 U.S.C. § 152(3).
9. *Rubin v. American Sportsmen Television Equity Soc.*, 254 P.2d 510, 511 (Cal. 1953).
10. *Rubin v. American Sportsmen Television Equity Soc.*, 234 P.2d 188, 189 (Cal. Ct. App. 1951), *aff'd* 254 P.2d 510, 511 (Cal. 1953).
11. *Id.* at 190.
12. 29 U.S.C. § 654(a)1.
13. 29 U.S.C. §§ 206, 207.
14. 29 U.S.C. § 2612(a)(1).
15. *See, e.g.*, VA. CODE ANN. § 65.2–101.
16. NFLPA, Injuries & Workers Comp, https://nflpa.com/active-players/health/injuries.
17. David Cowley, Note, "Employees vs. Independent Contractors and Wrestling: How the WWE is Taking a Folding Chair to the Basic Tenets of Employment Law," 53 *U. Louisville L. Rev.* 143, 143 (2014).
18. David Shoemaker, *The Squared Circle: Life, Death, and Professional Wrestling* 361 (2013).
19. NFLPA, Injuries & Workers Comp, https://nflpa.com/active-players/faq/are-nfl-players-eligible-for-workers-compensation.
20. "Football Players Yielding Hundreds of Thousands in Workers' Compensation," *eGeneration Marketing*, Aug. 31, 2017, https://www.egenerationmarketing.com/blog/football-players-workers-compensation.
21. Contract between WWE and Nelson Frazier (Nov. 11, 2007), https://61a84

bb3-a-62cb3a1a-s-sites.googlegroups.com/site/chrisharrington/mookieghana-prowrestlingstatistics/wwe_contracts/nelson_frazier_2007_contract.pdf?attachauth=ANoY7crTvy1rErqxLp8gMj3wiWyORWoXxBALAqMSosieRgoEh-QmoV2r2Th1m5QrAfZ_mnP1ZAb-B056gto0pHovi76WGjuYq63iYhkoL-rr3_Kf-fAPZRhaBwrDsU2q7rUdXn-He-c7VQDWRlKDE1kv3CEf2fwK-4IuT-4N_0rLBuXWfr_x8iJnXW163mc-jsKYV-QfNbkY4UsLlHnz5JSPTRb-WhzQmzvAxlSzWaEZcsWghNDhAunbUlKgeorcoUe74SCbDXj-N29QC39UW-CxBty8d6KXL_Ke-miW_1t9aJykuZrd5Y-N51awtQ1D1Jv78pxATrwE2I2VjTs5&attredirects=0.

22. Contract between WWE and Chavo Guerrero, Jr. (April 5, 2010), http://ia802906.us.archive.org/32/items/gov.uscourts.ctd.113085/gov.uscourts.ctd.113085.1.5.pdf.

23. CONN. GEN. STAT. ANN. § 31–51ll.

24. *See* Jonathan Gelber, "Why Professional Wrestlers are More Likely to Die Young," *Salon*, March 14, 2021, https://www.salon.com/2021/03/14/why-professional-wrestlers-are-more-likely-to-die-young/.

25. Christopher W. Herman et al., "The Very High Premature Mortality Rate among Active Professional Wrestlers Is Primarily Due to Cardiovascular Disease," *Plos One*, Nov. 5, 2014, https://www.ncbi.nlm.nih.gov/pmc/articles/PMC4220919/.

26. Benjamin Morris, "Are Pro Wrestlers Dying at an Unusual Rate?," *Five Thirty Eight,* https://fivethirtyeight.com/features/are-pro-wrestlers-dying-at-an-unusual-rate/.

27. Raymond Hernandez and Joshua Brustein, "A Senate Run Brings Wrestling Into Spotlight," *N.Y. Times*, July 15, 2010, https://www.nytimes.com/2010/07/16/nyregion/16mcmahon.html; WWE, Talent Wellness Program Summary, https://corporate.wwe.com/who-we-are/talent.

28. Contract between WWE and Chavo Guerrero, Jr. (April 5, 2010), http://ia802906.us.archive.org/32/items/gov.uscourts.ctd.113085/gov.uscourts.ctd.113085.1.5.pdf.

29. *Who We Are: Talent Wellness Program Summary*, WWE, https://corporate.wwe.com/who-we-are/talent.

30. CONN. GEN. STAT. § 31–146.

31. *Massey v. Jim Crockett Promotions, Inc.*, 400 S.E.2d 876, 880 (W. Va. 1990) (per curiam).

32. *Massey v. Jim Crockett Promotions, Inc.*, Plaintiffs' Petition for an Appeal from a Final Order of the Circuit Court of Raleigh County, West Virginia, *28, Oct. 12, 1989.

33. Francoise Carre "(In)dependent Contractor Misclassification," *Economic Policy Institute*, June 8, 2015, https://www.epi.org/publication/independent-contractor-misclassification/.

34. *Id.*

35. David Weil, "Lots of Employees Get Misclassified as Contractors. Here's Why It Matters," *Harvard Business Review*, July 5, 2017, https://hbr.org/2017/07/lots-of-employees-get-misclassified-as-contractors-heres-why-it-matters.

36. *Levy v. World Wrestling Entertainment*, No. 08CV01289, Complaint (D. Conn. Aug. 22, 2008).

37. *See McCullough v. World Wrestling Entertainment, Inc.*, CIVIL ACTION NO. 3:15-CV-1074 (VLB), CIVIL ACTION NO. 3:15-CV-994 (VLB), CIVIL ACTION NO. 3:16-CV-1209 (VLB), 2018 WL 4425977 (Sep. 17, 2018) (dismissing wrestlers' claims on the grounds that Connecticut's statute of limitations had run and statute of repose had not been tolled); *Levy v. World Wrestling Entertainment, Inc.*, No. CIV.A.308–01289(PCD), 2009 WL 455258, at *4 (D. Conn. Feb. 23, 2009) (concluding wrestler's claim was barred by Connecticut's statute of limitations).

38. *McCullough v. World Wrestling Entertainment, Inc.*, Civil Action No.3:15-cv-001074 (VLB), Second Amended Complaint ¶¶ 325–57 (D. Conn. Nov. 3, 2017), http://wweconcussionlawsuit-news.com/wp-content/uploads/2017/11/FILED-LAURINAITIS-SAC-11.3.2017.pdf.

39. *Id.* ¶ 356.

40. *Haynes v. World Wrestling Entertainment, Inc.*, 827 Fed.Appx. 3 (2d Cir. Sep. 9, 2020).

41. IRS, Topic No. 762 Independent Contractor vs. Employee, https://www.irs.gov/taxtopics/tc762.

42. *Gale v. Greater Washington Softball Umpires Ass'n*, 311 A.2d 817 (Md. 1973).

43. RESTATEMENT (SECOND) OF Agency § 220 cmt. h (1958).

44. *Langness v. Ketonen*, 255 P.2d 551, 555 (Wash. 1953).

45. Internal Revenue Service Revenue Ruling 69–225 (1969).

46. *Silvia v. Woodhouse*, 248 N.E.2d 260, 262 (Mass. 1969).

47. *Id.* at 264.

48. *White v. Frenkel*, 615 So.2d 535, 537 (La. Ct. App. 1993).

49. *Id.* at 539.

50. Orly Lobel, "The Gig Economy and the Future of Employment and Labor Law," 51 *U.S.F. L. Rev.* 51, 61 (2017).

51. *See Razak v. Uber Techs., Inc.*, 2018 U.S. Dist. LEXIS 61230 (E.D. Pa. Apr. 11, 2018) (granting summary judgment in favor of Uber and holding that drivers were independent contractors, not employees); *Doe v. Uber Technologies, Inc.*, 184 F. Supp. 3d 774 (N.D. Cal. 2016) (concluding genuine issue of fact existed as to whether Uber driver was an employee for purposes of plaintiff's tort claim against Uber).

52. *Doe*, 184 F. Supp. 3d at 782–83.

53. Author interview with Tom Prichard, Jan. 11, 2023.

54. Cowley, *supra* note 16, at 155–56.

55. *See* David Robb, "SAG-AFTRA Settles Unfair Labor Practice Charges Against Telemundo Over Telenovela Actors," Oct. 23, 2017, https://deadline.com/2017/10/telemundo-labor-charges-settled-sag-aftra-telenovelas-1202193502/ (discussing settlement of dispute over whether Telemundo actors should be classified as employees instead of independent contractors).

56. Contract between WWE and Chavo Guerrero, Jr. (April 5, 2010), http://ia802906.us.archive.org/32/items/gov.uscourts.ctd.113085/gov.uscourts.ctd.113085.1.5.pdf.

57. *Tucker v. Sierra Builders*, 180 S.W.3d 109, 120 (Tenn. Ct. App. 2005).

58. *Dynamex Operations West, Inc. v. Superior Court*, 416 P.3d 1 (Cal. 2018).

59. *Id.* at 33–34.

60. *Id.* at 34.

61. *See Vogue v. Administrator, Unemployment Compensation Act*, 279 A.3d 727, 730–31 (Conn. 2022) (stating test is used for purposes of Unemployment Compensation Act); *Tianti, ex rel. Gluck v. William Raveis Real Estate, Inc.*, 651 A.2d 1286, 1290 (Conn. 1995) (stating test applies in the context of a wage claim).

62. *Dynamex Operations West, Inc. v. Superior Court*, 416 P.3d 1, 37 (Cal. 2018) (emphasis added).

63. *Id.*

64. *Id.* at 44.

65. Charlotte Alexander, "Anticipatory Retaliation, Threats, and the Silencing of the Brown Collar Workforce," 50 *AM. Bus. L.J.* 779, 781(2013).

66. *See Burlington N. & Santa Fe Ry. Co. v. White*, 548 U.S. 53, 68 (2006) (discussing Title VII); Alex B. Long, *Employment Retaliation and the Accident of Text*, 90 *Or. L. Rev.* 525, 580 (2011) (cataloging federal statutes).

67. Email interview with Lucas Middlebrook, Feb. 14, 2023.

68. *See, e.g.,* Matthew Wilkinson, *10 WWE Gimmicks That Were Meant as A Punishment*, The Sportster, Oct. 31, 2022, https://www.thesportster.com/wwe-gimmicks-meant-as-punishment/.

69. Alexander, *supra* note 64, at 802–03.

70. 29 U.S.C. § 158(a) (2018); *NLRB v. Q-1 Motor Express, Inc.*, 25 F.3d 473, 477 (7th Cir. 1994).

71. Email interview with Lucas Middlebrook, Feb. 14, 2023.

72. Jim Wilson, *Chokehold: Pro Wrestling's Real Mayhem Outside the Ring* 162–63, 178 (2003).

73. Alfred Konuwa, "AEW Dynamite Beats WWE NXT In Tuesday Ratings War With 752,000 Viewers," Forbes, Oct. 19, 2022, https://www.forbes.com/sites/alfredkonuwa/2022/10/19/aew-beats-nxt-in-tuesday-ratings-war-with-752000-viewers/?sh=64bc64554798.

74. Blake Oestriecher, "All Elite Wrestling Provides a Viable Alternative for WWE Stars Who Want Quality Contracts," Forbes, Jan. 18, 2019, https://www.forbes.com/sites/blakeoestriecher/2019/01/18/all-elite-wrestling-provides-a-viable-alternative-for-wwe-stars-who-want-quality-contracts/?sh=476e53f27276.

75. Sean Neuman, "AEW, Healthcare, and the Sweeping Change Wrestlers Hope Is Coming Next," fanbyte, Oct. 23, 2019, https://www.fanbyte.com/entertainment/wrestling/aew-healthcare-and-the-sweeping-change-wrestlers-hope-is-coming-next/.

76. Lobel, *supra* note 49, at 63–64.

77. Lobel, *supra* note 49, at 65–67.

Chapter 6

1. "The Winnah is—Rassler Rose!," *Herald and Review* (Decatur, Ill.), May 26, 1955, at 6.
2. Pat Laprade and Dan Murphy, *Sisterhood of the Squared Circle* 36 (2017).
3. *Id.* at 20, 36.
4. *Brown v. Board of Educ. of Topeka*, 347 U.S. 483 (1954).
5. *Bradwell v. People of State of Illinois*, 83 U.S. 130, 141 (1872) (Bradley, J., concurring).
6. *Id.* (Bradley, J., concurring).
7. "Sex, Discrimination, and the Constitution," 2 *Stan. L. Rev.* 691, 693 (1950).
8. *Id.* at 696.
9. *Id.* at 717.
10. *Bradwell v. People of State of Illinois*, 83 U.S. 130, 141 (1872) (Bradley, J., concurring).
11. *Id.* (Bradley, J., concurring).
12. *Radice v. New York*, 264 U.S. 292, 294 (1924).
13. "Lady Wrestler Wins bout with State in Court," *Chicago Tribune*, Oct. 21, 1954, at 80.
14. *Id.*
15. *Hesseltine v. State Athletic Com.*, 126 N.E.2d 631, 632 (Ill. 1955).
16. "Lady Wrestler Wins bout with State in Court," supra note 13, at 80.
17. *Hesseltine v. State Athletic Com.*, 126 N.E.2d 631, 632 (Ill. 1955).
18. "Lady Wrestler Wins bout with State in Court," supra note 13, at 80.
19. *Hesseltine*, 126 N.E.2d at 633.
20. *Id.*
21. Charles Stanton, "Wrestling Dispute," *News-Review* (Roseburg, Or.), March 29, 1955, at 4.
22. Beth Slovic, "Opinion: Vera Katz Took Office 50 Years Ago—and Legalized Women's Pro Wrestling to Change Oregon," *The Oregonian*, Jan. 3, 2023, https://www.oregonlive.com/opinion/2023/01/vera-katz-took-office-50-years-ago-and-legalized-womens-wrestling-to-change-oregon.html.
23. "Judge Says Women Can Enter Public Wrestling, "*Medford Mail Tribune*, Jan. 5, 1955, at 8.
24. "Wrestling by Women Faces Threat of Ban," *The World* (Coos Bay, OR), Jan. 31, 1955, at 10.
25. Slovic, *supra* note 22.
26. "House Outlaws Women Wrestling," *La Grande Observer* (La Grande, OR), April 14, 1955, at 6.
27. Or. Rev. Stat. § 463.130.
28. "Women Wrestlers Outlawed in Oregon," *Corvallis Gazette-Times*, May 6, 1955, at 9.
29. "Legal to Bar Women Boxers," *Capital Journal* (Salem, Or.), April 11, 1955, at 1.
30. "Notice to the Public," *Eugene Guard*, May 16, 1955, at 12.
31. *State v. Hunter*, 300 P.2d 455, 456 (Or. 1956).
32. *Id.* at 456–57.
33. *Goesaert v. Cleary*, 335 U.S. 464, 466 (1948).
34. *State v. Hunter*, 300 P.2d 455, 457 (Or. 1956).
35. *Id.*
36. *State v. Baker*, 92 P. 1076, 1078 (Or. 1907).
37. *Hunter*, 300 P.2d at 458.
38. *Id.*
39. Slovic, *supra* note 22.
40. "Midgets Will Wrestle Here for 1st Time," *Marshfield News-Herald* (Marshfield, WI), Aug. 7, 1957, at 13; "Live Texas-Style Wrestling," Eugene *Guard*, Jan. 28, 1957, at 13.
41. *Hoyt v. Florida*, 368 U.S. 57, 62 (1961).
42. *Id.*
43. *Calzadilla v. Dooley*, 29 A.D.2d 152 (N.Y. Sup. Ct. A.D. 1968).
44. "New York Commission Will Bar Women Fight Managers," *Chicago Tribune*, July 28, 1934, at 13.
45. "On Lawsuits for Licenses: The Fight for Women's Wrestling in New York, part 1," Finding Aid, Aug. 24, 2016, https://findingaid.wordpress.com/2016/08/24/fight-for-womens-wrestling-pt1/.
46. *On Lawsuits for Licenses: The Fight for Women's Wrestling in New York, part 2*, Finding Aid, Aug. 25, 2016, https://findingaid.wordpress.com/2016/08/25/fight-for-womens-wrestling-pt2/.
47. *Calzadilla v. Dooley*, 29 A.D.2d 152, 152–53 (N.Y. Sup. Ct. A.D. 1968).
48. "On Lawsuits for Licenses: The Fight for Women's Wrestling in New York, part 2," Finding Aid, Aug. 25, 2016, https://findingaid.wordpress.com/2016/08/25/fight-for-womens-wrestling-pt2/.
49. *Id.*

50. *Id.*
51. *Goesaert v. Cleary*, 335 U.S. 464, 466 (1948).
52. *Matter of* Whitehead v. Krulewitch, 25 A.D.2d 956 (N.Y. Sup. Ct. A.D. 1966).
53. *Calzadilla v. Dooley*, 29 A.D.2d 152, 153 (N.Y. Sup. Ct. A.D. 1968).
54. Associated Press, "Women's Lib Hits NY Wrestling Rule," *Herald News* (Passaic, NJ), Oct. 29, 1970, at 44.
55. *Calzadilla v. Dooley*, No. D-8187, Notice of Petition, Exhibit 1, at 24–25 (New York Supreme Court Appellate Division—Fourth Department).
56. *Calzadilla v. Dooley*, No. D-8187, Notice of Petition, Exhibit 1, at 28 (New York Supreme Court Appellate Division—Fourth Department).
57. *Calzadilla v. Dooley*, No. D-8187, Notice of Petition, Exhibit 1, at 16, 20 (New York Supreme Court Appellate Division—Fourth Department).
58. *Calzadilla v. Dooley*, No. D-8187, Notice of Petition, Exhibit 1, at 6 (New York Supreme Court Appellate Division—Fourth Department).
59. *Calzadilla v. Dooley*, No. D-8187, Appellant's Brief, at 25–26 (New York Supreme Court Appellate Division—Fourth Department).
60. *Calzadilla v. Dooley*, 29 A.D.2d 152, 155 (N.Y. Sup. Ct. A.D. 1968).
61. *Id.*
62. *Id. at* 157 (emphasis added).
63. *Id.*
64. *Id.*
65. *Id.* (quoting Tigner v. Texas, 310 U.S. 141, 147 [1940]).
66. Associated Press, "Women's Lib Hits NY Wrestling Rule," *Herald News* (Pasaic, NJ), Oct. 29, 1970, at 44.
67. Dick Wade, "Talk of the Times," *Kansas City Times*, Nov. 12, 1970, at 60.
68. *Id.*
69. "On Lawsuits for Licenses: The Fight for Women's Wrestling in New York," part 4, Sep. 2, 2016, https://findingaid.wordpress.com/2016/09/02/on-lawsuits-for-licenses-the-fight-for-womens-wrestling-in-new-york-part-4/.
70. LAPRADE & MURPHY, *supra* note 2, at 138.
71. Paul Zimmerman, "Let's Give the Girls a Ring," *New York Post*, March 9, 1972, at 70.
72. Greg Oliver, "Titi Paris Forced Women's Wrestling in New York State," Slam Wrestling, Feb. 6, 2023, https://slam-wrestling.net/index.php/2023/02/06/titi-paris-forced-womens-wrestling-in-new-york-state/.
73. Zimmerman, *supra* note 71.
74. *Seidenberg v. McSorleys' Old Ale House, Inc.*, 317 F. Supp. 593 (S.D.N.Y. 1970); *Commonwealth Alcoholic Beverage Control Bd. v. Burke*, 481 S.W.2d 52 (Ky.1972); *Sail'er Inn, Inc. v. Kirby*, 485 P.2d 529 (Cal. 1971); *Paterson Tavern & G. O. A. v. Hawthorne*, 270 A.2d 628 (N.J. 1970).
75. *Seidenberg v. McSorleys' Old Ale House, Inc.*, 317 F. Supp. 593 (S.D.N.Y. 1970).
76. *Id.* at 606.
77. *Id.* at 605.
78. *Id.* at 606.
79. *Id.*
80. *Reed v. Reed*, 465 P.2d 635, 638 (Idaho 1970), *rev'd* 404 U.S. 71 (1971).
81. *Reed v. Reed*, 404 U.S. 71, 76 (1971).
82. *Id.*
83. *1 for Women*, *Daily News* (New York, NY), May 9, 1972, at 26.
84. Oliver, *supra* 72.
85. "On Lawsuits for Licenses: The Fight for Women's Wrestling in New York, part 4," Sep. 2, 2016, https://findingaid.wordpress.com/2016/09/02/on-lawsuits-for-licenses-the-fight-for-womens-wrestling-in-new-york-part-4/.
86. Larry Fox, "Okay Gal Wrestlers," *Daily News* (New York, NY), June 6, 1972, at 68.
87. *Id.*
88. Marcia Kramer, "State Tosses in the Towel, Ladies Wrestle as Garden," *Daily News* (New York, NY), July 3, 1972, at 210.
89. Lillian Ellison, *The Fabulous Moolah: First Goddess of the Squared Circle* 130–37 (2002).
90. William Gildea, "Women Grapplers Start Push for Dates in Plush Garden," *Star-Gazette* (Elmira, NY), Sep. 20, 1970, at 37.
91. Oliver, *supra* note 72.
92. Laprade and Murphy, *supra* note 2, at 138.
93. Slovic, *supra* 22.
94. 429 U.S. 190 (1976).
95. *United States v. VMI*, 518 U.S. 515 (1996).
96. Catharine A. MacKinnon, *Sexual*

Harassment of Working Women: A Case of Sex Discrimination 32 (1979).

97. *Id.* at 40.

98. Frank Dobbin and Alexandra Kalev, "Why Sexual Harassment Programs Backfire," *Harvard Business Review*, May-June 2020, https://hbr.org/2020/05/why-sexual-harassment-programs-backfire.

99. Abraham Josephine Riesman, *Ringmaster: Vince McMahon and the Unmaking of America* 198 (2023).

100. *Id.* at 199.

101. *See Garcia v. Elf Atochem North America*, 28 F.3d 446 (5th Cir.1994); *Giddens v. Shell Oil Co.*, 12 F.3d 208 (5th Cir. 1993); *Hopkins v. Baltimore Gas & Elec. Co.*, 871 F. Supp. 822 (D. Md. 1994); *Vandeventer v. Wabash Nat'l Corp.*, 867 F. Supp. 790 (N.D. Ind.1994); *Goluszek v. Smith*, 697 F. Supp. 1452 (N.D. Ill. 1988).

102. *Oncale v. Sundowner Offshore Services, Inc.*, 523 U.S. 75 (1998).

103. *Faragher v. City of Boca Raton*, 524 U.S. 775, 778 (1998); *Burlington Industries, Inc. v. Ellerth*, 524 U.S. 742, 765 (1998).

104. *Faragher*, 524 U.S. at 777; *Ellerth*, 524 U.S. at 765.

105. RIESMAN, *supra* note 4, at 206.

106. *Bass v. World Wrestling Federation Entertainment, Inc.*, 129 F. Supp. 2d 491, 501 (E.D.N.Y. 2001).

107. *Id.*

108. Martin James Dickinson, "Sable's Lawsuit Against the WWE Explained," *The Sportster*, May 3, 2022, https://www.thesportster.com/sables-lawsuit-against-the-wwe-explained/.

109. *Oncale*, 523 U.S. at 81-82.

110. Adam Miller, "Lady Wrestler Settles Legal Fight Out of Ring," *N.Y. Post*, July 29, 1999, https://nypost.com/1999/07/29/lady-wrestler-settles-legal-fight-out-of-ring/.

111. Kati Cornell Smith, "She Gets Pinned—Lady Wrestler Loses Sex Case," *N.Y. Post*, Oct. 9, 2002, https://nypost.com/2002/10/09/she-gets-pinned-lady-wrestler-loses-sex-case/.

112. Joe Palazzolo and Ted Mann, "WWE Board Probes Secret $3 Million Hush Pact by CEO Vince McMahon, Sources Say," *Wall Street Journal*, June 15, 2022, https://www.wsj.com/articles/wwe-board-probes-secret-3-million-hush-pact-by-ceo-vince-mcmahon-sources-say-11655322722?mod=article_inline.

113. Joe Palazzolo et al., "WWE's Vince McMahon Agreed to Pay $12 Million in Hush Money to Four Women," *Wall Street Journal*, July 8, 2022, https://www.wsj.com/articles/wwes-vince-mcmahon-agreed-to-pay-12-million-in-hush-money-to-four-women-11657289742.

114. *Id.*

115. Michael Hill, "The Adult Survivors Act Launched Over 2,500 Sex Abuse Suits. Now, It's Expiring," AP, Nov. 20, 2023, https://apnews.com/article/sexual-abuse-lawsuits-new-york-6fd16aa4c-c992c089e91c6fef064f375.

116. Joe Palazzolo and Ted Mann, "WWE's Vince McMahon Settles with Ex-Wrestling Referee Who Accused Him of Rape," *Wall Street Journal*, Jan. 19, 2023, https://www.wsj.com/articles/wwes-vince-mcmahon-settles-with-ex-wrestling-referee-who-accused-him-of-rape-11674149751.

117. *Grant v. World Wrestling Entertainment, Inc.*, Civil Action No. 3:24-cv-90, ¶ 256, United States Dist. Ct. for the Southern District of New York, Jan. 25, 2024.

118. Greg Oliver, "Nick Kiniski Details Terry Garvin's Sexual Advances During His WWF Run," *SLAM*, Feb. 26, 2024, https://slamwrestling.net/index.php/2024/02/26/nick-kiniski-details-terry-garvins-sexual-advances-during-wwf-run/; John Pollock, "Nick Kiniski Speaks Out on Proposition by WWF Official," *Post Wrestling*, Feb. 26, 2024, https://www.postwrestling.com/2024/02/26/nick-kiniski-speaks-out-on-proposition-by-wwf-official/.

119. Tim Marchman, "McMahon of Sexually Preying on Wrestlers in Previously Unreleased Statement," *Vice News*, Feb. 9, 2024, https://www.vice.com/en/article/epv78z/ashley-massaro-wwe-vince-mcmahon-sexual-divas.

120. Dobbin and Kalev, *supra* note 3.

121. Lettie Rose et al., "State Regulation of Sexual Harassment," 24 *Geo. J. Gender & L.* 811, 829 (2023).

122. Matt Gonzales, "Five Years of #MeToo: Sexual Harassment Still Common in Workplaces," SHRM, Oct. 17, 2022, https://www.shrm.org/topics-tools/news/inclusion-equity-diversity/five-years-metoo-sexual-harassment-still-common-workplaces.

Chapter 7

1. Matt Schudel, "Craig Gilbert, Creator of 'An American Family,' Called the First Reality TV Show, Dies at 94," *Wash. Post*, April 18, 2020, https://www.washingtonpost.com/local/obituaries/craig-gilbert-creator-of-an-american-family-called-the-first-reality-tv-show-dies-at-94/2020/04/18/ea66b34c-7e4e-11ea-9040-68981f488eed_story.html.

2. *See Ledwell v. Ravenel*, 843 F. App'x 506, 507 (4th Cir. 2021); *Lundin v. Discovery Commc'ns Inc.*, 352 F. Supp. 3d 949, 953–55 (D. Ariz. 2018), *aff'd*, 796 F. App'x 942 (9th Cir. 2020); *Shapiro v. NFGTV, Inc.*, No. 16 Civ. 9152 (PGG), 2018 WL 2127806, at *1–2 (S.D.N.Y. Feb. 9, 2018); *Mossack Fonesca & Co. v. Netflix Inc.*, No. CV 19-9330-CBM-AS(x), 2020 WL 8510342, at *2 (C.D. Cal. Dec. 23, 2020); *Eckhardt v. Idea Factory*, LLC, 2021 IL (210813), at *1 (Ill. App. Ct. Sept. 30, 2021); *Klapper v. Graziano*, 970 N.Y.S.2d 355, 357–58 (N.Y. Sup. Ct. 2013).

3. Eriq Gardner, "Judge Set to Trim or Dismiss Lawsuit Over 'Keeping Up with the Kardashians,'" *The Hollywood Reporter*, Feb. 11, 2014, https://www.hollywoodreporter.com/business/business-news/judge-set-trim-dismiss-lawsuit-679460/.

4. Eriq Gardner, "Kardashians' Ex-Stepmom Claims Family's Reality TV Show Defamed Her," *The Hollywood Reporter*, July 12, 2013, https://www.hollywoodreporter.com/business/business-news/kardashians-stepmom-claims-familys-reality-584574/.

5. Bill Bradley, "The Coen Brothers Reveal 'Fargo' Is Based on a True Story After All," *HuffPost*, March 8, 2016, https://www.huffpost.com/entry/coen-brothers-fargo-true-story_n_56de-2c53e4b0ffe6f8ea78c4.

6. *Id.*

7. Guy Evans, *Nitro* 14 (2018).

8. *Id.* at 24.

9. *Id.* at 26.

10. Richard Sandomir, "TV Sports; ABC Losing its Hold on Monday Night Ratings," *N.Y. Times*, Sept. 25, 1998.

11. Paul Guzzo, "You Won't Believe How Hard They Once Worked to Make Professional Wrestling 'Real,'" *Tampa Bay Times*, March 19, 2020, https://www.tampabay.com/news/hillsborough/2020/03/19/you-wont-believe-how-hard-they-once-worked-to-make-professional-wrestling-real/.

12. Pro Wrestling Fandom.com, Glossary of Professional Wrestling Terms, https://prowrestling.fandom.com/wiki/List_of_professional_wrestling_terms#S.

13. https://www.wwe.com/videos/wwe-network-flyin-brian-vs-taskmaster-i-respect-you-leather-strap-match-wcw-superbrawl-vi.

14. EVANS, *supra* note 7, at 84–85.

15. https://www.dailymotion.com/video/xjf3j7.

16. EVANS, *supra* note 7, at 389.

17. *Id.* at 445.

18. *Id.* at 445–46.

19. *Bollea v. World Championship Wrestling, Inc.*, 610 S.E.2d 92, 97 (Ga. Ct. App. 2005).

20. EVANS, *supra* note 7, at 309.

21. *Id.* at 304.

22. https://www.youtube.com/watch?v=hJgiBsdHAUI.

23. EVANS, *supra* note 7, at 478.

24. https://www.dailymotion.com/video/x7apq6.

25. https://www.dailymotion.com/video/x7apq6.

26. https://www.dailymotion.com/video/x7apq6.

27. GA. CODE ANN. § 51-5-1.

28. Brief of Appellant, *Bollea v. World Championship Wrestling*, No. A04A1743., June 1, 2004, 2004 WL 5536502, *16.

29. *New York Times Co. v. Sullivan*, 376 U.S. 254, 288–91 (1964).

30. *Eidson v. Berry*, 202 Ga. App. 587, 588 (1992).

31. *Elias v. Rolling Stone LLC*, 872 F.3d 97, 104–05 (2d Cir. 2017).

32. *See, e.g., Greene v. Paramount Pictures Corp.*, 340 F. Supp. 3d 161, 170 (E.D.N.Y. 2018); *Bates v. Cast*, 316 P.3d 246, 251 (Okla. Ct. Civ. App. 2013).

33. *Smith v. Stewart*, 660 S.E.2d 822 (Ga. 2008).

34. *Id.* at 827.

35. https://www.youtube.com/watch?v=KdeIGyHgR60&t=319s.

36. https://www.youtube.com/watch?v=KdeIGyHgR60&t=319s.

37. https://www.youtube.com/watch?v=hJgiBsdHAUI.

38. https://www.youtube.com/watch?v=hJgiBsdHAUI.
39. https://www.youtube.com/watch?v=hJgiBsdHAUI.
40. *Bollea v. World Championship Wrestling, Inc.*, 610 S.E.2d 92, 97 (Ga. Ct. App. 2005).
41. *Id.*
42. *Id.*
43. *Milkovich v. Lorain J. Co.*, 497 U.S. 1, 21 (1990).
44. *Id.* at 17 (quoting Letter Carriers v. Austin, 418 U.S. 264, 284–86 [1974]).
45. *Id.*
46. *Id.*
47. Brief of Appellant, *Bollea v. World Championship Wrestling*, No. A04A1743., June 1, 2004, 2004 WL 5536502, *24.
48. *Id.* at *6.
49. *Id.* at *14–15.
50. *Bollea*, 610 S.E.2d at 96.
51. Kermit Hall, "Alabama in the 1960s," in *100 Americans Making Constitutional History: A Biographical History* 189, 191 (Melvin I. Urofsky ed., 2004).
52. *See id.* at 189.
53. *See id.* at 190.
54. Anthony Lewis, *Make No Law: The Sullivan Case and the First Amendment* 42 (1991); Glenn Harlan Reynolds, "Rethinking Libel for the Twenty-First Century," 87 *Tenn. L. Rev.* 465, 468 (2020).
55. *Sullivan*, 376 U.S. at 280. Originally, the Court held that the public official must prove that the statement was made with knowledge that it was false or with reckless disregard as to its truth or falsity. Over time, the Court clarified that this concept of "reckless disregard" included the situation in which the speaker entertained serious doubts about the truth of the statement. St. Amant v. Thompson, 390 U.S. 727, 731 (1968).
56. *Gertz v. Robert Welch, Inc.*, 418 U.S. 323, 345 (1974).
57. *Id.* at 351.
58. Brief of Appellant, *Bollea v. World Championship Wrestling*, No. A04A1743., June 1, 2004, 2004 WL 5536502, *19.
59. *Id.* at *14–15.
60. *Dworkin v. Hustler Magazine, Inc.*, 867 F.2d 1188, 1194 (9th Cir. 1989).
61. *Id.*
62. *Bollea v. World Championship Wrestling, Inc.*, 610 S.E.2d 92, 97 (Ga. Ct. App. 2005) (emphasis added).
63. *Hoppe v. Hearst Corp.*, 770 P.2d 203, 208 (Wash. Ct. App. 1989); *New Times, Inc. v. Isaacks*, 91 S.W.3d 844, 858 (Tex. Ct App.—Fort Worth 2002).
64. *New Times, Inc.*, 91 S.W.3d at 858.
65. Kelsey Sutton, "Gawker/Hulk Hogan Trial Report," *Politico* (Mar. 8, 2016), https://www.politico.com/media/tipsheets/media-pro/2016/03/politico-media-pro-hogan-takes-the-stand-v-gawkererin-andrews-wins-55-m-peeping-tom-suitif-bloomberg-had-run-000917/.
66. Eriq Gardner, "Hulk Hogan Grilled About Sex-Filled TMZ, Howard Stern Interviews at Gawker Trial," *Hollywood Rep.* (Mar. 8, 2016), https://www.hollywoodreporter.com/business/business-news/hulk-hogan-grilled-sex-filled-873435/.
67. Julia Marsh and Bruce Golding, "Hulk Hogan is Asked the Question Every Man Fears," *N.Y. Post* (Mar. 8, 2016), https://nypost.com/2016/03/08/hulk-hogan-i-do-not-have-a-10-inch-penis/.
68. Ryan Holiday, *Conspiracy* 245 (2018).
69. Maya Kosoff, "Why Gawker Filed for Bankruptcy," *Vanity Fair* (June 10, 2016), https://www.vanityfair.com/news/2016/06/gawker-filed-for-bankruptcy.

Chapter 8

1. *Bollea v. World Championship Wrestling, Inc.*, 610 S.E.2d 92, 97 (Ga. Ct. App. 2005).
2. *Hansen v. Wheaton Van Lines, Inc.*, 486 F. Supp. 2d 1339, 1346 (S.D. Fla. 2006).
3. *See, e.g.*, https://www.youtube.com/watch?v=AO736S26i_Y.
4. *NWA Southeastern Wrestling Inc. v. Garvin*, No. 66591, Trial Transcript at 27 (Knox County Chancery Court, Feb. 13, 1980).
5. Contract Between WCW and Bobby Walker, April 1996, https://61a84bb3-a-62cb3a1a-s-sites.googlegroups.com/site/chrisharrington/mookieghana-prowrestlingstatistics/wwe_contracts/Bobby_walker_Contract_1993-1999.pdf?attachauth=ANoY7cqVRzqNxRsUt-9g2OopuZeUDvSahD55ze3_2K5H-KXl67Jhskg0XEW812dXusut-VSqyyPzqL1-I9231JZat0tYJH66t-Beos9ONABVFbSWYYUNiq_9f6o-

tnol41TwuMlWUetkA8n9fXpf6R-WTYQKHNShXa4Te2xwAEcylE-CiRbUDzJ6TnNxRRq7JJ0Xaktf-muhRfLxzJ50yLLHK_1g7L2FudrRD-ZuFzwYPP-Giqf79jkIdnskIDRJu-Vc2iG7bCqKWZf0jcxv3WzxKYK3Y-seTWP4qBOLgQCXOtjru1SUgm-VN14Ak8IUuXULcdEPKIzCpasCiv-7ICS3N&attredirects=0. For a breakdown of modern WWE contracts, see Chris Smith, "Breaking Down How WWE Contracts Work," *Forbes*, May 28, 2015, https://www.forbes.com/sites/chrissmith/2015/03/28/breaking-down-how-wwe-contracts-work/?sh=ac141c46713f, For a treasure trove of wrestling contracts, see Indeed Wrestling, *Professional Wrestling Contracts (WWF, WWE, WCW)*, https://sites.google.com/site/chrisharrington/mookieghana-prowrestlingstatistics/wwe_contracts.

6. Shiven Sachdeva, "Eric Bischoff Gives the Exact Number of Times Hulk Hogan Used His Power of Creative Control in WCW," *Sportskeeda*, May 24, 2001, https://www.sportskeeda.com/wwe/news-eric-bischoff-reveals-exact-number-times-hulk-hogan-used-power-creative-control-wcw.

7. Contract Between WCW and Bobby Walker, April 1996 (emphasis added).

8. *Bollea*, 610 S.E.2d at 98.

9. *Guy Evans, Nitro* 267 (2018).

10. https://www.wwe.com/videos/jeff-jarrett-vs-hulk-hogan-wcw-world-heavyweight-championship-match-bash-at-the-beach-2000.

11. *Bollea*, 610 S.E.2d at 95.

12. *Id.*

13. *Id.* at 97.

14. *Id.*

15. *Id.*

16. https://www.youtube.com/watch?v=hJgiBsdHAUI.

17. *Bollea*, 610 S.E.2d at 97.

18. *Credible Behav. Health, Inc. v. Johnson*, 220 A.3d 303, 310 (Md. 2019).

19. *Id.* at 311.

20. *North Silo Resources, LLC v. Deselms*, 518 P.3d 1074, 1082 (Wyo. 2022).

21. Reply Brief of Appellant, *Bollea v. World Championship Wrestling*, No. A04 A1743, July 12, 2004, 2004 WL 5536504, *7.

22. *Bollea*, 610 S.E.2d at 98.

23. *Id.*

24. *Id.*

25. *Id.*

26. *Id.*

27. *Celebrity Cruises, Inc. v. Essef Corp.*, 478 F. Supp. 2d 440, 447–55 (S.D. N.Y. 2007).

28. Robert M. Lloyd, "The Reasonable Certainty Requirement in Lost Profits Litigation: What it Really Means," 12 *Transactions: Tennessee Bus. L.J.* 12, 24 (2010) (quoting cases).

29. *Id.*

30. William Dettloff, "Iconic Dempsey Exemplified the Roaring '20s," July 17, 2008, https://www.espn.com/sports/boxing/news/story?id=3492743.

31. *Chicago Coliseum Club v. Dempsey*, 265 Ill. App. 542, 549–50 (Ill. Ct. App. 1932).

32. http://indeedwrestling.blogspot.com/2014/02/deciphering-wcw-buyrates.html; https://wrestlenomics.com/resources/wcw-pay-per-view-buys/.

33. *Bollea v. World Championship Wrestling, Inc.*, 610 S.E.2d 92, 99 (Ga. Ct. App. 2005).

34. Id.

35. Mike Mooneyham, "Hogan Taking Another WWE Hiatus," The Wrestling Gospel According to Mike Mooneyham, July 13, 2003, http://mikemooneyham.com/2003/07/13/hogan-taking-another-wwe-hiatus/.

36. *Ventura v. Titan Sports, Inc.*, 65 F.3d 725, 727–78 (8th Cir 1995).

37. *Id.* at 730.

38. *Hesselgrave v. Harrison*, 435 N.W.2d 861, 863–64 (Minn. Ct. App. 1989).

39. *Schumacher v. Schumacher*, 627 N.W.2d 725, 729–30 (Minn. App. 2001).

40. *Frankson v. Design Space Int'l*, 394 N.W.2d 140, 140 (Minn.1986).

41. *Ventura*, 65 F.3d at 729–30.

42. *Id.* at 730.

43. *Id.* at 732.

44. *Id.* at 733.

45. *Id.* at 734.

46. *See* Contract between WWE and Chavo Guerrero, Jr. (April 5, 2010), http://ia802906.us.archive.org/32/items/gov.uscourts.ctd.113085/gov.uscourts.ctd.113085.1.5.pdf.

Chapter 9

1. "Study Suggests Brain Damage May Have Affected Benoit," ESPN.com, Sep. 5, 2007.

2. Jeanne Marie Laskas, "The Brain That Sparked the NFL's Concussion Crisis," *The Atlantic*, Dec. 2, 2015, https://www.theatlantic.com/health/archive/2015/12/the-nfl-players-brain-that-changed-the-history-of-the-concussion/417597/.

3. *Id.*

4. *Id.*

5. *Id.*

6. Joshua Piercey, Note, "Stop Playing Through It: Why Indiana Needs to Reassess Its Stance Towards Brain Injuries and Its Current Concussion Protocol in High School Sports," 17 *Ind. Health L. Rev.* 313, 319 (2020).

7. Ken Belson, "A Former W.W.E. Wrestler Taps in Against Concussion Deniers," *N.Y. Times*, Oct. 26, 2022, https://www.nytimes.com/2022/10/26/sports/football/chris-nowinski-cte-football.html.

8. Nick Eaton, Note, "Sacked by the Clock: Analyzing Statute of Limitations Defenses in the Context of Football-Related CTE Lawsuits," 88 *U. Cin. L. Rev.* 1149, 1150 (2019).

9. Piercey, *supra* note 6, at 319.

10. PBS, "Timeline: The NFL's Concussion Crisis," Oct. 8, 2013, https://www.pbs.org/wgbh/pages/frontline/sports/league-of-denial/timeline-the-nfls-concussion-crisis/ (citing Kevin M. Guskiewiecz et al., "Recurrent Concussion and Risk of Depression in Retired Professional Football Players," *Official Journal of the American College of Sports Medicine*, June 2007).

11. Stephanie A. Murray, Note, "The Misnomer of the NFL's 'Concussion Crisis': Don't Count on the NFL to Solve Football's Biggest Problem—and OSHA Regulation May Not Save the Game Either," 56 *Washburn L.J.* 181, 189 (2017); Mikayla Paolini, "NFL Takes A Page from the Big Tobacco Playbook: Assumption of Risk in the CTE Crisis," 68 *Emory L.J.* 607, 614 n.37 (2019).

12. PBS, "Timeline: The NFL's Concussion Crisis," Oct. 8, 2013, https://www.pbs.org/wgbh/pages/frontline/sports/league-of-denial/timeline-the-nfls-concussion-crisis/.

13. *Id.*

14. Paolini, *supra* note 9, at 614.

15. PBS, "Timeline: The NFL's Concussion Crisis," Oct. 8, 2013, https://www.pbs.org/wgbh/pages/frontline/sports/league-of-denial/timeline-the-nfls-concussion-crisis/ (citing Elliot Pellman et al., "Concussion in Professional Football: Epidemiological Features of Game Injuries and Review of the Literature—Part 3," *Neurosurgery*, Jan. 2004).

16. Alan Schwarz, "Dementia Risk Seen in Players in NFL Study," *N.Y. Times*, Sept. 29, 2009.

17. Tom Goldman, "House Hears Testimony on Football, Head Injuries," NPR, Oct. 28, 2009, https://www.npr.org/2009/10/28/114253880/house-hears-testimony-on-football-head-injuries.

18. PBS, "Timeline: The NFL's Concussion Crisis," Oct. 8, 2013, https://www.pbs.org/wgbh/pages/frontline/sports/league-of-denial/timeline-the-nfls-concussion-crisis/.

19. Alan Scwharz, "NFL Acknowledges Long-Term Concussion Effects," *N.Y. Times*, Dec. 20, 2009.

20. PBS Frontline, Interview with Chris Nowinski, PBS, June 12, 2013, https://www.pbs.org/wgbh/pages/frontline/sports/league-of-denial/the-frontline-interview-chris-nowinski/.

21. Greg Garber, "Doctors: Wrestler Had Brain Damage," ESPN, Dec. 8, 2009, https://www.espn.com/espn/otl/news/story?id=4724912.

22. *Id.*

23. *In re National Football League Players Concussion Injury Litigation*, 821 F.3d 410, 422 (3d Cir. 2016).

24. *Id.*

25. Steve Fainaru and Mark Fainaru-Wada, "NFL Board Paid $2M to Players While League Denied Football-Concussion Link," *PBS Frontline*, Nov. 12, 2016, http://www.pbs.org/wgbh/frontline/article/nfl-board-paid-2m-to-players-while-league-denied-football-concussion-link/.

26. *In re National Football League Players Concussion Injury Litigation*, 821 F.3d 410 (3d Cir. 2016).

27. Jesse Mez et al., *Clinopathological Evaluation of Chronic Traumatic Encephalopathy in Players of American Football*, 318 JAMA 360, 362 (2017).

28. *McCullough v. World Wrestling Entertainment, Inc.*, CIVIL ACTION NO. 3:15-CV-1074 (VLB), CIVIL ACTION NO. 3:15-CV-994 (VLB), CIVIL ACTION NO. 3:16-CV-1209 (VLB), 2017 WL 4400749, *2 (D. Conn. Sept. 29, 2017).

29. *Haynes v. World Wrestling Enter-*

tainment, Inc., Class Action Allegation Complaint, Case 3:14-cv-01689-ST (D. Or. Oct. 23, 2014).

30. CONN. GEN. STAT. ANN. § 52–584.

31. *Lagassey v. State*, 846 A.2d 831, 845 (Tenn. 2004).

32. *McCullough v. World Wrestling Entertainment, Inc.*, 172 F. Supp. 3d 528, 549–50 (D. Conn. 2016).

33. Jean Macchiaroli Eggen, "It's About Time: The Long Overdue Demise of Statutes of Repose in Latent Toxic Tort Litigation," 68 *Case W. Res. L. Rev.* 23, 31 (2017).

34. *Id.* at 32–34.

35. TENN. CODE ANN. § 29-28-103 (emphasis added).

36. *Id.* § 29-28-102.2.

37. *Montgomery v. Wyeth*, 540 F. Supp. 2d 933 (E.D. Tenn. 2008).

38. *See, e.g., Heath v. Sears, Roebuck & Co.*, 464 A.2d 288, 296 (N.H. 1983).

39. Eggen, *supra* note 26, at 40.

40. CONN. GEN. STAT. ANN. § 52–584.

41. *Id.*

42. *McCullough v. World Wrestling Entertainment, Inc.*, 172 F. Supp. 3d 528, 555 (D. Conn. 2016).

43. *McCullough v. World Wrestling Entertainment, Inc.*, No. 3:15-cv-01074 (VLB), No. 3:15-cv-00425 (VLB), 2018 WL 1525712, *2 (D. Conn. March 28, 2018).

44. *McCullough*, 172 F. Supp. 3d at 561.

45. *Id.* at 555, 556.

46. *Id.* at 539.

47. AP, "WWE Seeking to Block Concussion-Related Lawsuits," July 1, 2015, https://apnews.com/article/8e0c-9cb3f7d748b29fb1d4d595f9d7bd.

48. *McCullough v. World Wrestling Entertainment, Inc.*, CIVIL ACTION NO. 3:15-CV-1074 (VLB), CIVIL ACTION NO. 3:15-CV-994 (VLB), CIVIL ACTION NO. 3:16-CV-1209 (VLB) 2018 WL 4425977, *2 (D. Conn. Sep. 17, 2018).

49. *McCullough v. World Wrestling Entertainment, Inc.*, CIVIL ACTION NO. 3:15-CV-1074 (VLB), CIVIL ACTION NO. 3:15-CV-994 (VLB), CIVIL ACTION NO. 3:16-CV-1209 (VLB), 2017 WL 4400749, *2 (D. Conn. Sep. 29, 2017).

50. *McCullough v. World Wrestling Entertainment, Inc.*, CIVIL ACTION NO. 3:15-CV-1074 (VLB), CIVIL ACTION NO. 3:15-CV-994 (VLB), CIVIL ACTION NO. 3:16-CV-1209 (VLB) 2018 WL 4425977, *2 (D. Conn. Sep. 17, 2018).

51. *McCullough v. World Wrestling Entertainment, Inc.*, CIVIL ACTION NO. 3:15-CV-1074 (VLB), CIVIL ACTION NO. 3:15-CV-994 (VLB), CIVIL ACTION NO. 3:16-CV-1209 (VLB), 2017 WL 4400749, *1 (D. Conn. Sep. 29, 2017).

52. *McCullough v. World Wrestling Entertainment, Inc.*, No. 3:15-cv-01074 (VLB), No. 3:15-cv-00425 (VLB), 2018 WL 1525712, *3 (D. Conn. March 28, 2018).

53. *McCullough v. World Wrestling Entertainment, Inc.*, CASE NO. 3:15cv1074 (VLB) LEAD CASE, CASE NO. 3:15cv425 (VLB) CONSOLIDATED CASE, 2018 WL 2932354, * 4 n.4 (D. Conn. Feb. 22. 2018).

54. *McCullough v. World Wrestling Entertainment, Inc.*, No. 3:15-cv-01074 (VLB), No. 3:15-cv-00425 (VLB), 2018 WL 1525712, *3 (D. Conn. March 28, 2018).

55. *Id.* at *4.

56. *McCullough v. World Wrestling Entertainment, Inc.*, No. 3:15-cv-01074 (VLB) Lead Case, No. 3:15-cv-00425 (VLB) Consolidated Case, 2018 WL 4697285 (July 22, 2018).

57. No. 3:15-cv-1074 (JAM) CONSOLIDATED CASE, No. 3:15-cv-425 (JAM) CONSOLIDATED CASE, No. 3:15-cv-1209 (JAM) CONSOLIDATED CASE, 2021 WL 4472719, *1 (D. Conn. Sep. 30, 2021).

Chapter 10

1. Ryann D. Garza, "One Man's Fight Was A Fight For All: The Story of I.H. "Sporty" Harvey And His Battle Outside The Ring" (2021). *Methods of Historical Research*: Spring 2021, 7 (quoting Harvey), https://digitalcommons.tamusa.edu/hist4301_spring2021/7.

2. David Shoemaker, *The Squared Circle: Life, Death, and Professional Wrestling* 141 (2013).

3. *Id.* at 138.

4. *Id.* at 137.

5. 163 U.S. 537 (1896).

6. *Id.* at 552.

7. *Id.* at 551.

8. Louisiana Act No. 176 of 1908, §8 (cited in *State v. Lahiff*, 80 So. 590, 593 (La. 1919).

9. Felipe Tobar, "The Legacy Museum: Should Athlete Activists Receive More Attention?," *Sport Heritage Review*, https://sportheritagereview.com/2019/03/12/

the-legacy-museum-should-athlete-activists-receive-more-attention/.

10. *Id.*

11. *Id.*

12. *Dorsey v. State Athletic Commission*, 168 F. Supp. 149, 150 (E.D. La. 1958) (quoting LSA-R.S. 4:451 et seq.).

13. Steve Knopper, "Joe Dorsey's Big Fight: How An Unknown Boxer Knocked Out Segregation In Louisiana," *BuzzFeed*, July 1, 2016, https://medium.com/buzzfeed-collections/joe-dorseys-big-fight-how-an-unknown-boxer-knocked-out-segregation-in-louisiana-d0e8281b1efa.

14. Timothy Davis, "The Myth of the Superspade: The Persistence of Racism in College Athletics," 22 *Fordham Urb. L.J.* 615, 624 (1995).

15. *Id.* at 629.

16. Harry Edwards, "The End of the 'Golden Age' of Black Sports Participation?," 38 *S. Tex. L. Rev.* 1007, 1007 (1997).

17. Davis, *supra* note 14, at 296.

18. *Id.* at 297.

19. Edwards, *supra* note 16, at 1007.

20. Tobar, *supra* note 9.

21. John Kelly, "For Black Baseball Fans, Griffith Stadium Offered a 'Separate But Equal' Experience," *Wash. Post*, Nov. 2, 2019, https://www.washingtonpost.com/local/for-black-baseball-fans-griffith-stadium-offered-a-separate-but-equal-experience/2019/11/02/0e655be8-fcb0-11e9-8906-ab6b60de9124_story.html.

22. Nicholas Porter, Master's Thesis, "The Dark Carnival: The Construction and Performance of Race in American Professional Wrestling" 34 (Bowling Green) (August 2011), https://etd.ohiolink.edu/apexprod/rws_etd/send_file/send?accession=bgsu1308331340&disposition=inline.

23. Documentary, *Elliott Marquez, Black Sam's Statue* (2015), https://vimeo.com/120864245.

24. Charles Morrow Wilson, *The Magnificent Scufflers: Revealing The Great Days When America Wrestled The World* (2011).

25. SHOEMAKER, *supra* note 2, at 21.

26. Porter, *supra* note 23, at 43.

27. *Harvey v. Morgan*, 272 S.W.2d 621, 622 (Tex. Ct. Civ. App. 1954) (quoting Texas Penal Code Art. 614–11[f]).

28. *Dorsey v. State Athletic Commission*, 168 F. Supp. 149, 149 (E.D. La. 1958).

29. *Id.* at 152; *Harvey v. Morgan*, 272 S.W.2d 621, 623 (Tex. Ct. Civ. App. 1954).

30. Derek H. Alderman et al., "Jack Johnson Versus Jim Crow: Race, Reputation, and the Politics of Black Villainy: The First Fight of the Century," *Southeastern Geographer*, Volume 58, Number 3, Fall 2018, pp. 241, https://muse-jhu-edu.utk.idm.oclc.org/article/705472/pdf.

31. Lawrence M. Friedman, *American Law in the Twentieth Century* 113 (2004); Francine Sanders Romero, "'There Are Only White Champions': The Rise and Demise of Segregated Boxing in Texas," 108 *The Southwestern Historical Quarterly* 26, 29 (Jul. 2004).

32. Talgin Lee Cannon, Master's Thesis, *Impact of Battalion and Smaller African-American Combat Units on Integration of the U.S. Army in the European Theater of Operations During World War II*, at iv (2015), https://apps.dtic.mil/sti/pdfs/ADA623621.pdf.

33. Gerry J. Gilmore, "African-Americans Continue Tradition of Distinguished Service," U.S. Army, Feb. 2, 2007, https://www.army.mil/article/1681/african_americans_continue_tradition_of_distinguished_service; Cannon, *supra* note 31, at 105–06.

34. Edwards, *supra* note 16, at 1008.

35. *Id.* at 1012.

36. *See id.* at 1011 (stating that "[i]t was business, not brotherhood, that was the principal incentive motivating Branch Rickey" to sign Robinson).

37. "Top Moments: Earl Lloyd, Chuck Cooper, Nat Clifton Blaze New Path in NBA," NBA.com, https://www.nba.com/news/history-top-moments-earl-lloyd-chuck-cooper-nat-clifton-new-path-nba.

38. Edwards, supra note 16, at 1013.

39. "Firsts by African-Americans in the NFL," NFL.com, https://www.nfl.com/photos/firsts-by-african-americans-in-the-nfl-09000d5d826ca97b#6cf4c29f-4c4d-4df9-9005-a257cc00b2c6.

40. Porter, supra note 22, at 56; Jack Claybourne (1910–1960), https://sites.google.com/site/wrestlingscout/profiles-by-country/profiles/claybourne.

41. SHOEMAKER, supra note 2, at 133.

42. Porter, supra note 22, at 56 (quoting http://www.wrestlingperspective.com/blacklikeme.html), https://etd.ohiolink.edu/apexprod/rws_etd/send_file/send?accession=bgsu1308331340&disposition=inline.

43. John Cosper, *The Original Black Panther: The Life & Legacy of Jim Mitchell* (2019) (Location 407).
44. *Id.*
45. *Id.* at (Location 790).
46. Goodwin Liu, *State Courts and Constitutional Structure*, 128 *Yale L.J.* 1304, 1352 (2019).
47. Deborah L. Rhode, *Lessons From Iconic Leaders: Thurgood Marshall and Nelson Mandela*, 48 *Hofstra L. Rev.* 705, 709 (2020).
48. 339 U.S. 629 (1950).
49. *Id.* at 632.
50. *Id.* at 636.
51. 339 U.S. 637 (1950).
52. *Id.* at 639.
53. *Id.* at 639.
54. *Id.* at 640.
55. *Id.* at 641.
56. *Id.* at 642.
57. *Sweatt*, 339 U.S. at 636.
58. 347 U.S. 483 (1954).
59. *Id.* at 487–88.
60. *Id.* at 492.
61. *Id.* at 495.
62. *Id.* at 494.
63. *Id.* at 495.
64. *Harvey v. Morgan*, 272 S.W.2d 621, 622 (Tex. Ct. Civ. App. 1954).
65. *Strauss v. State*, 173 S.W. 663 (Tex. Ct. Crim. App. 1915).
66. *O'Connor v. Dallas Cotton Exchange*, 153 S.W.2d 266 (Tex. Ct. Civ. App. 1941).
67. Jan Jarboe Russell, "The Last Maverick," *Texas Monthly*, July 2003, https://www.texasmonthly.com/articles/the-last-maverick/.
68. *Id.*
69. Leonard S. Rubinowitza1, "A 'Notorious Litigant' and 'Frequenter of Jails': Martin Luther King, Jr., His Lawyers, and the Legal System, 10 *NW J. L. & Soc. Pol'y* 494, 510 (2016).
70. Russell, *supra* note 66.
71. Cary Clack, *The Bout, Truly Adventurous*, https://www.trulyadventure.us/the-bout-story.
72. Russell, *supra* note 66.
73. Garza, *supra* note 1, at 5 (quoting Harvey's lawyer), https://digitalcommons.tamusa.edu/hist4301_spring2021/7.
74. *Id.* at 8.
75. *Id.*
76. *Id.* at 14.
77. Clack, *supra* note 70.
78. Ryann D. Garza, "One Man's Fight Was a Fight for All: The Story of I.H. "Sporty" Harvey and His Battle Outside the Ring" (2021). *Methods of Historical Research*: Spring 2021, at 15–16, https://digitalcommons.tamusa.edu/hist4301_spring2021/7.
79. *Harvey v. Morgan*, 272 S.W.2d 621, 623 (Tex. Ct. Civ. App. 1954).
80. *Id.*
81. *Id.* at 624–25.
82. *Id.* at 623.
83. *Whitfield v. Cox*, 52 S.E.2d 72 (Va. 1949).
84. Porter, *supra* note 22, at 57; Shoemaker, supra note 2, at 133.
85. *Pat Laprade and Dan Murphy, Sisterhood of the Squared Circle* 55–56 (2017).
86. *Jim Mitchell vs. Gorgeous George*, Eat Sleep Wrestle, Sep. 23, 2005, https://eatsleepwrestle.com/?p=462.
87. Cosper, *supra* note 42, at 277.
88. *Jim Mitchell vs. Gorgeous George*, Eat Sleep Wrestle, Sep. 23, 2005, https://eatsleepwrestle.com/?p=462.
89. Jason Winders, *George Dixon: The Short Life of Boxing's First Black Champion, 1870–1908*, 124 (2021).
90. *Id.* at 127.
91. *Id.* at 126.
92. *Id.* at 127.
93. *Id.* at 129.
94. *Id.* at 130.
95. *Id.*
96. *Id.* at 135.
97. *Id.;* http://www.scrumptiouschef.com/2020/05/29/new-orleans-boxer-joe-dorsey-jr-fought-jim-crow-with-the-sweet-science/.
98. *Harvey v. Morgan*, 272 S.W.2d 621, 624 (Tex. Ct. Civ. App. 1954).
99. *Id.*
100. *Id.* at 625.
101. *Id.* at 625–26 (quoting Slaughter House Cases, 83 U.S. 36 [1872]).
102. *Id.* at 627.
103. Garza, *supra* note 1, at 16–17.
104. *Dorsey v. State Athletic Commission*, 168 F. Supp. 149, 150 (E.D. La. 1958).
105. "Joe Dorsey's Fight: The Fighter Who KO'd Louisiana's Jim Crow Law," *Jet*, Jan. 1, 1959, 58, https://books.google.com/books?id=d0EDAAAAMBAJ&pg=PA56&lpg=PA56&dq=%22joe+dorsey%22+jet&source=bl&ots=yfiJiGxuq

Notes—Chapter 10

B&sig=WshTTbk47Iz565yrGpMDvsnbo
Nc&hl=en&sa=X&ei=_nJ7U—sBsmvy
ASZ1YCQAg&ved=0CCgQ6AEw
AA#v=onepage&q&f=false.
106. *Id.*
107. Evelyn L. Wilson, "Louis Berry: A Man Among Men," 20 *Southern U. L. Rev.* 149, 173 (1993).
108. *Dorsey v. State Athletic Commission*, 168 F. Supp. 149, 150 (E.D. La. 1958) (quoting LSA-R.S. 4:451 et seq.).
109. *Id.* at 151.
110. *Id.* at 152.
111. *Id.* at 150.
112. *Id.* at 152–53.
113. Jurisdictional Statement on Behalf of Appellant, *State Athletic Commission v. Dorsey*, 1959 WL 101461, March 21, 1959.
114. *Id.* at *10.
115. *Ward v. Drennon*, 40 S.E.2d 549, 551 (Ga. 1946).
116. Jurisdictional Statement on Behalf of Appellant, *State Athletic Commission v. Dorsey*, 1959 WL 101461, *11–12 March 21, 1959 (quoting State v. Hunter, 300 P.2d 455, 457 [Or. 1956]).
117. *State Athletic Commission v. Dorsey*, 359 U.S. 533 (1959).
118. Wilson, *supra* note 105, at 174.
119. *Bynum v. Schiro*, 219 F. Supp. 204, 207 n.2 (E.D. La. 1963). Ironically, a federal court would use Dorsey's case to deny immediate relief to black plaintiffs who sued over statutes requiring segregated seating at places of public assemblage and that imposed criminal penalties for violations. *Reid v. City of Norfolk*, 179 F. Supp. 768, 771 n.5 (E.D. Va. 1960).
120. *Williams v. Eaton*, 443 F.2d 422 (10th Cir. 1971).
121. *Rybicki v. State Bd. of Elections of State of Ill.*, 574 F. Supp. 1082, 1131 (N.D. Ill. 1982) (Grady, J., concurring in part and dissenting in part).
122. *Brown v. Board of Education of Topeka*, 349 U.S. 294, 301 (1955).
123. Yuvraj Joshia, "Racial Transition," 98 *Wash. U. L. Rev.* 1181, 1193 (2021).
124. Allegra M. McLeod, "Police Violence, Constitutional Complicity, and Another Vantage," 2016 *Sup. Ct. Rev.* 157, 179 n.115 (2016).
125. Lia B. Epperson, "Resisting Retreat: The Struggle for Equity in Educational Opportunity in the Post-Brown Era," 66 *U. Pitt. L. Rev.* 131, 134 (2004).

126. "The History of Baseball and Civil Rights in America," Baseball Hall of Fame, https://baseballhall.org/civilrights; Jonathan Mayo, "From the Fields to the Stands," *Minor League Baseball*, Feb. 25, 2008, http://www.milb.com/gen/articles/printer_friendly/milb/y2008/m02/d23/c350776.jsp.
127. Rhonda Glenn, "Charlie Sifford: A Hard Road to Golf Glory," Feb. 3, 2019, USGA, https://www.usga.org/articles/2012/02/a-hard-road-to-golf-glory-21474845949.html#:~:text=Golf%20has%20long%20struggled%20with,-from%20competing%20on%20the%20PGA.
128. John Feinstein, "For Lee Elder, the First Black Golfer to Play the Masters, Import is not Measured in Wins," *Wash. Post*, Nov. 30, 2021, https://www.washingtonpost.com/sports/2021/11/30/lee-elder-appreciation-racism-john-feinstein/.
129. Mike Mooneyham, "Remembering the Past: Sailor Art Thomas was Wrestling Trailblazer," Nov. 13, 2021, https://www.postandcourier.com/sports/wrestling/remembering-the-past-sailor-art-thomas-was-wrestling-trailblazer/article_d2337766-422d-11ec-9f0f-47bb887ef2a3.html.
130. Archived *Sunday Punch* Columns, *Cauliflower Alley Club*, https://web.archive.org/web/20080919145320/http://www.cauliflowerallayclub.org/story4.htm; WWE Hall of Fame, Luther Lindsay, https://www.wwe.com/superstars/luther-lindsay.
131. Archived *Sunday Punch* Columns, *Cauliflower Alley Club*, https://web.archive.org/web/20080919145320/http://www.cauliflowerallayclub.org/story4.htm.
132. "Mixed Matches are Popular with Fans," *Ebony*, May 1962, at 46, https://classicwrestlingarticles.wordpress.com/2021/01/27/negro-wrestlers/.
133. *Id.*
134. Greg Garrison, "Pro Wrestler who Helped Integrate Sports in Alabama Dies," Alabama.com, Oct. 20, 2020.
135. Steven Johnson et al., *The Pro Wrestling Hall of Fame: Heroes and Icons* (ECW Press 2012); https://historyofwrestling.com/bobo-brazil/.
136. SHOEMAKER, supra note 2, at 135.
137. Javier Ojst, "Bobo Brazil, Bearcat Wright, and Art Thomas—Champion Pioneers," *Pro Wrestling Stories*, https://pro

wrestlingstories.com/pro-wrestling-stories/bobo-brazil-bearcat-wright-art-thomas/.

138. Mark Long, "Bobo Brazil," *History of Wrestling*, https://historyofwrestling.com/bobo-brazil/; "El Mongol," *Online World of Wrestling*, April 28, 2014, https://www.onlineworldofwrestling.com/profile/el-mongol/.

139. Ojst, supra note 133.

140. Bob Mehr, "Sputnik Monroe Used His Rock-'em-Sock-'em Star Status to Muscle the Way for Desegregated Seating in Pre-Civil Rights Memphis," *Memphis Commercial Appeal*, Nov. 11, 2006, at 73.

141. *Watson v. City of Memphis*, 373 U.S. 526, 528 & n.1 (1963).

142. *Id.*

143. *Id.* at 539.

144. Mehr, *supra* note 136, at 73.

145. John Sharp, "Sputnik Monroe was a Body-Slamming Civil Rights Pioneer," March 31, 2018, https://apnews.com/article/368a466a2ad84c44ad17354ec4f771f7.

146. Mehr, *supra* note 136, at 69.

147. Sharp, *supra* note 141.

148. *Id.*

149. *Id.*; David Williams, "Memphis Seized its Sputnik Moment," *Memphis Commercial Appeal*, Feb. 20, 2011.

150. John Beifuss, "The Beifuss File: Sputnik Monroe Was Out of This World," *Memphis Commercial Appeal*, March 19, 2017, at 6, https://www.commercialappeal.com/story/entertainment/2017/03/17/beifuss-file-sputnik-monroe-out-world/99248734/.

151. *Id.*

152. Mehr, *supra* note 136, at 69.

153. *Id.*

154. Robert Gordon, *It Came from Memphis* 35 (1995).

155. Mehr, supra note 136, at 69.

156. "Sputnik Wrestled Against Prejudice," *Wash. Times*, Dec. 2, 2006, https://www.washingtontimes.com/news/2006/dec/2/20061202-121718-9427r/.

157. Mehr, *supra* note 136, at 69.

158. *Id.*

159. Mehr, *supra* note 136, at 69.

160. "Sputnik Wrestled Against Prejudice," *supra* note 152.

161. 42 U.S.C. §2000a(b).

162. *Nesmith v. Young Men's Christian Ass'n of Raleigh, N. C.*, 397 F.2d 96 (4th Cir. 1968).

163. *Plaquemines Parish School Bd. v. U.S.*, 415 F.2d 817 (5th Cir. 1969).

Bibliography

Books

Assael, Shaun, and Mike Mooneyham. *Sex, Lies, and Headlocks*. Three Rivers Press, 2002.

Ellison, Lillian. *The Fabulous Moolah: First Goddess of the Squared Circle*. ECW, 2002.

Evans, Guy. *Nitro*. Published by the author, 2018.

Friedman, Lawrence M. *American Law in the Twentieth Century*. Yale University Press, 2004.

Gordon, Robert. *It Came from Memphis*. Atria Books, 1995.

Hall, Kermit. "Alabama in the 1960s", in *100 Americans Making Constitutional History: A Biographical History*. Melvin I. Urofsky, ed. C.Q. Press, 2004.

Holiday, Ryan. *Conspiracy*. Portfolio/Penguin, 2018.

Hornbaker. Tim. *National Wrestling Alliance: The Untold Story of the Monopoly that Strangled Pro Wrestling* 6. ECW, 2007.

James, Mark. *Memphis Wrestling History Presents: 1977 The War for Memphis*. Amazon, 2014.

Jarrett, Jerry, with Mark James. *The Best of Times*. CreateSpace, 2011.

Johnson, Steven, et al. *The Pro Wrestling Hall of Fame: Heroes and Icons*. ECW, 2012.

Laprade, Pat, and Dan Murphy. *Sisterhood of the Squared Circle*. ECW, 2017.

Lewis, Anthony. *Make No Law: The Sullivan Case and the First Amendment*. Vintage Books, 1991.

Shoemaker, David. *The Squared Circle: Life, Death, and Professional Wrestling*. Gotham Books, 2013.

Wilson, Charles Morrow. *The Magnificent Scufflers: Revealing the Great Days When America Wrestled the World*. Literary Licensing, LLC, 2011.

Wilson, Jim. *Chokehold: Pro Wrestling's Real Mayhem Outside the Ring*. Xlibris, 2003.

Winders, Jason. *George Dixon: The Short Life of Boxing's First Black Champion, 1870-1908*. University of Arkansas Press, 2021.

Journal Articles

Alexander, Charlotte. "Anticipatory Retaliation, Threats, and the Silencing of the Brown Collar Workforce," 50 *Am. Bus. L.J.* 779 (2013).

Collins, Wayne D. "Trusts and the Origins of Antitrust Legislation," 81 *Fordham L. Rev.* 2279 (2013).

Cowley, David. "Note, Employees vs. Independent Contractors and Wrestling: How the WWE is Taking a Folding Chair to the Basic Tenets of Employment Law," 53 *U. Louisville L. Rev.* 143 (2014).

Davis, Rochella T. "Talent Can't Be Allocated: A Labor Economics Justification for No-Poaching Agreement Criminality in Antitrust Regulation," 12 *Brook. J. Corp. Fin. & Com. L.* 279 (2018).

Davis, Timothy. "The Myth of the Superspade: The Persistence of Racism in College Athletics," 22 *Fordham Urb. L.J.* 615 (1995).

Donathen, Patrick. "Post-and-Hold Laws: Has the Second Circuit Authorized Liquor Cartels in the Face of the Sherman Antitrust Act?," 83 *U. Pitt. L. Rev.* 167 (2021).

Edwards, Harry. "The End of the 'Golden Age' of Black Sports Participation?," 38 S. Tex. L. Rev. 1007 (1997).

Eggen, Jean Macchiaroli. "It's About Time: The Long Overdue Demise of Statutes of Repose in Latent Toxic Tort Litigation," 68 Case W. Res. L. Rev. 23 (2017).

Epperson, Lia B. "Resisting Retreat: The Struggle for Equity in Educational Opportunity in the Post-Brown Era," 66 U. Pitt. L. Rev. 131 (2004).

Galligan, Jr., Thomas C. "The Tragedy in Torts," 5 Cornell J.L. & Pub. Pol'y 139 (1996).

Knauer, Nancy J. "Legal Fictions and Juristic Truth," 23 St. Thomas L. Rev. 70 (2010).

Lloyd, Robert M. "The Reasonable Certainty Requirement in Lost Profits Litigation: What it Really Means," 12 Transactions: Tennessee Bus. L.J. 12 (2010).

Lobel, Orly. "The Gig Economy and the Future of Employment and Labor Law," 51 U.S.F. L. Rev. 51 (2017).

Murray, Stephanie A. "Note, The Misnomer of the NFL's 'Concussion Crisis': Don't Count on the NFL to Solve Football's Biggest Problem—and OSHA Regulation May Not Save the Game Either," 56 Washburn L.J. 181 (2017).

Paolini, Mikayla. "NFL Takes a Page from the Big Tobacco Playbook: Assumption of Risk in the CTE Crisis," 68 Emory L.J. 607 (2019).

Piercey, Joshua. "Note, Stop Playing Through It: Why Indiana Needs to Reassess Its Stance Towards Brain Injuries and Its Current Concussion Protocol in High School Sports," 17 Ind. Health L. Rev. 313 (2020).

Reynolds, Glenn Harlan. "Rethinking Libel for the Twenty-First Century," 87 Tenn. L. Rev. 465 (2020).

Rhode, Deborah L. "Lessons from Iconic Leaders: Thurgood Marshall and Nelson Mandela," 48 Hofstra L. Rev. 705 (2020).

Romero, Francine Sanders. "'There Are Only White Champions': The Rise and Demise of Segregated Boxing in Texas," 108 The Southwestern Historical Quarterly 26, 29 (Jul. 2004).

Rubinowitza, Leonard S. "A 'Notorious Litigant' and 'Frequenter of Jails': Martin Luther King, Jr., His Lawyers, and the Legal System," 10 NW J.L. & Soc. Pol'y 494 (2016).

Warren, Samuel D., and Louis D. Brandeis. "The Right to Privacy," 4 Harv. L. Rev. 193 (1890).

Media Articles

Beifuss, John. "The Beifuss File: Sputnik Monroe Was Out of This World," Memphis Commercial Appeal, March 19, 2017, at 6.

Bierig, Joel. "Tug of War is on for Memphis Wrestling Limelight," The Commercial Appeal, March 20, 1977, at 37.

Bixenspan, David. "Starrcade vs. Survivor Series: The Fight for Thanksgiving that Changed Wrestling," Bleacher Report, Nov. 27, 2013.

Cobb, Ron. "Wrestling Camps Fight for Home," Memphis Press-Scimitar, April 28, 1977, at 23.

Encarnacao, Jack. "In City's Wrestling Prime, No Holds were Barred," Boston Globe, Sep. 26, 2004.

"'Express' Suit Settled," Times-Picayune, Aug. 19, 1991, at C-7.

Fox, Larry. "Okay Gal Wrestlers," Daily News (New York, NY), June 6, 1972, at 68.

Guzzo, Paul. "You Won't Believe How Hard They Once Worked to Make Professional Wrestling 'Real,'" Tampa Bay Times, March 19, 2020.

"House Outlaws Women Wrestling," La Grande Observer (La Grande, OR), April 14, 1955, at 6.

"Jarrett Suits Hit TAC, Gulas," The Commercial Appeal, Feb. 16, 1978, at 50.

"Joe Dorsey's Fight: The Fighter Who KO'd Louisiana' Jim Crow Law," Jet, Jan. 1, 1959, at 58.

"Judge Pins Fake Wrestling Scheme," Knoxville News-Sentinel, Feb. 13, 1980, at 46.

"Judge Says Women Can Enter Public Wrestling," Medford Mail Tribune, Jan. 5, 1955, at 8.

Kaplan, Peter W. "TV Notes: ABC Reporter May Sue Wrestler Who Sued Him," N.Y. Times, Feb. 23, 1985.

Kerr, Peter. "Now it Can Be Told: Those Pro Wrestlers Are Just Having Fun," N.Y. Times, Feb. 19, 1989, at A1.

Kramer, Marcia. "State Tosses in the Towel, Ladies Wrestle as Garden," Daily News (New York, NY), July 3, 1972, at 210.

Bibliography

Laskas, Jeanne Marie. "The Brain That Sparked the NFL's Concussion Crisis," *The Atlantic*, Dec. 2, 2015.

"Legal to Bar Women Boxers," *Capital Journal* (Salem, OR), April 11, 1955, at 1.

"Man Calls Wrestling Incident an Attack," *Beckley Evening Post*, Page 2 A, June 3, 1987.

Margolick, David. "Lawyers Go to the Mat in the Battle Between Hulk Hogan and a 98-Pound Comedian," *N.Y. Times*, Jan 5, 1990.

Mehr, Bob. "Sputnik Monroe Used His Rock-'Em-Sock-'Em Star Status to Muscle the Way for Desegregated Seating in Pre-Civil Rights Memphis," *Memphis Commercial Appeal*, Nov. 11, 2006, at 73.

Mooneyham, Mike. "Attempted WWE Fan Attack Evokes Memories of Bygone Era," *The Post and Courier* (Charleston, SC), Aug. 20, 2016.

"Notice to the Public," *Eugene Guard*, May 16, 1955, at 12.

"Poffos' Lawsuit Hits Promoters," *The Tennesseean*, Aug. 25, 1979, at 18.

"Promoter Gulas Retires from Wrestling Work," *The Tennessean*, Aug. 30, 1980, at 16.

Russell, Jan Jarboe. "The Last Maverick," *Texas Monthly*, July 2003.

Russell, Ron. "The Grapple Capital," *The Commercial Appeal*, Nov. 26, 1978, at 307.

Slovic, Beth. "Opinion: Vera Katz Took Office 50 Years Ago—and Legalized Women's Pro Wrestling to Change Oregon," *The Oregonian*, Jan. 3, 2023.

"Some Defendants Dismissed from Suit Against Wrestlers," *Beckley Register-Herald*, May 25, 1989, at 5A.

"Sputnik Wrestled Against Prejudice," *Wash. Times*, Dec. 2, 2006.

Strauss, Mahala. "Trial Date Set for Raleigh Man's Suit Against Tag Team Wrestlers," *Beckley Register-Herald*, Apr. 7, 1989, at 9A.

"Study Suggests Brain Damage May Have Affected Benoit," ESPN.com, Sep. 5, 2007.

West, Marvin. "Wrestling Rift's a Rather Tricky Affair," *The Knoxville News-Sentinel*, July 6, 1979, at 20.

"The Winnah is—Rassler Rose!," *Herald and Review* (Decatur, IL), May 26, 1955, at 6.

Woestendiek, John. "Wrestling's 'Outcasts' Looking for Respect, Riches," *Lexington Herald-Leader*, March 3, 1981, at 30.

"Women Wrestlers Outlawed in Oregon," *Corvallis Gazette-Times*, May 6, 1955, at 9.

Woody, Larry. "Mat Men: Gulas Pioneered the Sport," *The Tennessean*, July 10, 1985, at 11.

"Wrestler Ron Fuller Loses Court Tussle," *Knoxville News-Sentinel*, Feb. 4, 1980, at 4.

"Wrestler Sued by Spectator," *Knoxville News-Sentinel*, Dec. 29, 1983, at 10.

"Wrestling by Women Faces Threat of Ban," *The World* (Coos Bay, OR), Jan. 31, 1955, at 10.

York, Max. "The King of Wrestling," *The Tennesseean*, May 18, 1975, at 151.

Zimmerman, Paul. "Let's Give the Girls a Ring," *New York Post*, March 9, 1972, at 70.

Index

ABC Test 112–14
actual malice 163–65
Afflis, Richard 76
All Elite Wrestling (AEW) 88, 117–18
All Star Championship Wrestling 16, 23, 71–73, 77–78, 88, 90–91, 93–94
antitrust 52–54, 57, 59, 63, 75
Armstrong, Bob ("Bullet") 30–31

Baker, Ox 35, 44
Barnett, Jim 76–78, 80–84, 96
Bash at the Beach 153, 157, 160, 164, 166, 170–71, 176–77
Bass, Nicole 144–45
battery 33, 37, 47–48, 102
Battle for Atlanta 58, 78
Bayliner boat 16–18, 21, 22, 24, 27–28, 30
Belzer, Richard 5–7, 29
Benoit, Chris 181–83, 185–86, 191, 193–94
Bischoff, Eric 91, 153, 155–58, 174, 177
Bollea, Terry ("Hulk Hogan") 152–53, 157, 166–67, 172, 174, 176
Bollea v. World Championship Wrestling, Inc. 158–63, 166, 168, 172–177
Brazil, Bobo 196, 215, 216, 219
breach of contract 26, 63–64, 66–67, 87, 109, 155, 168–80
Brown, Bearcat 215
Brown v. Board of Education 121–23, 126, 201, 203, 205–06, 210, 212, 214, 216, 217, 219
Bryant, Vanessa L. 187, 191–95

Calzadilla, Silvia 131–34
Calzadilla v. Dooley 131–35
Chatterton, Rita 147
Chicken Challenge 88, 91, 93–94
Chokehold 116
chronic traumatic encephalopathy (CTE) 181–88, 190–91, 193–4
Cole, Tom 142–44

consent decree (DOJ) 57–58, 60–62
Cornette, Jim 33–37, 45–47, 50
Crockett, Jim 34, 37–40, 44–50, 86–87, 102–03

defamation 37, 147, 150–67, 168, 177
Dixon, George 209–10
Dorsey, Joe 211–13, 219
Dorsey v. State Athletic Commission 211–13

Eaton, Bobby ("Beautiful") 34–36, 45, 77

Fabulous Moolah 139–41
Fair Labor Standards Act (FLSA) 99
Family and Medical Leave Act (FMLA) 99, 101
Farhat, Ed ("the Sheikh") 76, 78–84
Flair, Ric 13, 15
fraud in the execution/fraud in the factum 169, 180
fraud in the inducement 180
Fuller, Buddy 66, 69, 71, 76
Fuller, Ron ("the Tennessee Stud") 16–32, 71–73, 74, 77, 88–94, 170

Gagne, Vern 76, 84
Garfield, Ron and Don 63, 66, 68
Garvin, Ronnie 16–29, 71, 73, 77
Garvin, Terry 142, 148
Gawker 1, 166–67
Geigel, Bob 76
Gold Dust Trio 8
Graham, Eddie 76–77, 84, 96, 154
Grant, Janel 147–48
Grant v. World Wrestling Entertainment 141–49
Gulas, George 75, 77, 91
Gulas, Nick 60–71, 73–78, 91

Harvey, Sporty 196, 205–11
Harvey v. Morgan 205–11

247

Hesseltine, Rose 122–24
Hesseltine v. State Athletic Commission 122–24
Hogan, Hulk 1, 5–7, 29, 116, 150–77, 180
Hunter, Gerry 124–28, 140

independent contractors 96–119
interference with contractual relations 63–72, 86–87
International Championship Wrestling (ICW) 52, 73–74, 78, 85, 91

Jarrett, Jeff 157–58, 161, 171–72
Jarrett, Jerry 60–71, 73–78, 84–86
Jeffries, Jim 200, 209
Jim Crockett Promotions 34, 37–40, 44–50, 86–87, 102–03
Jim Crow 196–99, 201, 205, 211, 213, 216, 219
Johnson, Jack 200, 209

kayfabe 5, 7–14, 16–17, 20, 27–30, 32, 36, 44, 82, 107, 109, 154
Knoxville 16–17, 27, 30, 44, 59, 71–73, 77, 92
Knoxville Five 71, 73, 92
Kyros, Konstantine 187, 191–94

labor and employment law 95–119
Lane, Stan ("Sweet") 34–37, 45, 47–50, 102–03
Laurinaitis, John 146–48
Lawler, Jerry 63, 66, 75, 78, 84–85
Levesque, Stephanie McMahon 191, 193–94
Levy, Scott 100, 103, 113
Lewis, Ed ("Strangler") 8
Lindsay, Luther 215–16

Major League Wrestling 87–88
Malenko, Boris ("Professor") 17, 44, 71, 92
Martin, Andrew ("Test") 185–86
Marshall, Thurgood 204, 219
Massey, Roy 36–40, 44–51
Matter of Whitehead v Krulewitch 129–32
Maverick, Maury, Jr. 206–07, 219
McCullough v. World Wrestling Entertainment, Inc. 181–95
McMahon, Linda 191
McMahon, Vince, Jr. 11–12, 29, 35, 58, 85–87, 91, 100, 115–17, 139–40, 142–44, 146–48
McMahon, Vince, Sr. 58, 85, 139, 152
Memphis 59–62, 68, 70–71, 86, 90, 216–18
Mero, Rena ("Sable") 145

Midnight Express 33–38, 45, 50, 102–03
Mr. Wrestling 15
Mitchell, Jim (the Black Panther) 203, 208–09
Monroe, Sputnik 216–19
Morgan, M.B. 207, 210–11
Munn, Ed ("Big") 8
Myers, George ("Sonny") 56–57

Nashville 33, 59–60, 70–71
National Football League (NFL) 100–01, 182–87, 191, 194, 202–03, 215
National Labor Relations Act (NLRA) 97–99, 118
National Wrestling Alliance (NWA) 10, 16, 18, 25, 27, 34, 36, 41, 48, 54–61, 68, 71, 74–78, 80, 85–87, 116, 215
negligence 9, 39, 46, 108–09, 189–90
Niccoli, Betty 135–137, 140–41
Nowinski, Chris 184–85, 190–91, 193–94
NWA Southeastern Wrestling, Inc. v. Garvin 15–30

Occupational Safety and Health Act (OSHA) 99
Orton, Bob, Jr. 16, 71, 88

Paris, Titi 136, 138, 140
Patterson, Pat 142–43
Phillips, Mel 142–43
Plessy v. Ferguson 197–98, 203–205, 210
Poffo, Angelo 73, 77
Poffo, Lanny 73–74
Poffo, Randy 3, 52, 73–74, 76–77, 91, 168
Poffos 73–78, 80, 84–85

race discrimination 196–219
rational basis review 128, 140
Raven 100, 103, 113
retaliation 100, 114–18
right of publicity 88–94
Robinson, Jackie 214
Rock 'n' Roll Express 33–34, 36–37, 45
Roop, Bob 16, 29, 57, 71, 73, 77
Rubin v. American Sportsmen Television Equity Society 98–99

Savage, Randy ("Macho Man") 3, 52, 73–74, 76–77, 91, 168
Schultz, Dr. David 5, 7, 29
segregation 197–98, 201–05, 209, 210–14, 215, 218
sex discrimination 120–41
sexual harassment 141–49
Silvia v. Woodhouse 107
Skelly, Jack 209

Index

Small, Viro 200, 219
Snyder, Wilbur 76
Southeastern Championship Wrestling 16–28, 71–74, 76, 78, 88, 90, 92, 94
Starrcade 86–87
State v. Hunter 124–28
statute of limitation 147, 188–90
statute of repose 188–90, 192
Stossel, John 5–7, 29
strict scrutiny review 123

Thomas, Sailor Art 215
Title VII 141, 143–46
Title IX 138, 141

unclean hands 15, 16, 25–30
unemployment insurance 99–100
unjust enrichment 178–80

Ventura, Jesse 116, 178–80
Ventura v. Titan Sports, Inc. 177–80
vicarious liability 47, 50, 102, 108

Webster, Mike 182–83, 187
Welch, Edward 66, 69, 71, 76
Welch, Ronald 16–32, 71–73, 74, 77, 88–94, 170
Welch, Roy 60–61
White v. Frenkel 108–09
Whitehead, Ethel 129–32
Wilson, Jim 116
Woods, Tim 15
workers' compensation 99, 100, 105
World Championship Wrestling (WCW) 87, 91, 100, 152–57, 160–63, 165–66, 168–77, 219
Wright, Bearcat 215–16
Wright, Ron 44, 71, 215

www.ingramcontent.com/pod-product-compliance
Ingram Content Group UK Ltd.
Pitfield, Milton Keynes, MK11 3LW, UK
UKHW041937140426
5217IPUK00014B/521